RENÉ COUDR

THE
ROSWELL
MESSAGE

50 YEARS ON - THE ALIENS SPEAK

RENÉ COUDRIS

THE ROSWELL MESSAGE

50 YEARS ON - THE ALIENS SPEAK

Translated from the German
by Effi and Jeffrey McCabe

Gateway Books

First published in English in 1997
© by Gateway Books
The Hollies, Wellow,
Bath, BA2 8QJ, UK

First published in German in 1996
as »Die Botschaft von Roswell«
© by F. A. Herbig Verlag, Munich

Translated by Effi and Jeffrey McCabe
© World rights by Studio Phoenix Austria
A-4810 Gmunden, P.O.Box 8

Distributed in the USA by
Access Publishers Network
6893 Sullivan Road,
Grawn, MI 49637, USA

Book design and
composition of pictures by René Coudris
Digital photo processing by Alexander Rudolph
Set in Garamond 11 pt on 13
Printed and bound by WBC of Bridgend

British Library Cataloguing in Publication Data
A catalogue record for this book is
available from the British Library

ISBN 1-85860-039-1

Contents

The Telepathic Roswell Commentaries

The Roswell Contacts – Condensed Scenarios

The Roswell Controversy – Conclusions

Epilogue

The Roswell Affair – A Declaration

Hubble Telescope Views into Space

Chapter Illustrations

Since 1995 the NASA Space Observatory has gazed 12 billion light years distant and viewed clusters upon clusters of stars, many of which are much older than our own sun. In each one of these spirals or ellipses in this sea of time and space could, according to latest studies, exist planets capable of supporting life and on which extraterrestrial beings may be living.

Photographs by Hubble Space Telescope

We Are Not Alone

»Whether through the unconscious eyes
of the collective mind
or through the eyes of hyperrationality,
we should examine what is alive
from ever-changing viewpoints,
thus permitting the far reaches of creativity
even more room to act in.

Every conceivable concept
which provides striving humanity
a furtherance and enrichment of its visions,
is good and useful in that context.

When significant aspects of life are raised,
it does not matter in the end
whether they are objective
or subjective realities;
far more important is
how the human being integrates them.

Extraterrestrial contacts help humankind
to perceive anew its lost heritage:
that archaic knowledge
of its inseparable interconnectedness
with the structure of the entire universe.

From that arises a legacy
of unequivocal memories
which contain both a store of truth
and its future possibilities.

In the cosmic reaches of space
live many millions of fascinating beings,
thus, it is today more important than ever
to take such extraterrestrial encounters
into consideration in our discussions.

Someday people will recognize
the universe as multifariously populated,
thoroughly alive,
and inhabited by many types of consciousness.

Their sense of loneliness will decrease,
and earth will no longer be experienced
as the only real center.

The more humankind opens itself to this fact,
that it does not exist alone,
the deeper it will link up with
cosmic consciousness
and the less it will postulate strange
theories about the superior
status of human beings.

Soon it will no longer be questionable
whether these truths exist or not,
but it will become more and more important
to imagine them and accept them
as a possible reality.

As the Bible says:
›Be as children, and you will enter
the kingdom of heaven...‹
I think that herein lie the emotion,
liveliness and the peopling
of the visible and invisible worlds,
in order to profoundly
experience their existence,
to examine and to savor them.

For, everything consciousness can experience
is an authentic reality,
just as our dreams depict a real world.

»Carl Gustav Jung«, 10 August 1995, as transmitted from the beyond

Foreword

A Mega X-File Solved

What could an Austrian parapsychologist who has never been near the place possibly have to say about Roswell? Can he contribute anything new to a subject about which everything seems already to have been said in a whole series of books and video documentaries? Why should he, of all people, have found a solution to one of the most confusing enigmas of the 20th century?

These are good questions. Frankly, it was only by chance that I got involved in this research. I was as surprised as anyone. It was probably a combination of my rather personal ambitions with some strange coincidences that led me into a series of bizarre experiences.

My abiding interest in the existence of life beyond our five senses has led me – after personally experiencing lots of strange phenomena – to fill in some of the blank spots on the colorful map of the unknown. After a UFO encounter of the first and fifth kind* about 17 years ago, as related in this book, the subject of alien life forms has never let me go. Indeed, it has become more and more a focal point in my life.

The research I have done in the parapsychological institute which I founded has led me to ever more profound and unusual experiments. Together with my gifted wife, Mirabelle, who has often acted as a trance channel for me, I have been able to delve deeply into all sorts of paranormal investigations.

After publishing half a dozen books on the subject of transcommunication, I happened to stumble again on the long-forgotten Roswell case. When the alleged US Alien Autopsy Film was spotlighted in the international media, I could not restrain an urge to help solve the riddle. So Mira, the medium, and I conducted several exploratory sessions to try to get into telepathic contact with the crashed aliens, on the assumption that they have some kind of conscious mind which, from time to time, is materially embodied. It was an enterprise which fortunately worked out far better than we could have anticipated.

Since the information obtained fitted so well with a new interpretation of the goings-on at Roswell in July 1947, and because there had been incessant efforts by the media to discredit and stamp as a fraud the Roswell autopsy footage made public by British film agent Ray Santilli – publishing this document and its conclusions became a must for me.

Although my own solution to the Roswell puzzle is not verifiable, its overall quality speaks for itself. To this day, no one else has been able to explain how all the strange pieces fit together and complete the picture.

These findings were only possible with the help of the medium and our telepathically communicating alien friends whose attempted visit to our planet failed so tragically. It is no exaggeration to describe it as the unfolding of an earthly and cosmic drama, right before our eyes.

* The following classification of sightings has become customary:
a) unknown nightlights, b) daylight sightings, c) radar sightings,
d) encounters of the first kind: close-up confrontations,
e) encounters of the second kind: with physical effects,
f) encounters of the third kind: with observations of crew members,
g) encounters of the fourth kind: with abduction,
h) encounters of the fifth kind: with telepathic contact.

Nonetheless I would suggest that readers regard it as a means of providing a variety of possible answers to the following puzzling questions: How many discs and aliens came down during that hot summer 50 years ago?

If there was only one UFO, how could it have created three crash sites? Why did the autopsy aliens have no navels and look so much alike? Why, after five decades, is the US government still hiding the truth from the public despite the clear evidence revealed by dozens of documents?

Is there a powerful secret group running the land of unlimited opportunity, apart from the President?

If your own and other conventional answers prove unsatisfactory, I would ask you to at least take our unique unravelling of the riddle into consideration. But be aware of the consequences because, as astonishing as my solutions are, they might force you to change your entire system of beliefs. Whatever your thoughts on the matter are, you will have to face the fact that so-called UFOs, which might more accurately be described as lightships, and the beings piloting them, have played an interesting part in our ancient history and will play a major part in the future of our planet Earth.

On the threshold of the third millennium, one should strive for an informed and aware viewpoint of the silver disc phenomenon which, at its core, is a spiritual one. Whatever its individual purpose might be, its overall one is to make us more aware of what it means to live consciously on our small blue planet, a tiny speck in the myriad systems revolving in eternity.

That said, I would like to invite you to immerse yourself in one of the most fascinating events of the 20th century, this top secret mega X-file which, according the US Air Force, doesn't exist, even though the circumstantial evidence is overwhelming. Despite all the disinformation and cover-up attempts, it is to be hoped that »Roswell« will mark a turning point in UFO policy at some point in the future. I am sure that most of the more advanced aliens focusing their attention on planet Earth are pleased to see that people are becoming increasingly willing to overcome their resistance to shaking hands with friends from other worlds, times and dimensions – no matter how far they have travelled.

After 50 years, during which the majority of the world's citizens have been arrogantly patronized by an exclusive group of military-minded power people, the facts can no longer be swept under the carpet. Human beings are mature enough to cope with the truth.

If you agree with this sentiment, many like-minded people would be grateful if you would sign the International Roswell Declaration. You will find a coupon at the end of the book.

Gmunden am Traunsee,
March 1997   *René Coudris*

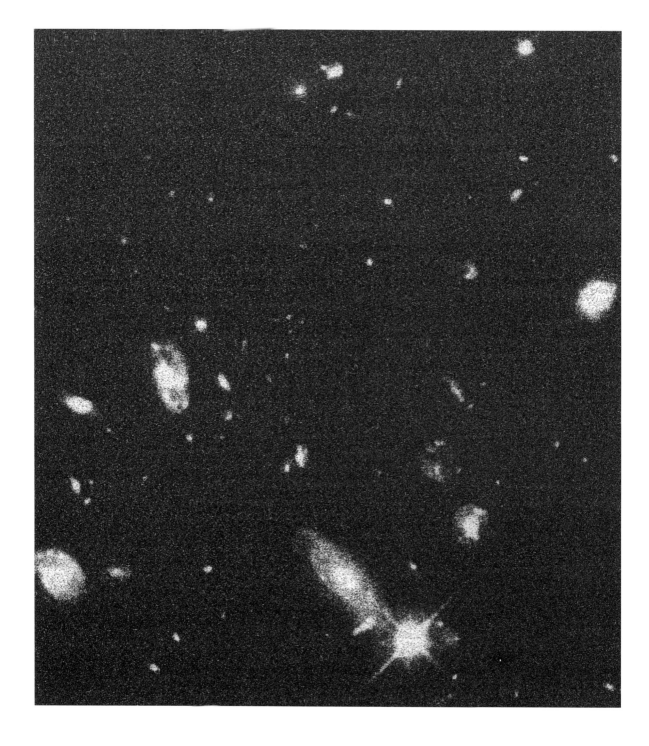

Worlds Upon Worlds All Around Us

Fascinating Heavens

On any clear and starry night, the heavens fascinate us anew. Since the beginning of time, they have posed countless questions to some of us and struck others dumb with awe at their infiniteness. Still others find themselves touched almost with a kind of longing for an eternal home.

Lie back on the grass on a summer night, hands folded behind your head. Allow yourself to slip off into that panorama of star-studded darkness, extending out towards distant worlds without limit. Almost 8000 suns are said to be visible to the naked eye, though what interests most of us more are the mysterious depths lying beyond even those heavenly bodies.

This much is known with relative accuracy today: in our Milky Way alone, more than 100 billion life-giving spheres of light describe individual paths in orbits we can see illuminated in very long photographic exposures. How many of these cosmic power cells gaze down on other forms of life in their own flock of planets? According to latest research, as many as every 24th star might possibly be surrounded by its own population of orbiting spheres. That amounts to an estimated 60 billion sun offspring, of which ten per cent could be similar to Earth – that is, moist and of temperate climate. Based on these figures, our immediate vicinity – from a cosmic point of view – must be positively teeming with alien life forms; not to mention all the possible forms of lively intelligence in parts of the universe quite unknown to us. We don't even today have any idea how far the cosmos extends.

Bearing in mind these unfathomable numbers, for someone to argue that there is definitely no life »out there« just demonstrates infinite stupidity and worldly ignorance. To begin with, the enormous, unimaginable depths and distances of outer space have hardly been calculated or explored by our scientists. Leaders of orthodox research who, of course, turn up their noses at the very mention of anything extraterrestrial, have to face the fact that they have not yet managed accurately to define the meaning of life or the nature of Nature. And how could they, when they themselves are inside the very thing they are trying to define? As they must know only too well, the only things which can be defined with anything approaching objective accuracy are those observed from outside.

Despite this highly awkward situation for science, the majority of experts, at the end of this century, still wear blinkers and go on defending their position that what's not permitted to exist doesn't!

Neither do the great religions on our planet have much of any relevance to say on the subject of extraterrestrial life. Our spiritual leaders are clearly reluctant to share their hard won positions of power with any sort of intelligence from outer space.

They have chosen to ignore evidence, handed down since the beginnings of humanity, that religion once had to do with »reconnecting oneself to the One/Whole – that is, the Cosmos«.

The inevitable outcome of such a narrow view will be the continuous decline of our churches – and of our politicians. There may be some who have the vision to look beyond the end of their noses but, in the main, these few don't occupy the positions of power, where international lobbies hold sway. Shortsighted profit-guaranteeing projects are much dearer to industry than the development of interplanetary concepts which might establish our position in a much larger, perhaps galactic, community. In financial terms, it is much easier for them to go on supplying their lethal toys to the powerful military in their sandbox wars based on projected stellar dangers.

The only field to have challenged this head-in-the-sand attitude, even if in a rather shallow manner, is the entertainment business. Little green men and their cohorts can be found everywhere one looks, in every imaginable type of entertainment – from children's books and amusing satires to cosmic adventure stories and spine-tingling alien thrillers. Cruel martial ETs, simple, endearing ETs or, less often, highly developed and intelligent ETs are all leaving their imprint on the media these days – though newspapers are generally more driven by the copies sold than any serious investigation of the intergalactic theme. Even the world of advertising has developed its own curiously populated cosmos.

Despite this ET boom of recent decades, one thing is still lacking: an open, serious coming to grips with the subject in the context of our global landscape. It is difficult for extraterrestrials to find a voice on that level, since most countries on Earth are too busy fighting off foreign influences within their own culture to look beyond.

Whoever persists in investigating the subject quickly becomes labelled as a fanatic. Periodic surveys show a huge jump in the number of »UFO believers«. A growing number of those who have an inkling and even those who know from personal experience are beginning to stand their ground against the ivory tower leaders of the church, government and big business. But even today, extraterrestrial fans haven't got it easy, since almost all the available evidence consists of eyewitness accounts of hardly verifiable sightings or subjective perceptions which often share only one characteristic: resistance to the traditional order. Even psychiatry which does its level best to march in step with the powers-that-be, has a hard time defining and/or dismissing cosmic creatures, as was demonstrated by a series of recent studies by a Harvard professor about abductions by extraterrestrials. When his affirmative conclusions were published, they remained at the top of best-seller lists for weeks in the US.*

To write a book like that one or the one you are now holding in your hand continues to mean risking one's entire credibility in the community. However, compared with established university professors, we para-experimenters have little to lose. I speak from experience, having exposed myself and my wife to public ridicule for years, albeit on a smaller scale.

Ever since the publication first of our sensitive conversations with our unborn son and then our trance dialogs with »Carl Jung«,** most people have dubbed us irrational. Our recently published survey in the discarnate realms which, according to »Jung« are simply an aspect of human unconsciousness, really took the biscuit as far as the orthodox were concerned. Based on two dozen trance interviews with celebrities who had passed on, we were able to illuminate, among other things, what the individual experience of death is like, as seen from the other side, as well as the subtle causes of what have become known as out-of-body experiences. This is a subject which also has a certain relevance to the extraterrestrial theme.

* John E. Mack, see bibliography.   ** see author's books, p. 218

It is no coincidence that most reported ET encounters take place in a more or less dreamlike state. There is much more going on in our own subconscious, unconscious and super-consciousness than science, a hundred years after Freud, dreams of. There are good reasons that many contact experiences can only be lifted to conscious level by hypnotic regression. If your everyday consciousness doesn't like being thrown off track by unknown things, the same applies to our over-rational science.

Our not having received any form of official support during our many years of work in this field shows, incidentally, just how difficult it still is to conduct alternative research in such areas.

The fact that we have not yet been able to discover animated life on Mars or Venus or anywhere else – at least not officially – does not mean that we are alone in the cosmos. Besides, certain intelligently placed signs on the red planet and elsewhere indicate that there may have been life here and there at least once before. The small-minded idea that the apparently deserted emptiness of outer space is filled with nothing but solitary heaps of floating, lifeless matter can safely be thrown into the dustbin of history as a caricature of homocentric claims to omnipotence.

Even the American space agency NASA recently declared research into extraterrestrial life as one of its most important tasks in the coming century; though this was merely in order to assure its own future existence. Billions of dollars have already gone down the drain on its amateurish, high-tech project to track down intelligent radio signals (SETI) as if higher forms of life felt any necessity, billions of years ago, to constantly send out signals »Here we are«.

Unfortunately it doesn't occur to NASA chiefs that extraterrestrial intelligence might not limit itself to our rough-hewn radio frequencies, or that aliens do not seek contact with us with a fanfare of trumpets. Just because the possible fact of extraterrestrial life could shake up a lot of social structures is not sufficient reason to make it taboo.

In Geneva, for example, astronomers have quite recently succeeded in at least indirectly extrapolating from the movements of the 45 light years-distant sun Pegasus 51 the existence of a single planet (of about 1000° C) beyond the bounds of our solar system. The ecstatic front page story about it in the distinguished German news weekly »Der Spiegel« is marked by such embarrassingly superficial commentaries that one could cry...and if it weren't all in vain, one would feel called upon to retort with a dozen books. Tied and bound by scientific dogma, many people can no longer see the forest for the trees. Most scientists find it exceedingly hard to admit that, despite all the knowledge we have accumulated, we still haven't the slightest notion of the origins of the universe and that reality recognized or acknowledged by science is not reality itself, but only the best possible picture drawn from it hitherto. It is at least admitted that no more than one per cent of the radiating celestial bodies of the universe have been discovered; and that what we see is nothing more than a reflection of the far distant past. What all these galaxies look like today, no one knows. Even the Big Bang theory, the rate of expansion of the universe and thus, its presumed age have already been put into enormous doubt by the latest information from the Hubble telescope. Moreover, the history of human perceptions shows us again and again that what we term true today will show itself as a thin crust of ice tomorrow. What was it Newton said 300 years ago: *What we know is a tiny drop, what we don't know, a great ocean.*

The deeper we dip into the reaches of space, the more we begin to recognize that countless secrets still slumber there. If, for purposes of comparison, we take the number of species of fauna in Earth's tropical rain forests which are also still more or less unknown to us, and project them as a kind of microcosmos onto the starry roof, we begin to get an idea what richess of variations in cosmic life forms the still undiscovered universe may yet offer us. If the rule that the macrocosm is a mirror of the microcosm is applied to psychic worlds, then new vistas open up. For example, something like time travel could be recognized as comparatively easy. That is the point at which the question arises whether, where and when the development of the creative potential of the human being – provided we don't annihilate ourselves beforehand – will end.

What does it mean to be human? Where is the seat of intelligence? What constitutes time? What do the stories, legends and depictions handed down to us from many different cultures about gods coming down from heaven really mean? And finally, what about all these sightings we hear about today, which are then tersely termed UFOs and X-filed away in the records? The spirit of the time is ready to dare to have a go at these enigmas, even if it is with the help of extraterrestrial intelligence.

Thus, this book is not a matter of hauling out the already well-known facts surrounding the Roswell case just once more. They but serve as the prerequisite backdrop for our transcommunicative experiences. Whoever wants to delve deeper into historic details and get to know individual researches in detail should turn to the special UFO literature referred to in part in the appendix of this book.

Despite the fact that all the experiments and thought processes shared in this book are necessarily subjective, they strike me as valuable enough to present to a larger audience. If the sceptical reader can at least agree with this premise by the end of the book, its purpose – to help the reader toward an enriched personal vision of life – will have been more than fulfilled.

We mustn't forget that the tree of knowledge is a constantly growing spiritual-organic creation. Like the reality which it mirrors, it is continually evolving.

Gmunden am Traunsee,
October 1996   *René Coudris*

PS: In 1996 several scientific events were made public: at the CERN atomic particle center in Geneva, Switzerland, a German physicist succeeded in producing for a few short moments the world's first anti-matter atoms. In thirty billionths of a second, the anti-world was proven to exist. The implications of this breakthrough cannot yet be calculated. If it should really turn out that anti-matter behaves differently from normal matter in Earth's gravitational field, long recognized principles of physics would start to totter.

American astronomers have (mathematically) sighted more planets in distant solar systems. A mere 35 light years away even earthlike life forms are possible. On one of the two calculated planets, each of which is larger than Jupiter, a mean surface temperature of 85° C is supposed to reign. The existence of water and other organic compounds appears highly probable. Thus, at their polar caps, even we might just manage to survive. As a result, the claim that there is no life possible as we know it anywhere else in the universe has had to give way to more advanced knowledge....

Welcome to the Genetic Age

Fierce discussions are now raging in almost every country in the world about the wisdom of genetic technology. The collusion between our scientists and the new biotechnology industry becomes even more transparent through the messages of the Roswell aliens. The shocking truth is that our present genetic meddling could well drag mankind into far deeper crisis than it is at present.

Unless we start reorienting towards a holistic world-view, a genetic catastrophe is inevitable. As long as it is possible for commercial interests to take over genetic tools, the situation could get out of hand, and all the more dangerously should criminal elements try to develop molecular biology as a weapon. The few medical benefits that could be derived from it are disproportionate to the increased risks latent in genetic technology.

At present no controls exist to prevent the unwitting transfer of artificial components from genetically altered plants entering the human DNA chain. As breakthroughs continue to be made in genetic cloning of animals, human cloning will inevitably follow, in spite of the fact that some governments theoretically prohibit it.

The crucial area to research is that of the interaction in the human body of the psyche and the genetic structure, where there lurk unknown dangers.

Molecular biology already has a rudimentary knowledge of how to intervene at the core of the human organism and mass produce the cells, but it does not have the remotest idea of the consequences. The Roswell aliens, speaking from their own experience, sound a clear warning to us:

Genetic technology combined with nuclear energy could – through an unforeseen biogenetic-radiological chain reaction – lead us into an evolutionary dead-end, out of which we may not be able to find our way for eons to come!

If you recognise that the future of our species is seriously threatened by our entry into the genetic age, you ought to demand that our so-called democratic institutions take a closer look at how this question will affect future generations. Only when a sufficiently large number of countries become aware of the dangers can safeguards be put in place to avoid catastrophe.

If we try to improve on Nature in our evolutionary direction, it will have the last word, having been at this game a lot longer than we have.

Scenario I: The Roswell UFO Crash

A Silvery Find

It goes without saying that tracking down the objective truth about something that happened fifty years before isn't easy. Most of the firsthand information has already been passed on from one generation to the next, to the extent that cogent details have been passed on at all. Rumors, memory gaps, dressing up what one knew with attractive additions, as well as intentional smoke screens have all played a part in the many attempted reconstructions of the events. The confusion surrounding this mystery is even greater today because contradictory evidence and testimony seem to point to two, or even three, UFO crashes in the vicinity of Roswell.

In the following reconstruction of the events, I stick primarily to the researches of the following people: nuclear physicist Stanton T. Friedman; science writer Don Berliner; private researchers Charles Berlitz and William L. Moore; retired Air Force Captain Kevin D. Randle and Donald R. Schmitt of the Chicago Center for UFO Studies; the towering figure of UFO research, Leonard H. Stringfield, and certain other sources named in the appendix. The details of these accounts unfortunately differ so vastly that it is, at times, unnerving. The handed down and reconstructed chronicles, on the other hand, bear sufficient resemblance to one another that it would seem logical to begin by relating in chronological sequence the common ground contained in these overlapping versions.

All this has to be prefaced by another incident. Throughout the summer of 1947, there was a continuous wave of UFO sightings which simply would not let up. It all began only a week before the crash in Roswell. On June 24, recovery pilot Kenneth Arnold, on a search mission for a missing plane in the area between Mount Rainier and the Cascade Mountains in Washington, sighted an airborne flotilla of illuminated objects which, after having »flashed« at him, attempted to pursue him for a short time. Local newspapers got wind of it and interviewed Arnold, who described the remarkable discs as »flying saucers«. The press picked up the phrase, and it soon became entrenched in everyday vocabulary around the world. It just fanned the flames of UFO sightings when a newspaper subsequently offered a reward of $3000 for any hard and fast proof of such craft. Of these increased sightings, the Roswell incident is but the tip of the iceberg. Nonetheless, »Roswell« has long been the most controversial symbol of this phenomenon; it is both the holy grail and El Dorado of Ufologists, bringing forth strong emotions from both skeptics and believers.

According to documented eyewitness accounts and in many cases sworn affidavits in what appear to be serious publications, the infamous Roswell crash, mother of all UFO dramas, in all probability happened and entered the annals of our contact with extraterrestrial civilizations in the following way. (Any information showing a great disparity from mainstream data is put in parentheses.):

July 2, 1947, Wednesday

It was about 10:00 pm local time (according to others, in the early morning hours of July 2 or not until July 4). Darkness had fallen. In the area around Corona, about 70 miles northwest of the army base town of Roswell, there was a tremendous thunderstorm right at the time of the full moon. William W. »Mac« Brazel (48), sheepbreeder and old-style Western cowboy who at the time was leasing the Foster Ranch heard (according to other testimony together with his children) a loud noise, as if from an explosion, clearly distinguishable from a clap of thunder (the loud noise was also allegedly heard by the neighboring Proctor family, who at the time lived ten miles away in an equally simple ranch house). This short, unusual sound right in the middle of a raging thunderstorm disquieted the farmer only briefly, he was more worried about the well-being of his sheep.

At about 9:50 pm, right at the time of the mysterious bang, iron salesman Dan Wilmot and his wife observed from the veranda of their house in Roswell for a period of about 40 seconds a large, fiery, oval object flying at high speed and low altitude in the direction of Corona. In addition to this, 13-year old rancher's son William Woody observed, together with his father, a brightly shining white object with a flaming red tail from a spot southwest of the city; it was also moving in a northerly direction.

Two nuns from Roswell's Saint Mary's Hospital also observed something extraordinary: about 11:00 pm, a brightly shining object crashed to Earth in an arc to the north of them. The sisters assumed an airplane has gone down and proceeded to pray for the souls of those who had lost their lives.

Corporal E. L. Pyles first thought he had observed a shooting star of unusual brightness. But the object maintained a constant glow and approached the Earth much too slowly for a meteorite. It was, moreover, wrapped in an orange-colored light.

On Air Force radar screens in Roswell, Kirtland, White Sands and Alamogordo, military personnel (Steve McKenzie, alias F. J. Kaufmann, among others) sighted an object several times. Its radar blip first began to flutter, then seemed to somehow inflate. Then at 11:27 pm it suddenly disappeared from the screen in a flash of light. »The thing has landed or crashed«, one of the military observers cursed, »if only I knew exactly where«. Hectically, the military tried to locate the precise point of the possible crash (these events were recorded differently as having taken place on July 1 and July 4). At several military bases along the west coast, jet fighters were placed on alert, just in case more unknown aircraft should appear.

July 3, 1947, Thursday

At dawn, a worried Mac Brazel was in the saddle, accompanied by »Dee« Proctor, the 7-year old son of his neighbor, heading out over the grazing pastures near Corona to find out if the previous night's storm had caused any damage and whether his sheep were all right. Instead of storm damage, he found a field full of silvery fragments of what appeared to be a kind of metallic foil, »out of a material you could crush, and when you let it go, it would spring back to its original shape«. In the damp sand he also discovered strange, long fibers and several lightweight pieces of metal, in their own little self-made craters, where rainwater had already collected. Then he detected »little rods as if made of balsa wood, but which couldn't be cut with a knife or burned, with lavender symbols on them that weren't Japanese, more like petroglyphs of old American Indian tribes«. Accounts of the size of this field of wreckage differ widely today, from 100 x 400 yards to 90 x 1200 yards. When Brazel brought young Dee back to his parents, Floyd and Loretta Proctor both advised him to report the mysterious discovery to the authorities. The farmer drove his truck back to the scene and discovered on the north side of the field a furrow about 130 yards long and 8 in. deep. At the end of this apparent point of ground contact of some flying object, he found the largest piece of wreckage yet: more than 9 feet long (probably also of the same metal-like foil). Brazel loaded some of the glittering wreckage onto his truck and hid it in the sheep pen next to his property.

On the same morning, two Indian boys were out riding on a pony from the nearby Apache reservation in the direction of the Catholic Missionary School, when they discovered the wreck – probably the very first ones to do so. At first they thought it was an airplane that has crashed with all its passengers. They told Father Fox (investigations failed to find anyone by that name, only a red-haired Father Brown, who might have been nicknamed »Fox« for that reason), director of the Mission, who departed at once for the scene. Allegedly he quickly administered the sacrament of Extreme Unction to the dying UFOnauts before calling Kirtland Air Force Base near Albuquerque (this information is from Air Force Lt. Col. Wendelle C. Stevens).

July 4, 1947, Friday

Because of Independence Day, which conveniently fell on a Friday in 1947, enabling people to take a three-day weekend, ›Mac‹ Brazel postponed handing over his find to the Sheriff in Roswell. Since he didn't have a telephone, he couldn't even report it orally, so he simply left the silvery pieces of wreckage for the time being in his storage shed across from the ranch house. Interestingly, the sheep refused to cross the field covered with foil fragments, despite their thirst, forcing Brazel to load the confused animals onto his truck and bring them to the watering spot.

July 5, 1947, Saturday

In the morning, an archaeological excavation group led by Dr. W. Curry Holden of Texas Tech University approached the actual spot of the crash, about 45 miles north of Roswell, without having any idea of what had happened. The group, which was looking for pre-Columbian pottery, coincidentally stumbled onto the wreck. The students stared uncomprehendingly at the horrible motionless scene in the hot morning sun. The director of this group couldn't be tracked down by Roswell researchers until much later, when he was 96 years old. He then said, looking back on his experience, that it looked »like a crashed airplane without wings«, oval, »but with a pronounced rump«, and a diameter of little more than 30 ft. At the scene, they then spotted three lifeless bodies, two lying outside the wreck, the third visible inside through a hole in the wreckage. Allegedly, Prof. Holden then sent a student to report the incident to the fire department and the sheriff. In the meantime, the Army had overnight apparently pinpointed the spot of the crash, which was repeatedly sighted by radar. According to Holden, a military security team, upon arrival at the crash site, threatened him and his group, forced them to »look the other way« and escorted them away from the area like civilian disturbers of the peace. All this took place at a decidedly different spot from the one sheepbreeder Brazel originally referred to.

Intelligence Officer Frank J. Kaufmann was only now notified of the »floating« radar signals from July 2nd to 3rd. Stationed in Roswell and authorized at the highest level, he belonged to a special forces group. About 5:30 pm, two Army vehicles bearing Officer Kaufmann and his men turned off US 285 about 40 miles north of Roswell onto an old ranch road. The sight which greeted them was overwhelming: »The spaceship was split in two and lay in a crater it had created with its crash at the foot of a cliff. *Four corpses lay about, a fifth creature seemed to still be alive. They wore skin-tight, one-piece silvery uniforms and a kind of belt. They looked like human beings – but with more perfect proportions, larger heads and eyes, small noses, ears and mouths and completely without hair. The bodies were slender and pale.«* Medics, military police and necessary equipment for a recovery operation were ordered via walkie-talkie. (Kaufmann's account has to be taken with a grain of salt, since later statements changed significantly in all details and were riddled with contradictions.)

Campers James Ragsdale and Trudy Truelove were also in the vicinity and almost bumped right into the military. According to Ragsdale, the wreck was only partially visible, most of it being hung up on a steep precipice. *»Lying around everywhere were parts and fragments, more or less torn apart. I picked up a piece of the crushed stuff and it smoothed itself out again all by itself. There were also these bodies, lifeless and stiff. They looked like midgets, about 4 feet 8 inches tall at the most.«* When they spotted the approaching military convoy, the two eyewitnesses, stricken with panic, quickly left the area before they were noticed. (A recent version claims that the campers even heard and saw the crash, then tracked it down during the stormy night.)

Not until 1975 did a female archaeologist dying of cancer at St. Petersburg Community Hospital reveal to nurse Mary Ann Gardner the carefully guarded secret which she had kept to herself all through the years. She had *»gone on a mountain hike with a group and as they climbed down a hill, they found a big, round, shiny thing. Next to it was a tarpaulin which was covering something. When one of the hikers pulled the cover aside, there were little people lying underneath, with large heads and big eyes«.* Although the nurse was instructed to tell no one, since *»the government can find you anywhere«,* after seeing the NBC TV series »Unsolved Mysteries« about Roswell, she phoned the station and related her experience.

Grady L. Barnett, a field engineer working for the land protection agency of the government, was involved in some work in the desert at the time in question (to be specific, on the San Augustine Plateau, he said) when he noticed a bright reflection of light, as if from a metallic object. He, too, ran into the wreck and saw *»four creatures, clothed in a tight, silvery suit all the way to their hands and bald, pear-shaped heads, and a metallic object, a kind of disc, stainless steel, about 10 yards in diameter, torn apart«.* He, too, was put under enormous pressure by the military to leave the area at once and forget everything he had seen. Brady told his boss anyway, who just laughed at him, whereupon the witness kept his secret to himself for decades. He merely told a friend *»it is a national secret«.* A few weeks before his death, Barney Barnett told his neighbor he probably got cancer from getting too close to the strange wreck and its dead crew.

That evening, Brazel drove to Corona, the nearest town, to pick up some needed supplies. In a bar, he met some friends and told them what had happened. His listeners were also of the opinion that this stuff could be from a UFO and that he should bring his findings to the attention of the authorities right away. He took their advice seriously and proceeded to get himself and his truck ready for the trip to Roswell, 75 miles away, the next morning.

July 6, 1947, Sunday

In the early morning, rancher Mac Brazel took off with some of the pieces of wreckage (a different source claims he also took his children along) to report to Roswell. He arrived at the Office of the

Sheriff at about 11:00 am and told Sheriff George Wilcox his story. As proof, he showed him (and also the sheriff's wife and daughter, who were present) some of the foil and other pieces of wreckage. The sheriff thereupon sent two of his deputies to the Foster Ranch. They found no wreckage, but »*a large, round surface on the ground where the sand has turned to a vaporized black glaze*«. While Brazel was still talking to Wilcox about what he had seen, they were interrupted by the regular Sunday phone call from radio reporter Frank Joyce of Station KGFL, to inquire of the sheriff about any local news. The journalist absorbed the news and immediately took the bull by the horns, interviewed Brazel on the spot on the phone and broadcasted the first report of the incident on his radio station. (According to Joyce, he advised the farmer to call up the Roswell Army Air Field, which Brazel then did. He was put through to Security Officer Major Jesse A. Marcel.)

According to other stories handed down over the years, Sheriff Wilcox himself called the Air Field headquarters of the 509th Bomber Squadron, the only nuclear bomber unit in the US at the time. (It is possible he also telephoned the fire department.) Major Marcel then drove the short distance to the Sheriff's Office at about 1:00 pm, examined the foil fragments and was amazed at their looks, especially the way they behaved when compressed. He reported immediately to his commanding officer, Colonel William »Butch« Blanchard, a whole field covered with such tiny pieces of stuff possessing the strange capacity to resist all crushing and wrinkling.

Just a short time afterward, Jesse Marcel, Colonel Blanchard and counterintelligence officer Sheridan Cavitt all arrived once again at the sheriff's office. Together, they assiduously examined the rancher's findings. The material seemed so utterly strange to the commander that he ordered the other two men to drive out to the farm and have a look for themselves. Later on, these uncovered fragments were described by Bessie Brazel, the then 14-year old daughter of the farmer, as part »*heavily waxed paper and part very lightweight metal foil. Some of the pieces had a kind of number or letter on them that no one could identify. They were all in a row like addition. On other pieces there was a kind of sticky tape that had a flowery pattern you could see if you held it up to the light, but couldn't be peeled away from the foil.*«

Another version has it that Major Marcel immediately brought the foil-like material back to the base and received orders from Colonel Blanchard to drive out to the Foster Ranch with Captain Cavitt and Brazel. Blanchard then informed his superior officer, Brigadier General Roger Ramey, Eighth Air Force commander in Fort Worth, of the discovery, and he in turn passed on the report to the Pentagon without delay. Around 3:00 pm General Ramey's staff officer, Colonel DuBose, got a call from General Clements McMullen, Deputy Commander of Strategic Air Command (SAC), ordering him to have the confiscated scrap material promptly flown in courier pouches via Fort Worth to Andrews Air Field near Washington, from where it was to be brought personally to McMullen. According to DuBose, the foil, after further orders, ultimately landed on the desk of Brigadier General Benjamin Chidlaw at Wright Army Air Field in Dayton, Ohio.

After several hours driving in two cars over bumpy, dusty desert roads across the vast countryside, Major Marcel, Officer Cavitt and rancher Brazel arrived in the late evening at the Foster Ranch where they spent the night in sleeping bags. Marcel examined the wreckage parts stored in Brazel's shed with a geiger counter: no radioactivity was registered.

Around 5:00 pm the same day, without Marcel's or Cavitt's knowledge, search helicopters received orders from the Pentagon to inspect the field of wreckage from the air (according to other statements, Brazel was also on board one of these reconnaissance flights to help the military locate the spot). At about 7:00 pm they found what they were looking for: about 2 - 3 miles from the foil area (about 37 miles from the Army base) they caught sight of the wreck and of several crew members catapulted from the vehicle. Soon afterwards troops were called up to cordon off the area. A recovery operation was ordered for the following morning.

After the hapless explorations of his two deputies, Sheriff Wilcox decided to go and look at the field of discovery himself. He claimed to have personally located »wreckage and four space creatures«, of whom one appeared to be still alive, in the vicinity of the crash scene. The beings had »large heads with slanted eyes and wore silvery suits«, his widow Inez Wilcox told her granddaughter, Barbara Dugger, years later. »At the time it all happened, military police came to the Sheriff's Office and said they would kill him if he breathed so much as a word about it to anyone, and that went for his family, too. They weren't joking, they meant what they said. Grandpa was pretty done in after that happened, he didn't want to be sheriff anymore.«

July 7, 1947, Monday

Brazel, Marcel and Cavitt departed on horses in the early morning hours to the foil field, which was just a mile and a half from the house. There they found great amounts of the very thin metal. They also discovered some tiny colored rods, about 1/2-inch square, light as balsa wood, very hard, yet flexible, utterly non-flammable, with lavender-colored hieroglyphic-type inscriptions. They also found an extremely strong type of brown parchment paper.

For the next few hours, they went about collecting a large amount of fragments, loading them into Marcel's old Buick and the Army jeep. On the way back, Marcel insisted on showing his eleven-year old son, Jesse Jr., the things they had found, since »it's something he won't forget his whole life«. So sometime during late evening, he stopped in front of his house (according to another account, Cavitt departed earlier or didn't stop), woke his wife Viaud and his son and spread pieces of the collected wreckage out on the kitchen floor. While Marcel's son stared goggle-eyed at the items, his father said, »This is something really special. It doesn't come from this world. I want you to remember this your whole life.« The shiny, tin-colored foil fragments turned out to be non-scratchable, non-bendable and altogether quite indestructible. Not even a sledge-hammer could make a dent in them.

In 1989, J. Marcel Jr., medical doctor and pilot, son of Major Marcel, now living in Helena, Montana, voluntarily submitted to hypnosis, from which state his memories were corroborated. He recognized anew the beige double I-beams with the strange »series of geometric patterns embossed on the inner surface of a fragment«. There even exist signed sketches with the foreign-looking symbols on them, which Marcel Jr. drew from memory. In his opinion, neither the »racks« nor any of the other wreckage could have come from a weather or other type of experimental balloon.

His father, Marcel Sr., also admitted in a video interview shortly before his death that he »as a former pilot was confronted with something completely foreign that had nothing whatever to do with a crashed weather balloon. It was all pretty mysterious«.

Shortly after Major Marcel's report on the wreckage parts found by Brazel and the strange pieces of foil, Colonel Blanchard ordered military police to erect street barriers on all the approach roads. Close to a hundred soldiers were sent to the field of wreckage to form an airtight cordon and pick up every single piece of foil. When the deputy sheriffs turned up a second time, they found their way blocked by the Air Force and declared a prohibited military zone. A bevy of MPs barred the way to all civilians wishing to enter the area. Brazel's neighbor, Bud Payne, and William Woody Sr. and Jr., who also wanted to have a look at the scene, since they had seen »*a huge ray of white light with a red tail gliding slowly toward the west like a shooting star for about 20 to 30 seconds*«, several days earlier, were brought to a halt at the barrier 22 miles north of Roswell on highway 285, and stopped again 10 miles north of there at the intersection with Route 247.

At the main scene of the crash, a scientist in a radiation-proof suit checked again for radioactive contamination for about 15 minutes. Only after the check had proved negative were nine specially trained military men permitted to approach the wreck. Intelligence officer McKenzie (pseudonym for Frank Kaufmann) was one of them. »*We were shocked for a minute and incapable of even moving. We just weren't prepared for the sight. The aircraft had got stuck on a steep slope, initial measurements showed it to be 8 - 10 yards long. There was wreckage everywhere. It was already clear from the start that these were extraterrestrials. They were about 4 feet 8 inches tall, slim and their heads somehow didn't go with the tiny bodies. Their eyes were bigger than human eyes. There were two dead bodies outside the wreck. One lay stretched out on the ground, the other maybe survived the crash and was in crouched position on the ground. Inside the wreck itself, there were three other aliens. One sat on a kind of seat, tipped slightly to the side. Another lay on the floor. Later, another body is supposed to have been discovered inside.*« (This event is dated by others as having happened on July 8.)

At about 1:00 pm Glenn Dennis, 22 at that time, of the local Ballard Morticians, got a call from the Roswell base. He was asked about the »*smallest hermetically sealable coffins that he has in stock...and how long it would take to get them.*« Asked what they were for, the officer answered that these were only for eventualities.

At 1:55 pm, a highly confidential meeting took place in the Pentagon between General Curtis LeMay* and Air Chief of Staff General Hoyt S. Vandenberg concerning »flying saucers«. At the same time, General Nathan F. Twining changed his plans and prepared for an unscheduled trip to New Mexico. Nearly an hour later, the same inquisitive base officer called the mortuary back and asked »*how to prepare corpses that have been lying a long time in the desert, and whether the chemicals used would change the body tissue or blood composition*«. The mortician recommended freezing and offered personal assistance, which was refused. He later found out that large amounts of dry ice had been ordered by the military from the local dairy and already delivered.

In the meantime, the alien bodies were brought in body bags to the Army base, where they were examined by the doctor on duty (Dr. Jesse Johnson?) and declared dead. For the planned dissection, two other doctors were flown in. The unidentified bodies were later brought to a shed in Hangar 84 and kept there overnight under military guard and floodlights.

As Mr. Dennis also ran an accident emergency service, he was called during the afternoon by a soldier who required assistance for a broken nose. After administering first aid, Dennis took him to the Army hospital, arriving just after 5:00 pm. They parked next to an army ambulance, the door of which was wide open. Dennis saw various pieces of metal

* Deputy Chief of Staff for Research and Development of the Army Air Force.

sticking out, »*of which one looked like the rump of a canoe, about one yard long, as if of stainless steel, but reddish, as if it had been exposed to high temperatures. It was covered with a semi-circle of hieroglyphs, resembling the Egyptian ones*« He went into the lounge to drink a coke and met a nurse he knew, who was just emerging from one of the examination rooms. The 23-year old whispered through her mask, »*My God, get out of here, if you don't you'll be in a lot of trouble!*«. A captain who seemed disturbed by Dennis's presence came up. He first told him to stay in the room and then asked two MPs to escort him home. As they left, an Afro-American officer shouted after them, »*We're not finished with that son-of-a-bitch. Bring him back here!*«. He then shouted at Dennis, »*You didn't see anything! There was no crash, or you're in big trouble!*«. Dennis replied boldly, »*Hey, mister, I'm a civilian. You go to hell. You've got nothing on me.*« The officer replied, »*You wanna bet? If you mention anything of this, someone will uncover your bones in the sand.*« Another sergeant is supposed to have added his two cents: »*They would make good food for the dogs. Get him outta here.*«

How much one's own memory can play tricks is shown by two different video interviews I stumbled on by chance, each with an apparently serious Mr. Dennis speaking about the above incident. In the more recent of the two, he relates the incident slightly transformed: this time the robust sergeant shouts, »*Bring the a--hole back here! I'm not finished with him yet!*« This detail demonstrates the blurriness of the facts handed down in the Roswell matter.

One of the two pathologists who were flown in, Dr. Major Sanford and Dr. Major Sullivan, who evidently directed the initial examinations, later gave one of his colleagues some hints about the anatomy of the extraterrestrials. Len Stringfield, for many years a researcher of the Mutual UFO Network, was able to find this man. According to his account, »*the corpses had no hair, and no hair follicles, no fully-formed noses, no upper lips and a mouth slit of only about 1.5 inches. The bones of the upper arm are supposed to have been longer than human ones. Nothing was found which gave any indication of a nutritive system, also no digestive system, no rectal area, no lymph glands and no muscle strands. Instead of blood, nothing but colorless liquid without red blood corpuscles was found.*«

It appears that even the local fire department was called out during the night of the crash, since a fire was reported. Because of the extremely harsh threats of the military, Frankie Rowe, who repressed her personal memories for a long time, now recalls »*that a policeman showed her a rolled piece of metal in the fire station at the time, which she also touched*«. She remembers »*that it spread itself out without any folds, completely smooth, like mercury. The piece was only about 12 inches long, a very thin silvery foil.*« Her father, Dan Dwyer, who together with other local firemen was called out to the »fire«, allegedly saw one of the beings involved in the crash brought, still alive, walking on his own two legs, into the military hospital.

Jack Rodin, son of a professional photographer who was involved in the affair, remembers a talk about Roswell. In very taciturn fashion, his father had repeated several times to him: »*They killed it!*«, and refused to say any more.

July 8, 1947, Tuesday

Marcel met Colonel Blanchard very early, just after 6:00 am, to show him some more recovered wreckage. The Counter Intelligence Corps agent returned to the Foster Ranch with two other CIC men and two military police to look for and remove other parts of the wreck and to keep an eye on Mac

Brazel. A staff meeting was scheduled for 7:30 am in the office of Colonel Blanchard to discuss necessary decisions which were pending.

At about 9:00 am, Sheriff Wilcox visited Glenn Dennis's father, who was a friend of his, and told him: »*It seems your son is in trouble. Tell him that he doesn't know anything and didn't see anything. The Army already asked me your name and your wife's and the names of your other kids.*«

Also at about 9:00 am, Commander Blanchard ordered a bit of damage control to pre empt any further rumors from being born. To distract the public from the discovery of the dead crew, he issued a press release. He personally dictated the following information to his communications officer, Lieutenant Walter G. Haut: »*The many rumors regarding the flying disc became a reality yesterday when the intelligence office of the 509th Bomber Group of the Eighth Air Force, Roswell Army Air Field, was fortunate enough to gain possession of a disc through the cooperation of one of the local ranchers and the Sheriff of Chaves county.*

The flying disc landed on a ranch nearby Roswell sometime last week. Not having phone facilities, the rancher stored the disc until such time as he was able to contact the Sheriff's office, who in turn notified Major Jesse A. Marcel, of the 509th Bomber Group Intelligence office.

Action was immediately taken and the disc was picked up at the rancher's home. It was inspected at the Roswell Army Air Field and subsequently loaned by Major Marcel to higher headquarters.«

Around 11:00 am, this text was distributed personally by Lt. Haut to the nearby radio stations KGFL and KSWS, as well as to the local newspapers »Roswell Daily Record« and »Morning Dispatch«. The former reported the news the same day as its front page story, adding critically, that »*no details with regard to construction of the saucer were divulged*«.

Toward the back of the same edition it is reported that several pilots and the owner of a private airfield near Carrizozo, 5 miles southwest of Brazel's ranch, had observed a similar object at about 10:00 pm the same evening. It later turned out that a number of other inhabitants of the area had also seen and heard something unusual in the sky at the same time.

A little before noon, a very upset nurse called up Glenn Dennis: »*I have to talk to you right away, but first you have to swear that you will never mention my name to anyone.*« Dennis promised and they agreed to meet for lunch at the Officers Club. The girl (described as a small attractive brunette) was an honest, deeply religious woman and said »*nothing horrible like this had ever happened before in her life*«. Two doctors had required her assistance with the initial examination of the dead bodies at the hospital. She saw three bodies, two of them badly mutilated and everyone present got pretty sick from the smell. But her emotions were battered far more. The woman, clearly still in a state of shock, was unable to eat one bite of her food. Glenn later reported, »*she was totally upset and thought she was going crazy and then she drew me a picture of the body and arm of the aliens*«. As far as he is able to recall her description, the hairless beings had deep-set eyes, a small, toothless slit of a mouth and no thumb on their long, thin arms, only four fingers. His girlfriend, about whom Dennis had very serious intentions, also spoke of small concavities on their fingertips, »*a kind of suction cup like an octopus has*«. Their noses hardly protruded at all and consisted of just two tiny holes, also the ears were only noticeable as two little bulges. She saw three bodies, each about four feet tall, two of them quite mutilated.

The doctors had told her: »*We've never seen anything like it. Nothing in our textbooks looks anything at all like this.*« As they began to be afraid the smell might permeate through the whole hospital, the air conditioning was turned off. But that just made it worse for her and the two doctors. In the end, they had to transfer the autopsy to a flight hangar.

Over the next few hours, events came hard and fast, especially after the news had gone out over the ticker tape from the radio station to Associated Press at 2:26 pm and from there, around the world. The telephones at Station KSWS, which broadcast news bulletins every hour, rang continuously. Around 30 different evening newspapers, including the »Chicago Daily News«, »Los Angeles Herald Express« and »San Francisco Examiner«, printed headlines about the incident the very same day. Sheriff Wilcox's office and Roswell Army Base were bombarded with phone calls from Hong Kong, London, Rome, Paris, Hamburg and all over the world. But when news anchorman Frank Joyce, who had already brought the story on Sunday over the local station, telegraphed the report via »Western Union« to »United Press«, he got a call shortly thereafter from Washington. A colonel named Johnson roughly demanded to know where he had got his information. When Joyce named Lt. Haut as his source, the unfriendly colonel hung up without another word. Shortly afterwards, an official call declared to all the local newspapers that the press release about the incident had been an error. The big morning papers »New York Times«, »Washington Post« and »Chicago Tribune« published only the hurriedly fixed-up balloon cover-up story.

What happened behind closed doors during these hours at the Air Force and in the Pentagon can only be guessed at. Every possible scenario, from urging calm, to panic-stricken horror to paranoid espionage and Russian invasion fantasies was played through in minute detail. On the telephone, in telexes, in confidential meetings, those presumably bearing responsibility in such situations – and part of the problem was that it was never really clear just who really had ultimate authority – desperately sought some feasible solution. To understand the atmosphere one has to put oneself in the shoes of the people at that time, when there was far less clarity about UFO matters than there is today. There were literally no scientific researches being carried out, nor were there psychological or sociological studies of how the public might react to such an event, even if they were properly informed. No one had any idea about the technical stage of development one might be confronted with, and from which certain military implications might be deduced. In other words, one was totally in the dark. How, in such a situation, was one supposed to arrive at a tenable solution?

In any case, it was finally agreed to cover up the affair with every method and maneuver at their disposal. The same day, a general military news blackout was declared, and a more or less 48-year long holding action, covering up or veiling everything that had happened, and ordered by the highest authorities, began to take its course.

The Cover-Up

Despite initial efforts to impose a news blackout, news of the day's events spread like wildfire. Local authorities at the scene and citizens from the area all contributed to this. High ranking military at the Pentagon continued to react hysterically. It isn't surprising that all this, taking place during the Cold War, unleashed a certain panic. On the one hand, echoes of unusual flight movements had been sighted over New Mexico on the radar screens for days; on the other, the military was made especially nervous by the nearness of the incident to, of all places, the strictly off-limits White Sands Missile Range testing zone, where, under conditions of strictest secrecy, V2 rockets taken from the Nazis and state-of-the-art military aircraft of every type were being tested. The atomic laboratory of Los Alamos, where two years earlier the first nuclear bomb had been detonated in a test, was also not far away. And, to top it all, the most highly trained, 509th elite squadron was stationed in Roswell.

Despite the increased buzzing of civilians whose curiosity had been piqued, the strictly off-limits military recovery operations now came into full swing. All unauthorized persons in the areas of the crash were immediately identified, severely intimidated, their patriotism appealed to and chased away.

July 8, 1947, Tuesday

Johnny McBoyle, reporter from KSWS radio, drove out to the barriers in order to do a little investigating of his own. At about 4:00 pm, he phoned the secretary at his larger associate station, KOAT, in Albuquerque, and dictated his findings to her. *»A flying saucer crashed near Roswell...I saw it myself, it looks like a beaten up soup pot...some rancher discovered it and the Army is trying to pick up all the pieces...the whole area is hermetically sealed...they're talking of little men on board...«* Lydia Sleppy typed the hot scoop into the telex, but just as the first lines began to go out over the ABC wire to all broadcasting stations in the country, the interrupter rang and the telex came to an abrupt halt. A minute later, the machine began to operate again, but what came out in print was an entirely different report:

»ATTENTION, ALBUQUERQUE, THIS IS THE FBI. END THE REPORT! REPEAT: STOP THE REPORT! MATTER OF NATIONAL SECURITY. AWAIT FURTHER INSTRUCTIONS.«

Lydia asked McBoyle, who was still on the phone, what she ought to do. After a moment's reflection, he said with resignation, *»Forget it! You never heard a thing. Don't talk to anyone about it.«*

At about this time, a plane full of experts and photographers from Washington landed at Roswell Army Air Field. The scene of the crash was carefully mapped by several experts and the whole region simultaneously flown over by small airplanes taking aerial photographs (these events, according to other accounts, took place on July 7).

Sergeant Melvin E. Brown's curiosity got the better of him. Despite strict orders, he couldn't hold himself back from approaching a certain truck. Together with a pal, he awaited a propitious moment, then hoisted the tarpaulin and gazed in upon the dead extraterrestrials. He was obviously severely interrogated and intimidated for this bold act, since it was not until he lay on his death bed that he at long last confessed to his wife, Ada, *»They were small, had big heads, were in suits of shiny material and had yellow-orange colored skin«*. His daughter, Beverly Bean, even heard him talking of his experiences in his sleep. On the day he died, Brown was of clear mind as he spoke of something else: a secret bank account in Roswell into which he had received hush money. However, no trace of either the bank account or the money was ever found.

The order to the soldiers was specific: not even the tiniest fragment from the wreck was to be left behind. Each piece, be it ever so minute, was catalogued, numbered, labelled and packed up. The entire loading operation took no more than six to eight hours. The larger pieces of wreckage were flown to Wright Field in Dayton, Ohio by military pilot Captain Oliver »Pappy« Henderson. Just before departure, he succeeded in stealing a glance at the extraterrestrial corpses which had, in the meantime, been packed in dry ice in Hangar 84. Not until 1982, upon reading a false report in the magazine »Globe« that the ban of secrecy had been lifted from the affair, did he admit to his wife Sappho »having delivered the damaged saucer to Dayton at the time of the incident«.

Towards 3:00 pm, Major Marcel was ordered to Air Force Base Fort Worth, and some pieces of wreckage went with him. Once there he was debriefed by General Roger M. Ramey about what he knew. Ramey led him to the map room for purposes of pinpointing the exact spot of the crash. Marcel subsequently went to the officers club. At a press conference convened at 6:00 pm, then later on local radio, Ramey tersely declared the saucer from Roswell to be the remains of a meteorological measuring device. As proof, he permitted himself to be photographed with the »wreck«, which was not the original brought to him in a crate by Major Marcel, but a genuine, quickly bashed-up weather balloon and a radar search device. A dumbfounded Major Marcel saw with his own eyes how his crash find was passed off to the journalists as a big error.

Both the posed photo set-ups and the »corrected report« by First Sergeant Irving Newton, from the weather station at the Fort Worth base, declaring it to be a normal weather balloon which had crashed to earth, hit the morning papers all over the country the next day. The whole nation found it all highly entertaining...and the Roswell incident had officially never happened. The world returned to its daily routines. Even in Roswell itself, a small town in the middle of a big desert, the waves, after a few more ripples, calmed down and people lost interest in the matter. But although the rush job of poorly-assembled disinformation worked for a while, it couldn't last forever. It was soon destined to cause the next officers in line, promoted to positions of authority, sizeable headaches. Here is a selection of post-earthquake rumblings.

About noon, the editor-in-chief of the »Roswell Morning Dispatch« sent reporter Jason Kellahin and photographer Robin Adair out to Foster Ranch. They found Brazel at about 4:00 pm with his family. He told them »it was a big mistake to tell the authorities. Next time he wouldn't say a thing to them, because it is a bomb.« The newspaper people also bumped into some officers who were still looking for leftover wreckage fragments and strangely enough didn't hinder them from trespassing into the field. (It can be assumed that either the journalists were fibbing or the military had by this time staged a new, phony scene of the crash.) After their return that evening, the reporters tried to interview Sheriff Wilcox, who, however, refused to talk, »because the military forbade him to say anything about the incident«.

At 6:17 pm, the Dallas FBI sent a telex to Director J. Edgar Hoover in Cincinnati that »Major Curtan, Headquarters Eighth Air Force, telephonically advised this office that an object purporting to be a flying disc was recovered near Roswell, New Mexico, this date. The disc is hexagonal in shape and was suspended from a balloon by cable, which balloon was approximately twenty feet in diameter...Disc and balloon being transported to Wright Field by special plane for examination...«. Another telex of that day notes an interesting addendum: »Residents near the ranch on which the disc was found reported seeing a strange blue light several days ago about three o'clock in the morning«.

At 7:30 PM, »Associated Press« interrupted its broadcast about the hijacking of a disc with the dry remark »that the flying saucer of Roswell was nothing but an exploratory balloon«.

Somehow in all the melee at the time, the Army lost track of Mac Brazel. Radio reporter Joyce found him and took him to the house of Walt Whitmore, majority shareholder of Station KGFL, where a new interview was taped and made ready for broadcast.

Farmer Brazel was brought back to the Roswell AAF base, very severely intimidated and forced to relate a completely different version in yet a third interview for Station KGFL with Frank Joyce that same evening, *»if he doesn't want to land in some really big difficulties«*. Following the interview, military personnel waited for him in the lobby of the station and escorted him away. The Proctors observed Brazel on the street with bowed head, being marched off in the custody of two MPs. He was taken to and detained at a »guest house« on the base, interrogated with relentless thoroughness all week long by various military experts and questioned by Prof. LaPaz. Purportedly, Charles Lindbergh, the flying pioneer, also visited Roswell on July 9, 1947.

That evening, Mr. Dennis found the local paper with its article about the recovery of a flying disc in his mailbox. He wanted to call his girlfriend about it next morning, but was told by the base that she was unavailable. The most puzzling thing of all to Dennis was that he was unable to reach his girlfriend by phone for the next three days. Weeks later he found out by chance that she had been transferred to England. A letter he sent to her was returned to him with the notice »Return to Sender – Addressee deceased«. In spite of enormous efforts to find out what had happened to her, he couldn't ascertain anything, and never heard from her again. The rumor made the rounds that she, together with four other nurses, was killed in a plane crash while on maneuvers. In a subsequent interview for the magazine »Omni«, in an article titled »The Chief Witness«, Dennis says her name was Naomi Maria Selff, but this could well be a cover name, since it isn't listed in any military archives. Incidentally, Glenn Dennis, together with retired Lt. Haut, is today the director of the second Roswell UFO Museum.

First Lieutenant Payne Jennings of the 509th Bomb Squadron, who was witness to the whole Roswell enigma, was also killed in a plane crash. Yet another soldier was later found dead a mere 300 yards from the scene of the UFO crash, allegedly run over by his own car. And this was not to be the last sudden death of a Roswell witness.

Also worthy of mention is a certain Army photographer with the pseudonym F. B., who *»in the second week of July 1947 was ordered to a tent at the crash scene in order to photograph four identical alien bodies«.*

All these sightings, observations and other events represent but a small selection of hundreds of eye witness accounts.* The divergent accounts unfortunately permit a great deal of leeway for the wildest speculations, which of course is no help toward an ultimate objective assessment. Nevertheless, despite the many information leaks and the likelihood of some additionally introduced disinformation, more than enough circumstantial evidence remains bearing solid witness to the fact that somewhere outside Roswell something inordinately strange and eerie, or spectacular, or explosive occurred, which, despite all the trouble it caused and continues to cause, has led the United States government to drape a veil of silence over the matter to this day.

According to Stanton T. Friedman, a few representatives of the governments of France, Great Britain, Canada and Germany have been kept fully informed about the crash ever since 1947, with the stipulation of strictest secrecy. To maintain this screen of secrecy has become and will continue to become more and more difficult for the authorities in question, insofar as they are still alive. And their successors will not have it any easier. For the days of darkness and cover-up of this cosmic Watergate, or rather, UFOgate, are numbered...dawn is drawing near.

* All in all, there are by now close to 500 people who had, directly or indirectly, some connection with the Roswell incident.

The Secret Commando

From then on, everything moved with the precision of a military operation. The pressure for secrecy had become so intense that for a time nothing whatever leaked out. Nonetheless, through meticulous detective work and with the collaboration of many UFO researchers, the subsequent course of events was pieced together.

July 9, 1947, Wednesday

Colonel Blanchard visited the crash scene in the morning, personally supervising the wrap-up of the recovery operation. Military police and inspectors flown in from Washington monitored the loading of all the wreckage parts into three C-54 transport planes. Around 3:00 pm the planes took off in the direction of Kirtland Air Base, near Albuquerque, where General Nathan F. Twining had arrived a few hours earlier for the inspection of the recovered materials. General Leslie Groves, Commander of the weapons development project in Los Alamos, NM, and General Montague, Commander of the Army Guided Missile School south of Fort Bliss, NM, took off together for Washington.

The morning papers continued to spread the news of the weather balloon, while UFO parts continued to arrive at the Roswell base, where they were immediately packed into shipping crates. In the presence of a military escort, Brazel, according to instructions, gave his newest version to the »Roswell Daily News« with the next day's headline: »*Harassed Rancher who Located ›Saucer‹ Sorry He Told About It*«. Now, all of a sudden, it appeared that he discovered the wreckage on June 14 with his children and had already found weather balloons twice before!

In a morning phone call from the office of Congressman Clinton Anderson of New Mexico, Walt Whitmore was prohibited from broadcasting the Brazel interview he had recorded the day before. *»We assure you that it is quite possible that your broadcasting license will be revoked if you do.«* Two further phone calls, one from Senator Dennis Chavez personally, followed with similar threats. Station owner Whitmore and his reporter »Jud« Roberts tried to get back to Foster Ranch, but were thwarted by street barriers.

At about 10:00 am, a high ranking intelligence officer, the personal representative of President Harry S. Truman, landed in Roswell. While this was going on, the President met New Mexico Senator Carl Hatch in Washington. Both generals Jimmy Doolittle and Hoyt S. Vandenberg meanwhile discussed the matter with Secretary of Defense Stuart Symington. Shortly thereafter, the discussion continued in the headquarters of General Dwight D. Eisenhower with both Eisenhower and General Lauris Norstad present.

At 12:00 noon, while General Vandenberg was updating the President by phone, the alien bodies in Hangar 84 at the Roswell base were being prepared for transport. Vandenberg and the Defense Secretary met again and stopped in at a hurriedly convened meeting of the Joint Chiefs of Staff at 12:57 pm. A third short crisis meeting was called between General Vandenberg and Secretary Symington.

Sometime during the late afternoon Air Force Brigadier General George F. Schulgen informed the FBI in a telex that the weather balloon declaration was a hoax and that the disc originated neither with the Army nor the Navy. The cooperation of the FBI was requested in the telex, to which the response of its apparently not all-powerful Director, J. Edgar Hoover, was: *»I would do it, but before agreeing to it, we must insist upon full access to discs uncovered* (plural!)*«*.

At the same time, all radio stations and newspaper editorial offices in the vicinity of Roswell were sought out by the military to make sure the hasty press release of the previous day by Lt. Haut was withdrawn entirely.

The extraterrestrial corpses were flown to Fort Worth and Washington on two separate flights. MPs, intelligence men and the mortician from Fort Worth took over the consignment at 6:00 pm. Major Marcel flew straight back to Roswell. A crew member remarked heavily, »*We just made history*«.

July 10, 1947, Thursday

Generals Leslie Groves and Robert M. Montague met Generals Hoyt S. Vandenberg and Curtis LeMay in the Pentagon for a hectic discussion. A meeting with President Truman, General Vandenberg and General Jimmy Doolittle had been scheduled at short notice for 12:15 pm at the White House. While General Nathan F. Twining was on his way to Wright Field from New Mexico, another emergency session between War Secretary Robert P. Patterson and Generals L. Groves and R. M. Montague took place.

July 11, 1947, Friday

The crash scene and the field of wreckage were subjected to a massive clean-up designed to leave behind no trace of what had happened. To the world at large, the event was over. In final instructions, an officer emphasized to all the soldiers participating in the recovery as well as to all the eyewitnesses – addressed in one small group at a time – that this was a matter of national security which, furthermore, fell under the highest classification. After swearing them to secrecy, the officer issued severe threats to them not to speak to anyone about any-

thing they had witnessed; that it was their duty to the country to forget everything they had seen and heard. As a further security measure, a few weeks later all military police in any way involved in the incident were transferred to other bases.

The illegally detained civilian, Mac Brazel, was also warned repeatedly before being permitted to return to his ranch. His immediate neighbors were bewildered to see Brazel, who had never had a penny to spare before, show up in a brand new truck and shortly afterwards purchase a house in Tularosa and a cooling container for his mutton in Las Cruces.

It was initially presumed that the disc was but a tiny part of a large-scale fleet. It goes without saying that the Russians were initially suspected to be behind it all. It was thought they had developed a new type of espionage system, a theory which turned out to be absurd. As only became known in 1952 through Russian double agent Yuri Popov, Stalin had been informed by his KGB operatives in the US within three days of Lt. Haut's press statement that the balloon story was a mere ruse. Stalin ordered his own military secret service to conduct concrete UFO research*, since sightings of unidentified flying objects had also increased in the Soviet Union.

Three Weeks Later

On July 26, 1947, a meeting of the National Security Council was called, something quite unusual in times of peace. To this day, there has been no satisfactory explanation for the convening of this meeting, despite repeated inquiries. At the time, it was

---

* The three specialists called upon, distinguished mathematician Mstislav Keldysh, chemist Alexander Topchiyev and space physicist Sergey Korolyov, all came to the conclusion that »flying saucers are not a threatening alien secret weapon, but a completely realistic phenomenon«.

decided that a whole series of new organizations ought to be established to deal with these secret areas. Even the newly-established CIA, founded under the aegis of Admiral Hillenkoetter and consolidated in the wake of the Roswell incident*, was instructed »to proceed in a program which pursues both scientific and appropriate espionage activities to solve the problem of instantaneous positive recognition of unidentified objects«.

Two Months Later

After things had settled down a bit, the Army had the blackened circular surface in the desert, where the sand had melted, examined and analyzed by the astronomer and meteorite expert Dr. Lincoln LaPaz. The scientist, in the presence of CIC Sergeant Lewis S. Rickett, attempted to calculate both speed and flight path of what he himself concluded to be an »outer planetary object«. Judged by the evidence it left behind, he thought »the unmanned object (a reference to the explorer probe attached to the underside of the disc?) must have briefly bounced on the ground here«.

On September 24, 1947, President Truman established the super secret »Operation MAJESTIC 12«. As only became clear when documents were anonymously brought into play in 1984, its primary purpose was to coordinate the evaluation of the Roswell findings. The genuineness of the identically named anonymous document is, naturally enough, still in dispute, but is accepted by and large as authentic.

Brigadier General Schulgen composed a memo, classified as secret information, dated October 30, 1947, in which he gave Air Force intelligence the assignment of gathering and ordering everything known about »flying saucers«.

* The CIA was formed in 1947 from the CIG, itself an outgrowth of the OSS which was active in World War II. Both directors of the CIG and the first CIA director belonged to the inner core of the secretive MAJIC Group, assigned to the well-concealed investigation of the UFO phenomenon.

Subsequently, the technology became known as »composite or sandwich construction utilising various combinations of metals, metallic foils, plastics... unusual fabrication methods to achieve extreme light weight and structural stability«. This corresponded precisely to the reports of Roswell eyewitnesses and provided confirmation that the Army considered the object to be a »saucer«, and by no means a weather balloon. General Schulgen even emphasized in the end »that it is the opinion in some circles that these objects are in fact interplanetary spaceships«.

Two Years Later

As Secretary of Defense, James Forrestal was too much of an idealist. In spite of his professional obligation to keep the matter secret, he began to talk to congressmen and congressional leaders about the »extraterrestrial problem«. On May 22, 1949, he fell to his death – quite possibly with a little help from federal agents – from the window at a hospital where he was being treated for »depression«.

Sometime in September 1949, Brazel's teenage son Bill talked a little too much at a bar in Corona about the fragments he had found later in his fields. The next day, he was visited by a Captain Armstrong and three other military personnel, who confiscated his little collection of fragments in the interests of national security.

Three Years Later

Unverified rumors were rife that more flying discs had crashed and been recovered. In a telex of March 22, 1950, the FBI informed its director for the first time about something the Air Force had known for a long time: »An investigator for the Air Force stated that three so-called flying saucers had been recovered in

New Mexico. They were described as being circular in shape with raised centers, approximately 50 feet in diameter. Each one was occupied by three bodies of human shape but only 3 feet tall, dressed in metallic cloth of very fine texture. Each body was bandaged in a manner similar to blackout suits used by speed flyers and test pilots.

According to Mr. XXXXX (censored), *an informant, the saucers were found in New Mexico due to the fact that the government has a very high powered radar set-up in that area and it is believed the radar interferes with the controlling mechanism of the saucers.*«

At this moment in time, a cemetery-like quiet began to reign over the Roswell affair and lasted for decades, at least officially, as if nothing had ever happened.

Seven Years Later

Under conditions of strictest secrecy, most of the Roswell wreckage was supposed to have been brought overland to what was then Muroc, today Edwards Air Force Base. Recent incontrovertible evidence has proved that a mysterious, inordinately large shipment was transported via low-bed trailer and crane at the time.

The brief disappearance of President Dwight D. Eisenhower for several hours on February 20, 1954 also points in this direction. On a golfing holiday in Palm Springs, less than 100 miles from Edwards Air Force Base, the President, who was literally under observation around the clock, suddenly disappeared from right under reporters' noses for an entire day. Certain evidence points to his having inspected the UFO wreck and perhaps also the preserved corpses of the crew during this interval. A hastily prepared press release, pasted together after the fact, with the flimsy explanation that Eisenhower had

required emergency treatment at a nearby dentist's never really convinced anyone. The wife of the local dentist the president was supposed to have seen, Dr. Purcell, refused to say anything about the matter even years later, which in the case of such a prominent patient was unusual, to say the least.

15 Years Later

In connection with new technological aircraft sighted by civilians, the name of top secret AREA 51, also referred to as Dreamland, repeatedly comes up. According to accounts of former employees, nine extraterrestrial discs were allegedly stored in a hangar in the S-4 section of this isolated area in the Nevada desert – discs which were occasionally flown by US test pilots. A whole collection of various ET corpses deep-frozen in glass coffins is also said to be kept there. Yet officially, there is no such thing as AREA 51. The name was only seen in print once, on a card destined for President Kennedy, who demonstrably visited this restricted area in 1962.

In the early sixties, Senator (and ex-Governor) Barry Goldwater also tried to gain access to the secrets of Roswell. Goldwater, a general in the reserves, had long been deeply interested in UFO-related matters. On a stopover at Wright-Patterson Base, he went to see his old friend, Curtis LeMay, and asked to be allowed to view the items in storage. The Senator from Arizona was quickly sobered by LeMay's furious response: *»Never ask me about that again!«*

18 Years Later

In June 1978, Leonard Stringfield, an old hand in UFO research, gave a lecture at the annual meeting of the American UFO organization MUFON on *»Recovery Operations of the Third Kind – A Case Study* *of Apparent UFOs and their Occupants in Military Custody«.* He had meticulously investigated and analyzed a whole host of eyewitness accounts and come to the conclusion that the reports ought to have been taken seriously. After press reports on the lecture had appeared, several people in the know from military, intelligence and scientific circles contacted Len Stringfield and, being assured of confidential treatment, eventually handed over additional informational material. The evidence began to accumulate.

31 Years Later

Not until Stanton T. Friedman's evening lecture »Flying Saucers Exist« was promoted in various radio and television interviews in 1978 did the subject of UFOs pick up steam again. He received a hint from a station director that he should talk to Jesse Marcel Sr., who had years earlier seen a disc close up. The next day Friedman called Major Marcel, now retired and living in Houma, Louisiana, who stuck to his account of having been involved in the Foster Ranch crash investigation and even gave a video interview on the subject. The long silence began to crack.

In the interview, many of the facts already related here came to the surface again. One clue led to another, one researcher met another, and ever so slowly over the next eighteen years, a half-dozen well researched non-fiction books on the subject of Roswell were written and published.

34 Years Later

Senator Barry Goldwater, despite his high-ranking position as Chairman of the Senate Committee on Intelligence, gave up trying either to gain access to the so-called »Blue Room« Archives or to inspect the pertinent documents. In a letter to UFO researcher Lee Graham of October 19, 1981, he wrote, *»To tell you the truth...this thing has gotten so highly classified...it is just impossible to get anything on it«.* The fact that not even a man of Goldwater's standing and influence could break through the government's wall of UFO secrecy, gives one ample food for thought.

37 Years Later

Things became exciting once again in 1984, when the film producer Jaime Shandera received anonymously in the mail the mysterious MAJESTIC-12 documents, probably retrieved from disloyal intelligence circles, on negative film. These were materials from which other UFO reporters had been shown excerpts over the years. They included the unconfirmed report of President Eisenhower's UFO briefing of November 18, 1952, in which he was informed of identified and unidentified alien aircraft and the investigations conducted in connection with them by the super secret group known as MAJIC 12.

When more UFO sightings were also reported in Canada, the military attaché at the Canadian Embassy in Washington upon his government's orders managed to find out that »...

a. The matter is the most highly classified subject in the United States Government, rating higher even than the H-bomb.

b. Flying saucers exist.

c. Their ›modus operandi‹ is unknown but concentrated effort is being made by a small group headed by Dr. Vannevar Bush.

d. The entire matter is considered by the United States authorities to be of tremendous significance.«

The MAJESTIC document, written by the first director of the CIA, Admiral Roscoe Hillenkoetter, had the task of initiating the new President into the deepest secrets of that period. The MJ 12 group was set up by President Harry S. Truman in September 1947, on the recommendation of Defense Secretary James Forrestal. This elite team comprised – and apparently still does today – a dozen top scientists and intelligence authorities who were all in key government positions. After first listing the members of the group the strictly classified papers relate the Roswell incident from the first discovery of the wreckage to the examination of the recovered corpses. On page 3, one reads the following:

»On 07 July, 1947, a secret operation was begun to assure recovery of the wreckage of this object for scientific study. During the course of this operation, aerial reconnaissance discovered that four small human-like beings had apparently ejected from the craft at some point before it exploded. These had fallen to earth about two miles east of the wreckage site. All four were dead and badly decomposed due to action by predators and exposure to the elements during the approximately one week time period which had elapsed before their discovery. A special scientific team took charge of removing these bodies for study. (See Attachment »C«.)

The wreckage of the craft was also removed to several different locations. (See Attachment »B«.)

Civilian and military witnesses in the area were debriefed, and news reporters were given the effective cover story that the object had been a misguided weather research balloon.«

It was then admitted that the cryptic signs on the UFO could not be deciphered and that the vehicle was most likely a short-distance exploratory craft from Mars or from another solar system. It was only possible to speculate about the nature of the power unit, since the parts concerned were presumably all destroyed in the crash. The original document then goes on:

»A similar analysis of the four dead occupants was arranged by Dr. Bronk. It was the tentative conclusion of this group (30 November, 1947) that although these creatures are human-like in appearance, the biological and evolutionary processes responsible for their development has apparently been quite different from those observed or postulated in Homo Sapiens. Dr. Bronk's team has suggested the term ›Extraterrestrial Biological Entities‹, or ›EBEs‹, he adopted as the standard term of reference for these creatures until such time as a more definitive designation can be agreed upon.«

Evidently, the beings were looked upon as a kind of bio-robot because of their mongoloid facial features, which appeared so identical to one another that they seemed to have been cast from the same mold. The instructions came to a close with an account of another crash on the Texas-Mexican border and the mention of an emergency plan. Furthermore, it is interesting that investigations into the genuineness of these explosive documents proved that a member of the group of 12, a Dr. Menzel, subsequently wrote letters to John F. Kennedy in which he offered Kennedy certain data kept under lock and key apparently about just such activities of the intelligence agency. Besides the Roswell film which later came to light, the MAJESTIC 12 document, which is today considered by some to be phony, and by others to be genuine, is the most important »proof« that the US government recovered at least one, if not more, UFOs in 1947 and is still desperately trying to get behind the technical/physical power secrets buried in the object, or the remains thereof.[*]

42 Years Later

A scientist who formerly worked in top secret AREA 51 by the name of Robert Lazar, who could no longer bear the psychological pressure and the incessant stress of supervisory control, went public in an

---

[*] Not even the earth invention of the Reichian Orgone energy motor, which is fully operable, albeit disassembled, could be reconstructed.

exclusive TV interview in Las Vegas in 1989, revealing those sparse technical details which could be deciphered and utilized from the recovered UFOs. It goes without saying that he was immediately termed wacky and his information fully discredited.

Another informant who concealed his identity behind the cover name »Falcon« went even further, saying that in the caverns of these ultra-secret areas three living extraterrestrials from the stellar grouping known as Zeta Reticuli collaborated with the US government and that one of them was still doing so. The first cooperative ET was allegedly the one and only survivor of the Roswell crash and was supposed to have died in 1952.

Also from Hangar 18 on Wright-Patterson Air Base, where, according to rumors, archives of UFO fragments were being kept in the »Blue Room«, there was more news:

Norma Gardner, an employee on the base who retired early in 1959, had access to a fair amount of top secret material, it being her responsibility to catalogue and document the recovered artifacts. She once disclosed to close personal friends »that she knew more about government involvement with ›flying saucers‹ than was kosher to some people in high positions«. She also saw »how one day two of the alien corpses preserved in liquid chemicals were transferred from one laboratory to another. They were between 4 and 4 1/2 feet tall and had conspicuously large heads and huge black eyes.« It was Mrs. Gardner, incidentally, who typed autopsy reports for the Army.

A mysterious scientist with the pseudonym of Dr. Cris, to whom materials for testing were given at the time on the pretext that they were Russian space research materials, recognized »foamed metal and metallic materials that demonstrated pyramid-like structures in nanometer regions and were made with technology which certainly did not exist at the time«.

43 Years Later

It was embarrassing for the guardians of silence in the Pentagon when such a leading Establishment figure as General Arthur E. Exon, former commander of the present Wright-Patterson Air Force Base, spoke so frankly in an interview with Roswell investigators Schmitt and Randle in 1990 about what happened at the Wright-Patterson laboratories: »...Everything from chemical analysis, stress tests, compression tests, flexing...they knew they had something new in their hands...the metal and material was unknown to anyone I talked to... the overall consensus was that the pieces were something from space.« General Exon was also certain that the material is still being kept at Wright-Patterson, most likely in the building for alien technology. He also confirmed the establishment of an investigating group comprising those top scientists, CIA directors and intelligence officers (»the MAJIC 12«) who to insiders are sarcastically known as »the Unholy 13« – and included President Truman. Apparently these are the men who gave the troops their orders to do such a thorough job of destroying evidence.

In addition, the man who was flight security officer at the time, Lieutenant Robert J. Shirkey, confirmed, even if rather late, that he was one of the chief witnesses on the base of the loading of the wreckage into the plane: »...approximately five people...carrying parts of the crashed flying saucer...saw pieces of metal: there was one piece that was 18 x 24 inches, brushed stainless steel in color.«

Lieutenant Robert E. Smith, of the 1st Air Transport Unit in Roswell, testified that, among other things, »the largest (wreck) crate was roughly 20 feet long, 4 to 5 feet high and 4 to 5 feet wide. It took up an entire plane...There were a lot of people in plain clothes all over the base...They were ›inspectors‹...When

38

challenged, they...flashed a card, which was different from a military ID card...I'm convinced, that what we loaded was a UFO that got into mechanical problems...«

Intelligence Officer Frank Kaufmann's job was to escort the bodies. He reported that they were first brought to Washington, where they were inspected by President Truman and various generals, before being brought to Wright Field. *»The spaceship seems to have no motor, but to get its power out of a kind of cell. Some of the secrets of the subsequently developed stealth bomber were gained from an analysis of this UFO technology. Modern night vision technology was developed from the analysis of the UFO sight hatch, which consisted of a very unusual prismatic glass.«*

The evaluation of this technology was, in the opinion of Kaufmann, the main reason for the strict secrecy and *»was probably ordered by the control group MAJIC 12. The fact that he had stood eyeball to eyeball with these beings changed his life and moved him inwardly so much that he almost looked upon it as a mystical experience.«*

45 Years Later

Much to the chagrin of the Army, retired Brigadier General Thomas Jefferson DuBose confirmed, voluntarily and candidly, in an affidavit to American UFO researchers in 1991: *»The weather balloon explanation for the material was a cover story to divert the attention of the press.«*

During an intensive pre-investigation in the years 1992-93 for Steven Schiff, present Senator from New Mexico, 25 notarized sworn statements containing explosive information were compiled from important Roswell eyewitnesses who are still alive. As member of the Committee for Control of Government Activities, Senator Schiff, after having been put off brusquely by the Secretary for Defense, ordered an investigation of the Roswell incident by the General Accounting Office, the agency monitoring the finances of Congress. After a year, a disappointing 20-page GAO final report was the only result. The GAO had thereby neatly removed itself from the affair.

All the data collected by the Air Force seemed to be stored in the data processing center of Wright Patterson Base: in 1992, NBC TV reported on its news show »Dateline« that a hacker had gained access to the main Air Force computer. One of the data banks pictured the following: *»WRIGHT PATTERSON AFB/Catalogued UFO part list – an underground facility of Foreign Technology Division«.* The network was protecting the anonymity of the hacker, and no further details about him were forthcoming.

48 Years Later

In its premature official response to the GAO investigation on August 27, 1995, the Air Force stuck to its story of a balloon, though it was now *»experimental balloon no. 4 of the secret MOGUL Project, which was supposed at the time to track down Soviet nuclear bomb tests in the atmosphere«.* They, however, did not provide the slightest proof for this explanation and even refused to produce any documentation. Besides, the Pentagon issued the statement *»that in the nation-wide Air Force UFO research project ›BLUE BOOK‹, with over 12,000 reported UFO sightings, the Roswell one does not appear«.* Almost as an aside, it declared *»that all the files of the MOGUL incident were apparently destroyed, without there ever having been any order to do so«.* This is an unbelievable, downright ridiculous protective mantle. For, if official reports existed, in particular the courier reports between the Roswell elite division and its directors in Washington, this mystery could have been cleared up long ago. Significantly, however, masses of files with humdrum contents are still extant. On top of that, it has since been made public that the MOGUL espionage project was not started until 1949. Thus, there is only one explanation: somebody very high up wished to wipe out all evidence and in doing so became entwined in a large web of sticky contradictions.

The US Army also maneuvered itself into a »cul-de-sac« with its balloon story. In reality a helium-filled balloon such as the one described as having crashed could not have exploded: for the simple reason that helium does not burn. The pieces found by Brazel could only have come from a large-sized object which exploded in the air. Besides, the appearance of weather balloons, of which great numbers were sent up in those days, was something with which many people, civilians and military alike, were familiar. Getting it mixed up with other projectiles was out of the question. It is all too apparent that this, too, was a further attempt to cover up and deceive.

However, the many mysterious military flight movements of July 1947 permit no re-interpretation: here was a concentration of at least nine unusual flights in all, not counting the search planes. On July 6, the first wreckage parts were brought from Roswell to Fort Worth, then on to Washington D. C. On July 8, a group of special agents arrived from Washington. Shortly thereafter, the same plane brought wreckage parts from Roswell to Wright Field (today's Wright-Patterson Air Field Base) and continued the flight with Major Marcel to Fort Worth, Texas. Then, on July 9, just after General Ramey's explanation, three flights full of top secret crates took off for Los Alamos, and then another flight to Fort Worth. On July 10, a last flight in this affair took off from Wright Air Field to an unknown destination. All this activity just to transport a torn weather balloon?

The government offices involved in the cover-up campaign tried to learn swiftly from their mistakes. Documents which came into the hands of investigators show that since the sightings began, special high level US Air Force projects have been initiated aimed at coping better with such situations in the future. For example, the PANDO project (1949-1974) was established to collect and evaluate medical information pertaining to extraterrestrials; Project MOONDUST (since August 12, 1954) includes a detailed list of instructions with regard to the recovery of crash objects and what official channels the information should then be fed into. The task of Project AQUARIUS (since July 16, 1954) is to collect and assess any and all information on UFOs. In project SIGMA (since 1954) forms of communication with extraterrestrials are studied, developed and tried out. In Project REDLIGHT (which goes at least as far back as 1951) crashed and recovered UFOs are disassembled and reconstructed in order to test them in Project SNOWBIRD (since about 1972) flight trials. There was also a series of other relevant secret projects, with code names like SIGN, TWINKLE, GRUDGE and POUNCE, in which so-called »Blue Teams« and »Alpha Teams« were deployed.

At least some of these secret operations will be revealed in the near future, if President Clinton keeps his promise and insists on having the files finally released to the public.

49 Years Later

To the flood of military eye witness accounts that can be taken seriously was now added a document which came into the hands of UFO researcher, Leonard Stringfield. It probably came from General Nathan Twining, MAJESTIC 12 member and chief of technical intelligence of the Air Force. It is dated July 16, 1947 and entitled »*Air Accident Report on ›Flying Disc‹ Aircraft crashed near White Sands Proving Ground*«. It contains a mass of interesting details: »*According to the President's directive of July 9, 1947, a tentative examination of the recovered ›flying saucer‹ and a possible second disc* was conducted by a staff of experts of the AMC** Commando. The cited examinations were carried out by engineers of T-2 and the airplane laboratory of the engineering division T-3. Further data came from scientific personnel of the Jet Propulsion Laboratory at California Institute of Technology and the scientific advisory staff of the Air Force, under the direction of Dr. Theodore von Karman.*«

The investigating team came to the joint conclusion that »*the aircraft recovered by units of the Army Air Force was not manufactured in the US*«. This is supported »*by the lack of any external propulsion system*«. The object could not be identified as a secret German V-weapon. It is also very doubtful that the Russians constructed such a flight instrument, »*due to the complete lack of Identification numbers or Cyrillic instructions*«. According to Dr. Oppenheimer*** and Dr. von Karman, »*an area which was quite possibly atomically propelled was discovered*«. Also the possibility that parts of the craft may themselves constitute a power unit cannot be excluded, since »*there are no movable parts in the central system. This might be the activation of an electrical potential of a heavy water reactor, but that is just a theory at the moment.*

Above this power system, a spheric cockpit about 10 feet in diameter was discovered. The cockpit was surrounded by a series of mechanisms whose functions couldn't *be identified by our engineers. On the underside were four round concavities, cloaked in a softer, not identified material. These symmetric concavities seem to be movable, though it is uncertain how. In any case, their mobility is connected with the dome-shaped upper area. The main propulsion system is possibly a turbine without blades, comparable to what is presently being developed by AMC.*

Another possible theory has been postulated by Dr. August Steinhoff (a ›Paperclip‹-scientist*), Dr. Wernher von Braun** and supported by Dr. Theodore von Karman: the craft could, as it moves through the atmosphere, take on hydrogen by a kind of induction process, thereby generating a nuclear fusion reaction. The air outside the spacecraft would ionize and thus, propel the ship forward. Together with the circular boost during ascent, the ship could thereby attain an unlimited range and speed. That could also explain the lack of any noise, a fact which many witnesses attest to.«

Len Stringfield also documented the report of a sergeant from the Alamogordo base, which states that he was ordered by his commander, Colonel Paul F. Helmlek, in July 1947, to write a report about a crashed aircraft. The soldier was even permitted to see a photo of the disc, which is supposed to have gone down near Tularosa.

The estate of the above mentioned UFO researcher who died at the end of 1994 also brought to light some highly interesting papers on a chemistry professor from Florida. If one can believe the testimony of this lady, whose pseudonym is Edith Simpson, she, as a highly gifted student, got the chance in 1947 to spend the summer as Albert Einstein's assistant.

According to her own words, Einstein was so taken with this promising student that he took her

---

*It is highly probable that this »possible second disc« was one of the UFO-type unmanned probes like that attached to the underside of the main Roswell UFO used for reconnaissance.
** Air Material Command (later ATIC) of air technical intelligence at Wright Field, Ohio.
*** Nuclear physicist and »father of the atom bomb«

* Top-Nazi-V2-ingeneers, who worked furtheron in the USA..
** I had a five-minute channel contact with Wernher von Braun through my wife more than ten years ago, though on a more spiritual than technical level.

everywhere with him. She even accompanied the then 68-year old physicist from Princeton to an urgent crisis meeting with other top scientists and high military personnel at an Air Force base in the US Southwest. She recalled in an interview that the two of them were taken in a military jeep through the desert for about 60 miles to a base where in a heavily guarded hangar the bodies of extraterrestrial creatures were being kept. *Some of the specialists, including my boss, were permitted to get close to the bodies. All five of them looked alike to me. They were about 5 feet tall, hairless and had large heads with unbelievably black eyes. Their skin was grey, with a light green sheen, as far as one could see. Most of their bodies were in skin-tight suits. I heard that they had neither navels nor genitals.*

On one of the extraterrestrials, I saw a bilious, greenish liquid flowing slowly out of the nostrils. As soon as this nasal secretion was exposed to the air, it turned bluish, seemingly indicating something copper or cobalt-based. I wondered whether the being was still alive, but I wasn't close enough to perceive body movements or hear the comments of the doctors".

Mrs. Simpson was also able to see briefly the spacecraft wreck at the other end of the hangar. *It had a concave disc form and filled a quarter of the hangar floor".* She wasn't permitted to go any nearer to the wreck, so couldn't make out any details, merely that it was badly damaged on one side. Armed guards were standing all around and investigating specialists blocked her view of the wreck. *My reaction was half amazement and half curiosity, and maybe a little fear. No one told me any details. Prof. Einstein had full clearance and he wrote a report about it as well, which I never saw. I was merely told to keep my mouth shut".* Asked about Einstein's reaction, his temporary assistant said, *He seemed in no way unsettled when he saw all of it. I didn't make any notes of his responses, but he said*

something to the effect of not being surprised about their having come to earth, and that it gave him reason for hope to learn more about the universe. Such contact would be advantageous for both worlds. In the end, the propulsion system of the disc was what interested him most".* After her summer vacation, Mrs. Simpson, who was then still a student, was visited on campus by a *psychologist* and, unbeknownst to her, apparently interrogated while under snap-hypnosis. Then one day, long after Mrs. Simpson had, herself, become a professor, she was subjected to some highly unusual questioning by government officials. In addition, she was burglarized no fewer than seven times during this period. One can guess at the reasons behind all this.

Even after 50 years, eyewitnesses keep popping up: Don Ecker of *UFO Magazine* almost by chance bumped into an unknown eyewitness named Thomas Gonzales, 78, in the Roswell UFO Enigma Museum recently. The TV series *Roswell*, aired in summer '94, inspired the soldier, who had been stationed at the RAAF base at the time, to come forward. He was one of the men ordered to watch over the UFO wreck and the crew members who had been catapulted out of it. He showed the UFO researcher his military documents and the Roswell base yearbook of 1947 in which his photograph appeared. Gonzalez said that he had had a non-scratchable piece of metal from the UFO lying on his TV set for a long time, until it was lost when he moved house. He also mentioned that he had never been able to cope with the experience and nearly became an alcoholic because of it.

The Open Résumé

There have been many other statements from former military, scientific and civilian circles (authors Schmitt/Randle list 297 eyewitnesses) which unanimously unmask the counter-testimony of the Air Force as preposterous bluff. More detailed materials are on file at various UFO research organisations.

From the many documents which have gradually come to light, it is now beyond any doubt that massive attempts at prevarication and cover-up took place all around the events of July 1947. It is almost certain that something fell out of the sky which did not come from our little world. What major researchers from UFO societies have assembled over the years in countless hours of meticulous exploration, after sorting out facts from disinformation, permits no other conclusion. What's more, the piecing together of the puzzle has been filled in and amplified by fragments of information from people who could not possibly have colluded to produce such similar accounts which were so much at variance with the official one. The number of sworn oaths made under duress, threats and even murders could not prevent the assiduously hidden truth from slowly surfacing, piece by piece. But in spite of all the facts which have been assembled, a great deal remains a mystery. Even hardened skeptics must ask themselves:

• Why were there suddenly so many flight movements outside the normal and official framework, if nothing had happened?

• Why did 60 men drive out into the desert in trucks just to recover a crashed balloon which would easily have fitted into the trunk of a car?

• Why were radioactivity tests conducted on a crashed weather or espionage balloon?

• Why was Mac Brazel taken into custody for a whole week, when he was hardly in a position to say much about a weather or research balloon?*

* Even MOGUL Balloon engineer Charles B. Moore thought in a 1980 interview that anyone coming across the aluminum foil and balsa wood of a crashed measurement balloon would have a tough time getting it mixed up with something alien.

• Why were so many official agencies actively involved in things which officially didn't exist?

• Why did the 12 military police who cordoned off the wreck each receive $10,000 hush money to forget everything if there had been nothing of interest?

• Why were almost all soldiers and MPs who participated in the recovery of bodies and materiel transferred shortly afterwards in all directions of the compass?

• Why did Marcel, Blanchard and other military eyewitness receive such unusually rapid promotions?

• Why have nearly all reports on military movements of that time and the files of nearly all participants disappeared if they contained nothing but hot air on unimportant subjects?

• What was behind the Army's threats of imprisonment, deception, brainwashing, bribery and murder if there was nothing to hide?

• Why does the military even today maintain a policy of concealment and block all investigative efforts with contradictory explanations?

• Does a shadow government fear for the pre eminent role of the US as world policeman and/or its own power through the revelation of the UFO files?

• Is it being kept from us that enemies from the cosmos with little regard for human life have invaded?

• Is this knowledge being withheld because it would shake the foundations of science and religion, because anarchy and chaos could break out, or because the stock market would collapse?

• Would a sweeping revelation of the events erode the illusory security we feel in being sole masters of the world? Would it send tremors through established power and financial structures?

• Would human beings be unable to accept the existence of benevolent or sinister aliens who are possibly more advanced than we are?

• Is the US government trying to protect us from some other horrible knowledge relating to UFOs?

• Or, what is far more likely, are the crude fears of a powerful elite the real reason for protecting us from a hypothetical mass panic?

Certain documents point to Roswell's high level of top-secret classification being based on the fact that the motives of these visitors to Earth are still utterly unknown! Be that as it may, here on the threshold of the 21st century, it is high time for the US government to finally come out with the whole truth. The US owes the whole world an explanation.

Facts are the only things which can put pressure on the authorities. For that reason, batteries of citizens have taken it upon themselves to examine presumed crash sites with metal detectors and similar instruments in search of solid proof. Thus far, the search has been in vain. The only thing left of the Roswell incident is the myth, from which an entire small town is profiting. Two Roswell museums and mountains of kitschy UFO memorabilia draw no small amounts of tourist dollars to the desolate region. Roswell's mayor recently declared July 2 as the official remembrance day of the UFO crash.

To top it all, star emigrant German movie director Roland Emmerich (»Star Gate«) made a UFO movie called »Independence Day« which makes a mockery of the Roswell story. The science-fiction film which hit the movie theaters just in time for the 4th of July '96 holiday in the US (the opening in Europe was a few months later) was, according to the German magazine »Cinema«, based on »*the assumption that the US government is keeping an extraterrestrial spaceship hidden in a subterranean silo which, according to Ufologist research, crashed in the vicinity of the small town of Roswell. The horror begins on July 2nd. That day, huge flying discs appeared above Earth's cities. From the very start, the super-powerful aliens intentions were clearly hostile, as they opened fire without warning.*« Emmerich, who does not believe in UFOs, added this comment: »*My film begins where others leave off,*« and proceeded to describe the destruction of New York. »*The aliens continue their worldwide terror attack, resistance appears pointless. While the President, who is prepared to surrender, orders the evacuation of all the cities, a secret resistance forms. A small group of people led by computer specialist David Martin discovers a weak spot in the extraterrestrials' communication system. The ET battle to destroy Earth is decided on the 4th of July, America's Independence Day.*« Emmerich was probably quite indifferent to the fact that, in portraying this $70 million UFO massacre, with every possible cliché, he has merely stirred up traditional prejudices in the public unconscious.

On a more positive note there are encouraging reports that Steven Spielberg may be planning a 50-million dollar film about the UFO crash and the subsequent political intrigues. So-called »Project X« is said to contain never before seen footage from the crash site. Similar new film productions on »AREA 51« and the SETI Project are also being planned. Hollywood is placing bets on a mixture of reality and illusion which – who knows? – might hopefully increase tolerance of and understanding for extraterrestrial intelligence instead of just fanning fears of them.

To return to the historically documented Roswell reality. Just where in the hinterland of New Mexico was the real location of the incident, whether near Corona, near Socorro, near White Sands, at Tularosa or whether the craft crashed on one of the lonely rocks in the desert or elsewhere* is immate-

---

* From various sources, e.g. German border science »Magazin 2000«, it is being claimed that the precise crash site has been found, even though, 50 years after the fact, this borders on the absurd, since weather influences over the course of decades make it impossible to distinguish between a >>

rial; the fact remains, it was somewhere. Whether the craft first »touched down« and only miles further on actually crashed; which of the reported shapes and forms the UFO really had; exactly how many crew members were on board; the endless circumstantial evidence is by now, despite all discrepancies, overwhelming. However much the files were tampered with, or to what degree the eyewitness accounts contradict each other, it nevertheless happened! An object not originating in our world came to grief in summer 1947 with its entire crew in the desolate spaces of America and was unjustifiably put under lock and key by the US Army.

The question arises, what is the real purpose of the so-called (inter-)national security of the established powers? Is there a paranoid fear that the established order might crumble as soon as the general public realizes that in view of a higher intelligence all our earthly institutions die on irrelevance: These power broker's power world quickly melt away. Let us not forget what sums are involved in military armament. The egos of so-called statesmen, of whole nations are at risk. And the game depends only on the basis of institutional control of the people!

The military are mistaken if they believe the Roswell mystery has been erased through their secret conspiracies and cover-up. We are now in a time in history when no secret is safe and when all that is lodged in the unconscious will come out.* It is still too soon to hope that political and military authorities will see the light and put all the facts on the table.

Nevertheless, we are now approaching a time in which the term »world« will be increasingly understood as something which reaches beyond the boundaries of our solar system. The day is near when »life« will no longer be conceived as anything less than a whole string of pearls in a never-ending row of reincarnations. And you can bet that more spectacular sightings of extraterrestrial objects of unimaginable proportions will be recorded than ever before, and that these won't be swept under the carpet as easily as used to be possible. All this and more will force the subject of Roswell into the spotlight again and again, and will keep it from being forgotten.

When the critical mass has been reached, the gates to this particular truth will be thrown open, one way or another. Open contact with beings from the universe who have advanced beyond us in evolution will no longer be stoppable.

---

sheep watering hole and a crash crater. One also musn't forget that the military went to some effort to make the real crash site unrecognizable. Thus, every crash site found from now on in a desert where everything looks more or less alike, can only have been selected arbitrarily.

* Even the US Air Force investigation »BLUE BOOK« had to attest to the fact that of 3201 unusual aircraft sightings, 21.5% had to be classified as unidentified.

Scenario II: The Roswell-US Army Film

Santilli Ransoms a Film

Ray Santilli of London, together with his partner the present »owner« of the film fragments, has related in various interviews how he came into possession of documentary materials whose evolutionary relevance to the Roswell story has not been properly assessed to this day. He had been involved with the media since leaving school. Beginning with promotion and marketing, he later became a manager of musicians before establishing his own record company. He marketed the exclusive English rights of Disney movie soundtracks going on to specialize in the sale of rights and original recordings, while publishing books on the side. Today, his company, Merlin Group, is active in the sales and distribution of audio, video and literary productions.

In 1993, Santilli was in the States doing research for a music documentary. He was always on the lookout for early unreleased original recordings of singers like Bill Haley, Pat Boone and Elvis Presley. In his searches he met a cameraman who had, in the sixties, worked independently for a number of different agencies. In early 1955, on assignment from Universal News, this cameraman had filmed a string of rock 'n' roll concerts at various American high schools. He had been contracted for this work only because the Universal News camera staff was on strike at the time. He shot film footage which Santilli would be able to use, including some of the King himself, Elvis Presley, in his early years.

Another cameraman by the name of Jack Barnett (this is obviously a pseudonym, so I will refer to him as J. B., since it is possible that the initials are cor-

rect) was at that time a sprightly 80-year-old. He and his wife led a seemingly retiring life in a small house in a suburb of Cleveland, Ohio (or according to other accounts, in Cincinnati). The only thing we can be sure of is that Santilli first came into contact with autopsy film hawker J. B. via an ad that he (Santilli) had placed in a local newspaper in his search for old film material. Santilli paid J. B. in cash several times for his materials, soon establishing a working business association. J. B. liked it when everything was settled without complications or paperwork, freeing him from worrying about the Internal Revenue Service. Then one day at the end of 1993, it so happened that while they were having a couple of drinks together, Santilli casually raised the subject of UFOs.

For Santilli this had long been a subject of fascination, even though he had never paid overly much attention to it. He had merely thought that in the course of his usual business activities he might one day make a documentary on the theme. Reg Presley, a friend of his who played in the former hard rock group, The Troggs, had aroused his interest, having himself been an ardent follower of all the latest news on the subject for years. Presley had even sighted a UFO himself. The talk with Santilli gave J.B. a brain wave that very night. He had already been wondering how to scrape together the money to pay for his granddaughter's wedding when Santilli's expressed interest fell into his lap. According to a different account, the old man didn't come up with the idea until he had seen a kitschy TV program about the Roswell crash. That was when it dawned on him that this might be the perfect nest egg for his old age.

As Santilli was packing his bags and getting ready to leave the hotel the morning after they'd had drinks, the phone rang. It was J. B., with a tempting offer: *»Come on over, before you leave. I've got something for you here that's a lot more interesting than that Elvis stuff.«* Santilli called a cab and was at J. B.'s front door half an hour later. J. B. sat his guest down on the sofa and told him *»that he could offer him some footage of the autopsy of extraterrestrials, since he was thinking of doing something about UFOs«*. Santilli replied, *»that might be interesting, that's not the sort of thing you run into every day«*. J. B. left the room and returned in two minutes with a cardboard box full of 16mm films in tin filmreel cans.

»Ray, this is maybe the most explosive film material in the world. Have you ever heard of the Roswell incident?« Santilli hadn't. *»Back then, a UFO came down in a crash. We recovered the wreck and four corpses. And I was there filming it all! Here are some of the reels. The Pentagon just forgot to collect them.«* And J. B. proceeded to tell him the whole, mind-boggling story that sounded more like science fiction than anything else, projecting a few sequences of the footage onto the living room wall.

»You can have the stuff, all of it - but cash only, and nothing written down. And only if you don't tell anybody where you got it«. Santilli found the prospect understandably tantalizing. The first thing he did was call the Kodak company, right from J. B.'s, to ask how one could ascertain whether a given film was authentic. He was told one only had to examine the codes and markings. Santilli picked up one of the film reels and described what he found on it to the Kodak employee on the phone, both the writing and code consisting of a little black square next to a

similar small triangle. Right off the bat, the expert was able to say the film had to have been made either in 1927, 1947 or 1967.

Back in England, Santilli showed some leader frames he'd brought along to various Kodak experts, asking them to determine the year it was made. After listening to various expert opinions he came to the conclusion that the film had to be authentic. He then in all good conscience presented the film to Polygram, a company with whom he enjoyed a good business relationship, offering to provide the entire Roswell film material in J. B.'s possession. Polygram was quite interested in the deal and sent one of its top managers, Gary Shoefield, straight to the cameraman in order to settle the transaction as quickly as possible.

For a variety of reasons, the deal never came off. J. B. became seriously ill and had to go into hospital, while Shoefield waited for him at his hotel in vain. He called J. B. at home and heard from his wife what had happened. When he checked with the hospital, it confirmed the story. So the meeting never took place, but the Polygram people were still firmly convinced that J. B. existed. Finally, for legal reasons, Polygram broke off negotiations, reasoning that it could not afford to purchase film material from someone to whom it didn't really belong: it was and is still the property of the US military.

When the cameraman was released from hospital, he found out that the deal had fallen through. Santilli did not have enough money to purchase the material outright himself. Consequently, a rather ludicrous situation arose: Santilli had promised to pay J. B. (through Polygram), but no money changed hands and the elderly man lost confidence. It took all of eighteen months before Santilli succeeded in reopening negotiations. Between November 1994 and the beginning of 1995, with the financing help of music producer Volker Spielberg of Hamburg,

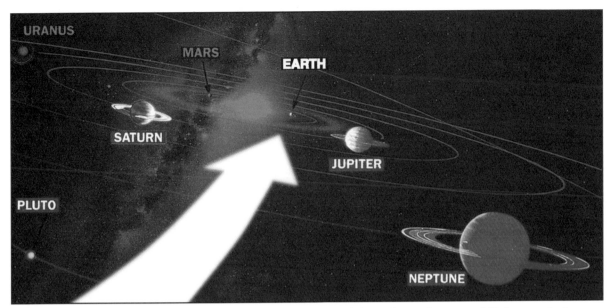

1 *The solar system's planetary positions on 2 July 1947 revealed themselves to be a sort of flight tunnel: the outer planets pointed the way towards Earth like pathmarkers.*

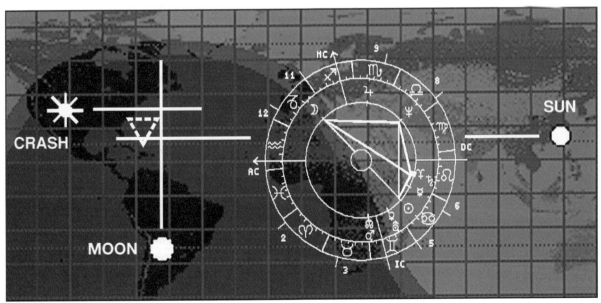

2 *The constellations on July 2, 1947, 9:50 pm local time: as night fell on New Mexico, full moon was at 65° longitude over Bermuda Triangle. Insert: The astrological space-time quality of the crash.*

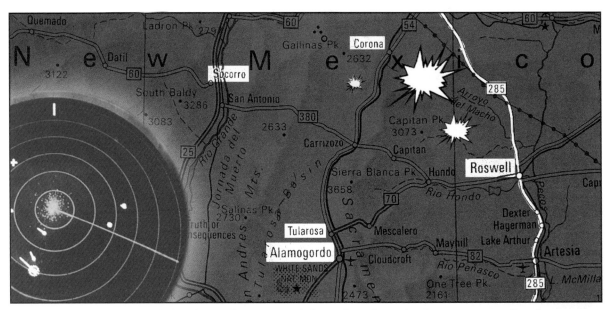

3 *Dozens of eyewitnesses observed something unusual descending from the skies near Roswell in late evening. Even radar personnel from nearby military bases expressed astonishment.*

4 *Farmer »Mac« Brazel took to Sheriff George Wilcox a few of the extraordinary items he'd found scattered over his sheep pasture. The case was passed on to Major Jesse Marcel.*

5 *American painter Jim Nichols' imaginary portrayal of the silvery saucer which crashed at Roswell, showing the first soldiers to arrive puzzling over the unknown object.*

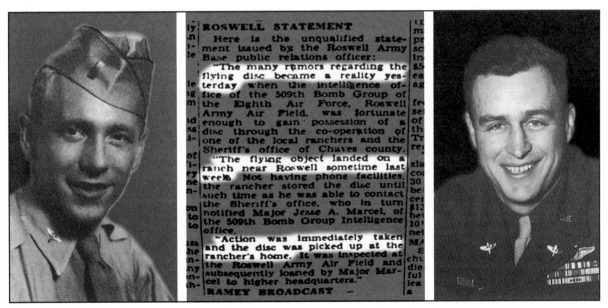

ROSWELL STATEMENT

Here is the unqualified statement issued by the Roswell Army Base public relations officer:

"The many rumors regarding the flying disc became a reality yesterday when the intelligence office of the 509th Bomb Group of the Eighth Air Force, Roswell Army Air Field, was fortunate enough to gain possession of a disc through the co-operation of one of the local ranchers and the Sheriff's office of Chaves county.

"The flying object landed on a ranch near Roswell sometime last week. Not having phone facilities, the rancher stored the disc until such time as he was able to contact the Sheriff's office, who in turn notified Major Jesse A. Marcel, of the 509th Bomb Group Intelligence office.

"Action was immediately taken and the disc was picked up at the rancher's home. It was inspected at the Roswell Army Air Field and subsequently loaned by Major Marcel to higher headquarters."

RAMEY BROADCAST —

6 *With the official announcement by the US Air Force, precipitately released to the press by Lt. W. Haut, on orders from Col W. Blanchard, the matter became public on 8 July 1947.*

7 *Reports of the UFO discovery and subsequent Pentagon denial appeared on the front pages of many newspapers, in US and worldwide.*

8 *Military disinformation promptly followed: reporters were presented with scraps of a weather balloon instead of original parts of the UFO wreck. From left to right: Major J. Marcel, General R. Ramey, Colonel T. J. DuBose.*

9 *A selection of major eyewitnesses from a gallery of several hundred civilians who observed events surrounding the UFO crash which officially never happened!*

10 *Hangar No. 84 on Roswell Army Air Field played a major part in the first days of salvage. Both wreckage and corpses were deposited here under utmost secrecy. Insert: Roswell Army Air Field in 1947*

Gen. R. M. Ramey · Gen. G. Kenney · Gen. C. Spaatz · Gen. M. F. Scanlon · Lt. Col. P. Jennings

Col. T. J. DuBose · Lt. R. Shirkey · Sgt. C. Stone · Maj. E. S. Easley · Sgt. L. S. Rickett

11 *Military witnesses, some of whom declared under oath that they took part in secretly salvaging the UFO wreck and its »exotic« crew.*

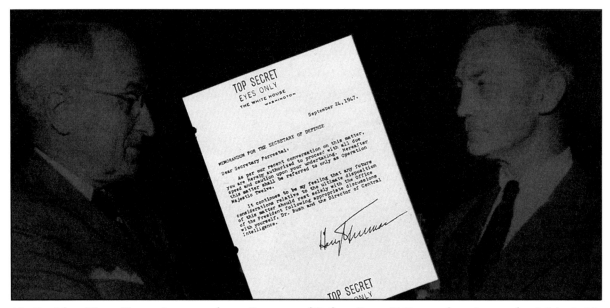

12 *President Harry Truman's secret orders to Secretary of Defense James V. Forrestal, setting up the »Majestic 12« group on 24 September 1947.*

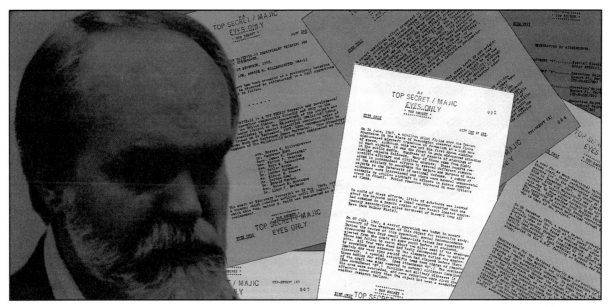

13 *The top secret »MAJESTIC 12« - document briefing President Eisenhower on the Roswell affair on 18 November 1952. It was mailed to filmmaker Jaime Shandera in 1984.*

MJ1 Adm. R. H. Hillenkoetter | MJ2 Dr. V. Bush | MJ3 Sec. J. V. Forrestal | MJ4 Gen. N. F. Twining | MJ5 Gen. H. S. Vandenberg | MJ6 Dr. D. Bronk

MJ7 Dr. J. Hunsaker | MJ8 Adm. S. W. Souers | MJ9 Mr. G. Gray | MJ10 Dr. D. Menzel | MJ11 Gen. R. M. Montague | MJ12 Dr. L. V. Berkner

14 *The members of the top secret »Majestic 12« - group, established by President Truman both to investigate and cover up the Roswell incident.*

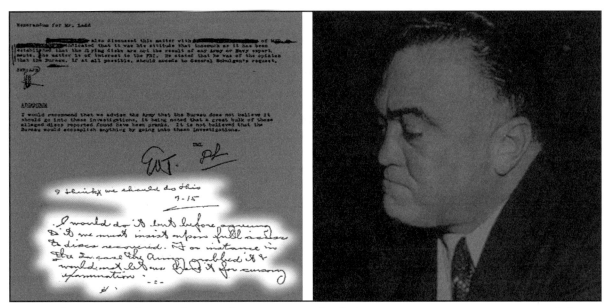

15 *Handwritten FBI directive from J. Edgar Hoover: »...but before agreeing to it we must insist upon full access to discs recovered...«*

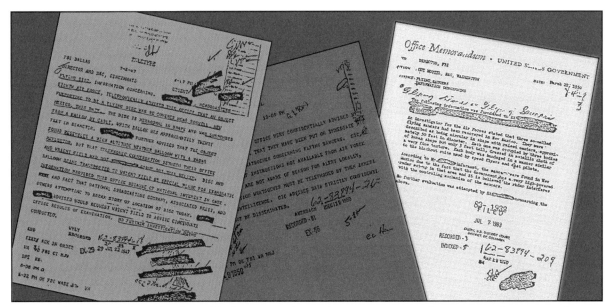

16 *FBI documents released to the public by court order: right, a memo to J. Edgar Hoover from 1950 claiming the Air Force was in possession of wreckage from crashed »flying saucers«.*

Germany, Santilli paid J. B. several installments and received in return 22 three-minute reels of film (other accounts speak of 14 or 15 reels of 10 minutes each). It is said he paid $150,000 for the entire 66-91 minutes of original film footage. (Other accounts maintain he paid $100,000 or $250,000; some sources also say he only received film copies from J. B.) The deal was evidently finalized in Orlando, Florida. The wedding of J. B.'s granddaughter was celebrated with all pomp and ceremony, one imagines.

In response to the question of what, besides the information from Kodak, convinced Santilli that the films were genuine, the new »owner« said it was primarily because he had known the cameraman personally for such a long time. *»I've known him now for more than two years, met him many times, went through his diaries, also his other files and even his photo album. I visited his house, his family, saw his collection of old cameras and heard the whole story of the incident first-hand from him. The man is genuine and honest.«*

J. B. also showed Santilli his military discharge papers from 1952 and photos from his period of service. *»I think the film is genuine for that reason, even though it can only be settled conclusively by the people who examined the material.«*

After a conscientious examination, instigated by Santilli, of some of the original frames by Bob Shell, a top film expert and photo-technical advisor of the FBI, as well as American court experts and two large Japanese companies* the tentative dating of the footage as 1947 was confirmed: *» The ›Roswell Film‹ is on Cine Kodak Super XX High Speed Panchromatic Safety Film, a film type introduced in the early 40s and discontinued in 1956-57...Since the edge code could be 1927, 1947 or 1967, and this film was not manufac-*

---

* In the meantime, it has become known that Santilli closed an exclusive contract with Shell for a book on Roswell and his film footage, including an exclusive interview with the cameraman. This, of course, effectively impedes his objectivity.

tured in 1927 or 1967, this clearly leaves us with only 1947 as an option. The photo quality, clarity and granular texture permit me to conclude that this film was shot and developed when it was rather fresh, that is, within three to four years. Based on this, I see no reason to doubt the cameraman's claim that the film was exposed in June and July 1947, and processed ›a few days later‹«.

Ultimately, Shell confirmed that he was 95% certain that the footage was genuine – though there was a 5% chance of its being fake. This could be authenticated by Kodak by identifying the »chemical signature« of the film. Concluding his expertise, he wrote: *»I don't set my name lightly to such a statement and am only prepared to do so now after extremly careful consideration and detailed examination of the film.«*

Santilli estimated that there was no chance whatsoever of the cameraman's going public in the near future, *»but that can change. I also didn't think he would be willing to talk about this subject to anyone else besides me, but he did just that recently. My original agreement with him was that we respect his anonymity. That was a fundamental part of our accord, without that assurance I wouldn't today have the film in my hands. Everything which still comes from him is real bonus,«* Santilli told Philip Mantle, chairman of BUFORA, the British UFO Research Association. Gary Shoefield, the initially interested Polygram manager, has in the meantime corroborated to reporters Santilli's version.

Although J. B. has emphasized to other people that he is not considering going public with what he knows, since *»he is somewhat unsure about the legal situation, because he sold films which didn't belong to him«,* in autumn 1996, he finally did appear on a Japanese television program, without however, presenting anything new. According to a secretary of

Roswell Footage Ltd. this was an 18-minute long home video made privately by or with the help of Mr. Santilli. That is to say, direct contact of reporters with the cameraman is even now being prevented (evidently in order to keep the IRS from learning his identity)

In the meantime it has become known that the cameraman had first attempted in 1972 to go public with his material. Air Force Colonel and UFO researcher W. C. Stevens heard at that time through the UFO researcher Mary Teal C. of a 62-year old man in Los Angeles who had in his possession film footage which he had taken himself of the autopsy of an extraterrestrial. When Stevens attempted to contact him, the man got scared, since agents were allegedly observing his house. According to Ray Santilli, his supplier really did live in L. A. from 1959 to 1973, since his wife came from there. The age given to Stevens would also tally. Mary Teal C., who could say more on the subject, today lives in a Buddhist monastery in Virginia and regrettably wishes to have nothing more to do with the subject of UFOs.

Now that Santilli was finally in possession of the reels, and of the Elvis concert films too, he had to have them restored individually in a professional photo laboratory he trusted, since the celluloid was in very bad condition. In January 1995, the first seven minutes of restored film footage emerged from the photo lab. Friends of Santilli said it shows a creature half covered with a kind of tarpaulin, lying on a table. For purposes of treatment, his skin-tight overalls had been removed. The setting appeared to be a tent or field hospital of sorts. Standing next to the being are two doctors in white gowns, without masks, who are uncovering the mid-section of the alien's arm. A third man in civilian clothing appears briefly. Santilli had this film fragment copied on

video, to give his closest friends a chance to view it. That's when events started to snowball.

A year later, it must be said, Santilli managed to tie himself up in all sorts of contradictory statements. Both he and his financier behaved in a manner that hardly commended them. Apparently the two owners had begun to get insecure about their case. This is the only possible explanation for their hindering, or attempting to hold up verification of the film by other independent UFO researchers. If, as they both admit, it was all a matter of money, it is understandable that they should try to cash in at every step of the way. They could always permit further verification tests to be made at some later date. Should the films then be declared a fake, at least they would have made some profit, and their objective would have been achieved. Or else, as Santilli's partner, Volker Spielberg, pithily affirmed in a phone call that was bugged, the two would have made so much money by that time that they wouldn't care less what the public thought.

UFO institutions are understandably nervous that if the contents of the films are not verified as authentic, all their efforts in reconstructing the Roswell incident will go down the drain. If the as yet unidentified Santilli alien girl were to turn out to be a fraud, the file of the most celebrated, best documented UFO contact of all time would be shelved for a long time, if not permanently closed. Everything vaguely connected with the subject would die a quiet death and, what's more, a final clarification of the loose ends of the incident might never be forthcoming. The insistent, impatient urging of Ufologists in this matter is therefore understandable.

On the other hand, it must also be rather nervewracking for the film owners to be hunted by the press for more than a year and see most of their own answers either twisted, changed or downright invented, making their statements all but unrecognizable in the media. If you surf through the Internet pages under Roswell and/or Santilli you can form your own impression of just how many controversial extremes the whole affair has provoked.

A number of thought-provoking points are raised: no one outside the owners, for example, has yet admitted in public having seen the original films and film reel cans. All the films were copied by an unidentified firm at Santilli's behest and digitally remastered onto video to improve their rough granular picture quality. The original color of the half-century old celluloid is allegedly brown and yellow, by the way, not black and white.

By now there are about 150,000 home videos of the alien autopsy in circulation in America alone. Worldwide television and photographic rights amount to many times that. In fairness to the public the owners ought to get on with untangling the mass of contradictions and respond to a series of questions still begging for clarification. That is, if it weren't for one very sensitive point...

It must not be forgotten that the Roswell affair might still have the same top secret classification in the Pentagon as it did decades ago. This means that if the early statements about President Truman's personal inspection of the UFO wreck and/or being on film with the aliens (statements later disclaimed by Santilli) turned out to be true, the potential explosiveness of the subject would be enormous. First of all, the incident would be verified as actually having happened; second, the fact would be exposed that several American administrations in an unparalleled cover-up campaign deceived the public for fifty years. At the very least, a government crisis of the first order would be unleashed.

Early on there were rumors flying about that Santilli had been severely intimidated by intelligence agents in the same way the eyewitnesses claim to have been. How does one react when the lives and well being of one's own family are subtly threatened, if one doesn't behave in a particular way? Nearly every reasonable person would abandon his principles and behave in a very restrained way from then on....

The Camouflaged Cameraman

Santilli is contractually obliged to keep secret the identity of the original autopsy filmmaker. In spite of rumors that the person is already dead, Santilli claims to still be in contact with his secret supplier; he gave a document written by the cameraman to the press. Under the pseudonym Jack Barnett, the cameraman made the following statement about »Operation ANVIL – now known as the Roswell Incident« during sales negotiations:

»I joined the forces in March of 1942 and left in 1952. The ten years I spent serving my country were some of the best years of my life. My father was in the movie business, which meant he had good knowledge about the workings of cameras and photography. For this reason I believe I passed a medical that would not normally allow me in, due to my having had polio as a child.

After my enrollment and training, I was able to use my camera skills and became one of the few dedicated cameramen in the forces. I was sent to many places, and as it was wartime, I fast learnt the ability of filming under difficult circumstances.

I will not give more detail on my background, only to say that in the fall of 1944, I was assigned to Intelligence, reporting to the Assistant Chief of Air Staff. I was moved around, depending on assignment. During the time, I filmed a great deal including the tests at White Sands (Manhattan project/Trinity*).

* Code name for the atomic development project.

I remember very clearly receiving the call to go to White Sands (Roswell). I had not long returned from St. Louis, Missouri where I had filmed the new Ramjet (»Little Henry«). It was June 1st when McDonald* asked me to report to General McMullan** for a special assignment. I had no experience of working with McMullan but after talking to him for a few minutes, I knew that I would never wish to be his enemy. McMullan was straight to the point, no messing. I was ordered to a crash site just southwest of Socorro. It was urgent and my brief was to film everything in sight, not to leave the debris until it had been removed and I was to have access to all areas of the site. If the commander in charge had a problem with that, I was told to get them to call McMullan. A few minutes after my orders from McMullan, I received the same instructions from Tooey,*** saying it was the crash of a Russian spy plane. Two Generals in one day, this job was important.

I flew out from Andrews with sixteen other officers and personnel, mostly medical. We arrived at Wright Patterson and collected more men and equipment. From there, we flew to Roswell on a C54. When we got to Roswell, we were transported by road to the site. When we arrived, the site had already been cordoned off. From the start it was plain to see this was no Russian spy plane. It was a large disc »Flying Saucer« on its back, with heat still radiating from the ground around it.

The commander on site handed it all over to the SAC medical team who were still waiting for Kenney**** to arrive. However, nothing had been done as everyone was just waiting for orders. It was decided to wait until the heat subsided before moving in as fire was a significant risk. This was made all the worse by the screams of the freak creatures that were lying by the vehicle.

What in God's name they were, no one could tell, but one thing is for sure, they were circus freaks, creatures with no business here. Each had hold of a box which they kept hold of in both arms close to their chests. They just lay there crying, holding those boxes.

Once my tent had been set up, I started filming immediately, first the vehicle, then the site and debris. At around 06:00, it was deemed safe to move in. Again, the freaks were still crying and when approached, they screamed even louder. They were protective of their boxes, but we managed to get one loose with a firm strike at the head of a freak with the butt of a rifle.

The three freaks were dragged away and secured with rope and tape. The other one was already dead. The medical team was reluctant at first to go near these freaks, but as some were injured, they had no choice. Once the creatures were collected, the priority was to collect all debris that could be removed easily as there was still a risk of fire. This debris seemed to come from exterior struts that were supporting a very small disc on the the underside of the craft which must have snapped off when the disc flipped over. The debris was taken to tent stations for logging, then loaded onto trucks. After three days, a full team from Washington came down and the decision was taken to move the craft. Inside it, the atmosphere was very heavy. It was impossible to stay in longer than a few seconds without feeling very sick. Therefore, it was decided to analyse it back at base, so it was loaded onto a flattop and taken to Wright Patterson, which is where I joined it.

I stayed at Wright Patterson for a further three weeks, working on the debris. I was then told to report to Fort Worth (Dallas) for the filming of an autopsy. Normally, I would not have a problem with this, but it was discovered that the freaks may be a medical threat, therefore, I was required to wear the same protective suits as the doctors. It was impossible to handle the camera properly, loading and focusing was very difficult. In fact,

* Major General George C. McDonald, deputy chief of staff of Air Force Intelligence.
** Major General Clements M. McMullen, deputy commander of SAC.
*** Nickname for General Carl Spaatz, Air Force chief of staff.
**** General George C. Kenney, commander of SAC.

against orders, I removed my suit during the filming. The first two autopsies took place in July 1947.

After filming, I had several hundred reels. I separated problem reels which required special attention in processing (these I would do later). The first batch was sent through to Washington and I processed the remainder a few days later. Once the remaining reels had been processed, I contacted Washington to arrange collection of the final batch. Incredibly, they never came to collect or arrange transportation for them. I called many times and then just gave up. The footage has remained with me ever since.

In May of 1949, I was asked to film the third autopsy.

The Pentagon thought that all the film material had arrived. Since the cameraman had a higher security clearance than his immediate superior, he wasn't even permitted to speak candidly with his own chief about the lapse. About Major General McMullen, General Ramey expressed himself very succinctly before he died: *»McMullan had everything under control, no discussion was allowed. It was more than top secret. The balloon story was intentional misinformation, no question about it.«*

According to J. B.'s account, the third extraterrestrial lived until 1949 and died of unknown causes. The last autopsy took place in Washington, DC in the presence of scientists from various western nations, including Britain and France, according to the filmmaker. Evidently, the military even succeeded in engaging in a form of non-verbal mental communication with the alien.*

* There are reports according to which a number of living extraterrestrials have been sighted on subterranean US military bases. These need not necessarily be Roswell aliens. Meanwhile, Major Ed Dames, director of the top security division of Army intelligence known as PSI-TECH, has confirmed that he has conducted espionage via mediums. He and his group, away from any official context, established contact with extraterrestrials. He considers the Roswell film to be a fake. In his position, however, he can hardly be expected to say anything else.

The French journalist Nicholas Maillard, on assignment for Channel TF1, tried to track down the life story of the apparently real person »Jack Barnett«. He found out that he was never in the Army and died, according to his death certificate, in 1959.

The Macabre Autopsy

Conscious of the extraordinary significance of the material and the possible consequences of such revelations, Santilli, on March 11, 1995, presented the film, or rather, the fragments which had been restored by then, in a private showing to an exclusive group of religious leaders in Great Britain, among them purportedly the Archbishop of Canterbury and Chief Rabbi of London. *»The result was absolutely negative, there was total rejection«*, Santilli said later. *»They thought I was a fraud, some of them even left in the middle of the showing.«* Evidently at the same time, CIA agents Dan Smith and Ron Pandolphi tried hard to thwart the showing, then to postpone it, allegedly because President Clinton was just about to release heaps of documents anyway, and the timing of the publication of the Roswell films didn't fit into these plans. Santilli seemingly paid no attention to these diversionary tactics.

On April 28, there was another showing of the 9-minute film footage of the first autopsy for a select circle. On May 5, a second, longer sequence of about 28 minutes was shown to about 80 people from various fields, journalists, scientists, filmmakers and UFO experts, in the auditorium of the London Museum. It was expressly forbidden to bring any photographic equipment into the hall; this was checked with electronic detectors. One UFO zealot distributed leaflets just before the showing accusing Santilli of fraud, though without giving any reasons. The showing itself seemed to be somewhat shorter than planned. Santilli disappeared prematurely, due to threats he received, and the guests at the premiere departed from the auditorium with mixed feelings, ranging from disbelieving astonishment to sceptical disappointment.

On May 16, a first report about it appeared in the Encounter Forum of CompuServe. When, in July, photos first surfaced in the world press, heated debates throughout the UFO scene were sparked off instantaneously. The general consensus was that either it had now definitively been proved that a UFO landed...or this was the cleverest hoax since the Hitler diaries. One side screamed »fake«, without ever having seen the film; the other could not restrain its enthusiasm. And so the brew of rumors boiled over.

Soon major magazines and newspapers all over the world also began to report on the film fragments, and published stills. Under the terms of the contract the film was allowed to be publicly aired on August 28 at the earliest by the highest bidding TV stations; several major networks proceeded to do this on the same day, amid great fanfare. But barely five minutes of pasted-together original footage was broadcast. On top of that, the commentary contained crass discrepancies, though whether intentional or not is hard to say.

Frustrated by the eyewash I saw on the private German television RTL, I obtained a video copy of the uncut original films being marketed by the Santilli company, Merlin Group, via various distributors and the Internet for £33.* For those unacquainted with the documentary films released thus far which, collectively are convincing in their authenticity, increasingly underpinning the most sensational story of the century, I will attempt to describe in words what is actually seen on the video tape.**

* now available through Gateway Books for £ 11.95 - see page 217.
** see stills in second photographic section of this book.

The original film sequence is in black and white, despite the fact that color film was available to the Army in 1947; it is heavily granular in texture and completely without sound. The video is entitled »Roswell – The Footage« by Santilli. According to the label, it was copyrighted by a company named »Roswell – The Footage, Ltd.«, even though it has still not been clarified to what extent possible Army property claims are still applicable. In the credits, it is stated – besides legal safeguards that the highest possible degree of authenticity cannot yet be guaranteed 100% and that the film does not have the quality of a movie reel – that Macrovision technology protects the video from being copied.

In the introduction, a collage of film clips, accompanied by dramatic kettle drums beating in the background, show historic facts about the 509th nuclear bomber squadron of Roswell Army Air Field as well as the wave of UFO sightings of the time. This is followed by brief historical interviews with eyewitnesses already mentioned in this book, such as radio reporter Frank Joyce, PR Officer Walter Haut, Mac Brazel's neighbor Loretta Proctor, UFO researcher Sgt. Stone and Major Jesse Marcel, who states definitively in front of the camera, 31 years after the incident and shortly before his death, that *»certainly no weather balloon went down at the time«*. Security officer Robert Shirkey and mortician Glenn Dennis, film owner Ray Santilli and BUFORA boss Philip Mantle also have their say. The statement of the cameraman quoted in full in the preceding chapter, follows; it is both read and shown in written form. A memo from Kodak confirming the age of the film and reel labels is shown. Top expert Bob Shell attests to the almost 100% authenticity of the film. Then without comment follow a few shots of UFO bits and pieces and instrumentation panels, to which I will return later.

It continues with newspaper clippings, the report of pathologist Dr. C. M. Milroy of the University of Sheffield is quoted, then a page of the MAJESTIC-12 briefing for President Eisenhower is shown and explained. Not until this 25-minute introduction is over does the actual autopsy part of the film begin. It starts with the limp excuse that for the time being only those alien sequences will be shown which have been verified to the film owners' full satisfaction as authentic. Evidently, a carefully worked out strategy of the new film owners is behind all this, for purposes of squeezing, bit by bit, maximum profits from this unique booty. The concept seems to be working.

The historical shots show, in accord with information we already have, the dissection of a humanoid, but not human, creature in an autopsy room of the military hospital at Fort Worth Air Force Base near Dallas, Texas. It was probably carried out by Dr. Detlev Bronk and one, sometimes two assistants (Dr. Willies?) in July, 1947. The original label of each of the twelve, voyeuristically silent film reels (reprinted below) appears in the credits for each film:

• **Reel No. 53 – Body No. 2** (about 2 min.): The naked, supine, apparently female body is seen in its entirety, laid out on a simple dissecting table, circled several times by the camera. On the right thigh, a serious and deep injury or burn is visible. Surgical instruments are visible on a tray, at the side off to the rear is a wall telephone with spiral cord hanging down from it. The clock on the wall shows the time to be 10:06. After a blurred close-up of the oversized bald head, someone in white protective clothing and some kind of cloth head-covering with rectangular glass eye-slits steps up and touches the bloated body. The heavily masked pathologist lifts the corpse's injured right knee and speaks into a microphone hanging from the ceiling. An observer with conventional mouth mask in normal surgical clothing is visible behind a large glass window in the background. It is now 10:20 on the wall clock.

• **Reel Un-numbered – Body/Leg** (about 2 minutes): The injured leg is once again examined by a heavily masked person and the body carefully felt all over. A second pathologist enters the picture. He indicates the intended dissection cut to the third person behind the window. The telephone with the spiral cord is clearly visible. The rudimentary female genitals are examined. It is 10:24 on the wall clock, a 1936 model with hour and minute hands. The already severed six-fingered right hand of the humanoid lies next to the stump of its lower arm. With surgical scissors and forceps, a 2-inch long (metal?) splinter is carefully removed from the thigh wound and placed into a dish held by a heavily masked assistant.

• **Reel No. 56 – Body/Leg No. 2** (about 1 min. 30 sec.): The left six-fingered hand and a six-toed foot are lifted and shown close up. Humanlike toenails are recognizable. With the scalpel a cut is made from the ears to the chest, the second pathologist assisting. Dark liquid flows slowly from the incision. The body is then opened with a vertical, overall Y-shaped cut along the abdominal surface down to the groin. It is 10:40 on the clock.

• **Reel No. 59 – Chest No. 2** (1 min. 30 sec.): Three heavily masked people stand around the corpse (the third is presumably a nurse). The abdominal wall is separated from the organs and laid to the side. At about where the diaphragm is, an almost circular, dark organ, 10-15 in. large, is visible, though blurred. The skin of the chest is lifted as far as the chin, exposing esophagus and trachea. A blurred close-up follows of exposed, unusual intestines. Some things have clearly been removed from the body cavity.

• **Reel No. 61 – Chest No. 2** (2 min.): Overall shot of entire opened body. Close up of head. In area of (non existent) navel, a small, apparently hard object is peeled out of the tissue, possibly a kind of crystal. The (probably female) assistant hands forceps to the pathologist. Another large, unknown organ is removed and laid into a tin dish.

• **Reel No. 62 – Head/Eyes No. 2** (2 min): Body tissue is again placed into a tin dish. Several containers already filled with various tissues are on a nearby table, also a case of autopsy instruments. A pathologist goes deep into the body to separate and remove more clump-like organs. Three persons are again in the picture. Another organ is placed into a dish. A kind of black membrane is removed from the eyes with forceps and placed into a glass dish filled with clear liquid. A blurry close-up of the head follows. The eyeballs of the being are rolled sharply upward, the iris barely visible. With a scalpel, a precise cross-sectional incision is made in the middle of the head.

• **Reel No. 63 – Head No. 2** (2 min.): The skin is removed from the skull, a pathologist peels it down over the forehead. The second heavily masked person holds the head steady while this is done. It is 11:28 on the clock. The following shot of the whole body again shows three people. The nurse lists one more organ removal while standing at a nearby table. On this piece of paper, the name of the doctor and MJ-12 member, Dr. Detlev Bronk, is purportedly visible in the better quality original film. Various beakers, test tubes, bottles and a Bunsen burner can be seen on the table. It is 11:30 on the wall clock.

• **Reel No. 64 – Head No. 2** (2 min.): More skin is removed from the skull. The camera moves around the body, searching for the best angle. The cranium is then sawn open with a hand saw. This appears to require great effort and to be performed rather amateurishly. The assistants try to hold the skull steady the while.

• **Reel Un-numbered – Brain** (1 min. 30 sec.): The oversized brain is loosened and removed from its cavity. The apparently half-disintegrated, dark, flaccid mass is set down onto a deep rectangular tray. A close-up of this scene is blurred. Additional brain parts are removed and placed into other containers. Again, a shot of the whole body. A pathologist talks with the man behind the window who wears a simple mouth mask, pointing into the brain cavity.

In three other labelled sequences of this Santilli Roswell video film, technical shots of the spacecraft wreckage are seen (details follow in the next chapter). The 50-minute long film is concluded with continuous slow-motion shots of already seen fragments, stretching the playing time to 75 minutes. The film document ends with credits. In the advertisements for this video in Germany, as well as in the Internet order form and on the video-cassette itself, it was claimed that the cameraman's complete material would be shown in this film, which, based on everything we know today, is a lie.

The film clearly shows that this more or less female being with oversized head, large eyes and small mouth, which seems to gape open in shock, manifests not the slightest sign of a navel.*

In place of breasts, nothing but barely perceptible elevations without nipples are seen. Gender is indicated by a hairless vagina which appears rather atrophied. The abdomen of this otherwise nearly human-looking, slightly heavy-set body about 5 feet tall is somewhat more voluminous looking than a prototype Homo Sapiens because of putrefaction gases which have a bloating effect. I estimate the brain volume to be about 30% higher than a human being's.

---

* It was also claimed that the not-visible navel could have been smoothed out by the bloated abdomen or fraudulently covered. But even during the opening of the body, as the pressure must have subsided, no sign of a navel was evident.

The facial features seem quite distinct, resembling those of no known race on Earth: wide-open, over-sized eyes, a rather delicate, rudimentary nose, almost lipless mouth slit and low-set rudimentary earlobes all present the picture of a rather doll-like creature. The limbs, apart from the twelve rather long fingers and twelve toes, are in proportion and the musculature very human-looking. The knees appear swollen. As far as skin color is concerned, the black and white film gives the impression of a mixed race coloring.

Unfortunately, all the close-ups are slightly to severely blurred (skeptics see this as intentional, of course) and the camera is sometimes moved too abruptly, making a medical diagnosis of the organs impossible. The cameraman is always at pains to find the best angle, but since he always follows the doctors, they often obstruct the view. The films are not a continuous sequence, as can be ascertained by the wall clock. Some phases of the autopsy are missing entirely. The rest of the film fragments appear to be somehow pasted together. According to the wall clock, which often appears in the film, it is evident the autopsy took about one and a half hours. The »DANGER« sign (»Maximum Exposure Two Hours«) near the telephone might indicate that the autopsy was carried out under ultraviolet irradiation. This would also explain the protective clothing, due to possible danger of infection. However, a host of top pathologists have viewed the film closely in the meantime. A few excerpts from their opinions and summaries follow.

The pathologist mentioned in the credits at the beginning of the Roswell video, Dr. Christopher M. Milroy, MBChB, MD, MRCPath, DMJ, Senior Lecturer for Forensic Pathology, University of Sheffield, made the following statement on June 2, 1995 after viewing the film:

»At the request of the Merlin Group, I reviewed a film which was claimed to show a post-mortem examination being carried out on an extraterrestrial being... Beside the autopsy table was a tray of standard autopsy instruments. The body was human in appearance and appeared to be female but without secondary sexual characteristics – no breast development or pubic hair was visible. The head was disproportionately large. No head hair was present.

The abdomen was distended. There was no evidence of decomposition. The overall external appearance was of a white adolescent female, estimated height 5 feet, tending towards a heavy build not abnormally thin or fat. There were six digits to each hand and foot. The eyes appeared larger than normal and the globes were covered with a black material which was shown being removed.

There was an extensive and deep injury to the right thigh. This was not shown in very close detail, but appeared to be burnt and charred down to deep tissues. No similar injury was present, although there was possible bruising down the left hand side of the body...The body was opened with a Y shaped incision, but the skin of the neck was not fully reflected. A close-up of the knife being drawn against the skin was shown, with blood coming from skin. This appeared to be an unusual amount of blood. The neck appeared to contain two cylindrical structures either side anteriorly. These could have been muscles (sternomastoid muscles) but were odd in appearance, though they were not shown in close up.

The skin of the chest was shown reflected, and the central rib cage and sternum block removed...There appeared to be a heart and two lungs...The abdominal organs were not clearly seen, though it did not appear that the person was pregnant, an explanation that had been proposed for the distended abdomen.

The scalp was...cut in a standard autopsy manner...What appeared to be the membranes covering the brain (dura) were shown being cut and the brain being removed...However the appearances were not those of a human brain...

The body shape was dysmorphic. No accurate determination could be made of organ structure because every close-up shot was out of focus. The injuries present on the body were less than those expected in an aviation accident. No injuries to account for death were shown. Whilst the examination had features of a medically conducted examination, aspects suggested it was not conducted by an experienced autopsy pathologist, but rather by a surgeon.«*

Expert pathologists were also requested by several TV stations to study the film and give their opinion. Besides Prof. Milroy (»This can't possibly be a human brain, it has a different color and shape.«), the US FOX television network also questioned Prof. Cyril Wecht, former president of the Association of Forensic Pathologists in the US. This specialist thought the heavily masked doctors in the film were »either pathologists or surgeons who had already carried out many autopsies«. He confirmed that the instruments employed corresponded to those in use in 1947. Deforming illnesses such as Turner Syndrome and the theory that the corpse might have been the victim of nuclear tests were discussed. At the same time, it was conceded that these hypotheses could, not by a long shot, explain all the traits of the being. Unanimously it was ruled out that the flesh wound on the leg was the cause of death. As regards the inner organs visible in the film, Prof. Wecht said, »he cannot define these structures in the context of a human abdomen. What might be a liver is not where the liver ought to be. I have great difficulty finding correspondences with human bodies I have seen. The brain is not like any brain I have ever seen before, neither those of

tumor, radiation nor trauma victims. It's hard for me to say for certain but what we see here seems to me not to be a human being. I would call it humanoid. However, although I cannot say that it has come from a distant planet, neither can I confirm that it is a member of the human race, as you and I know it. I don't think that someone has created a giant hoax here.«

The reputable and well known Munich pathologist Prof. Dr. Wolfgang Eisenmenger was asked by German RTL-Extra TV editors to watch the film together with colleagues and to make his comments before a running camera. He felt in general »that he would consider the possibility of life creation outside our solar system to be quite possible, based on the millions of permutations and combinations probable«. As to the circumstances of the autopsy, he thought that the piece of furniture »on which the dissected object was laid was not a typical dissection table. The edges should have been raised, so that no liquid could overflow. It is striking that a dark liquid flows (out of the body) with a certain regularity and one could conclude that this was blood, as pictured in a black and white film, but the way it flows so regularly out of the cuts does not seem to correspond with reality in my opinion. Blood and any other liquid would flow uncontrollably out of a human being, whereas this need not be the case for extraterrestrials.« In the further course of the discussion, the possibility of an inherited premature aging (progeria) is raised. »When you look at a body like this one, you might conclude that we are dealing with chromosomal defects. But those suffering from premature aging do not usually become very old, most often they die before they reach the age of 10.« Prof. Eisenmenger paraphrases his remaining doubts as to whether his critical analysis is justified with a reference to President Kennedy's autopsy: »President Kennedy should also have been dissected only by the greatest medical authorities. But when you read the dissection reports, it is still unclear from

* If it was really Prof. Bronk who carried out the autopsy, this allusion would be borne out, since he was not a pathologist, but a physiologist and biophysicist.

66

what side he was actually shot down. This means, that in America even something very important indeed is not necessarily handled by top experts. Especially in the military, it usually depends on a number of other factors.«

The Italian television network RAI DUE discussed the autopsy on three successive days in October 1995 on the program »Misteri« (»Mysteries«), calling, among others, on the well-known Italian pathologist Prof. Dr. Baima Bollone as their principal witness. Prof. Bollone said: *»When we look at the inside of the body, we don't see one organ that even remotely resembles those of the human body. The face of the alleged extraterrestrial has amazing anatomical details: very large eye sockets, a very flat nose bridge, a somehow wide mouth in which one can see the tips of two teeth.**

But the face is flat and seems to have no facial muscles, which are responsible for the facial expression of human beings. This being is characterized by several fundamental distinctions from the human species.« The possibility of a genetic defect was dismissed by Prof. Bollone: *»The film excludes this hypothesis definitively. To begin with, people suffering from Turner's Syndrome do not have six fingers, but rather a hypertrophy* (excessive growth) *of the fourth and fifth finger joints, which is not the case here.«* For that reason, he had to conclude *»that we have here, due to the lack of facial and hand muscles, a being which is related to our species but is nonetheless quite different from it. And that very thing excludes any possibility of fraud.«* Prof. Bollone believed he recognized a detail which corroborated the story of the cameraman: according to the cameraman's story, the being sustained injuries to the left temple, which may have resulted from a harsh blow, e.g. from a rifle barrel, which was indeed the case.

* Despite computer enlargement, I could not make out any teeth.

In a special documentary lasting several hours on French television TF1, two doctors appeared to comment on the Santilli film on October 23, 1995. Surgeon Patrick Braun gave voice to his conviction *»that the being was organic and not a kind of rubber doll, recognizable, among other things, through the exuding body fluid«.* The experienced coroner Jean Pierre confirmed *»that the heavily masked people in the film were assuredly doctors, but not coroners.«* Due to the first signs of putrefaction setting in, he also excluded the possibility of the creature being a trick doll.

At the end of October, 150 pathologists and coroners from Switzerland, under the direction of the head pathologist of the University of Basle, met in a lecture hall which was filled to capacity for analysis and discussion of the Santilli video. The general opinion was that this was an extremely ill human body, in any case a real living being and not a fabricated doll. A radioactive mutation was also considered.*

No explanation was found for the lack of a navel. With regard to the removed organs, Prof. Dr. M. J. Mihatsch uttered the opinion *»that one could not compare them with known human organs«.* He called the flow of blood *»advanced autolysis. In such a case, the blood would flow like water.«* Since the body lay in high temperatures for some days in the desert and should for that reason show strong signs of putrefaction, the professor tended to think it was a fraud. *»The face would assuredly be soon completely deformed through decomposition«.*

So much for this bevy of experts, complete with expected disagreements. It remains confusing that

* This theory cannot be entirely dismissed, since nuclear tests were being conducted at the time in New Mexico. However, the films would then have to be older than they were determined by experts to be; or else the Americans had already been conducting such nuclear tests for decades.

cameraman J. B. said his work at the scene of the crash was carried out on June 1, 1947 and the autopsy only three weeks later. Of course, this could be a simple memory lapse of an 82-year old man. But I find it disturbing that slightly different sequences are to be seen in the RTL (German) broadcast as compared to the Roswell video one can purchase. This might be explained by Santilli's exclusive sale of various scenes. One is reminded in that connection of the infelicitous – because it is so revealing – name he chose for his new firm which was to market the film material: International Exploitation Management. Once more it shows that Santilli and Co., in a society such as ours, may indeed entertain sincere motives, yet primarily they want to make as much money as possible. The autopsy film itself, however, in no way seems to have been produced with worldwide marketing in mind. Researches conducted thus far point to just the opposite.

It is highly probable that parts of the remaining film material, handed over by cameraman J. B. immediately following the crash and the autopsy to the US military, were shown between 1953 and 1956 to several groups of experts at various Air Force bases. A radar specialist from Fort Monmouth and an Air Force colonel from a radar base in Maine both said, in accord, they had been shown film excerpts of a silvery, disc-shaped object wedged into the desert ground and surrounded by soldiers; as well as three weird dead bodies stretched out on tables in a tent. Evidently, the showings were used as a psychological test, for the viewers were afterwards told to think about what they had seen, but to mention it to no one. Two weeks later, they were told to forget the film altogether, since it was all a joke. The descriptions, according to UFO researcher Len Stringfield, agree strikingly with the beings visible in the Santilli film footage. Stringfield's

third witness was allegedly shown the corpse of an extraterrestrial pilot in a glass coffin in a subterranean chamber on Wright Patterson Base. Sergeant Richard Doty, a former officer in Air Force Intelligence, maintains having been shown precisely that film a long time ago at Los Alamos National Laboratory, New Mexico.

Surprisingly, a Chinese delegation of UFO researchers, upon seeing the film in London, declared they had seen copies of the film two years earlier, which they had received from the CIA in exchange for some Taiwanese UFO films. One of Santilli's employees, Chris Cary, is supposed to have given private showings of the film on June 28 for a group of American senators and for the counter-intelligence wing of the FBI in Washington DC.

Bob Shell demonstrated at the latest American UFO convention in Mesquite, Nevada, where he showed 500 convention-goers seven new individual pictures from the first, two days-older autopsy film, that we are dealing with externally identical, evidently cloned* beings, to the extent that one can depend on the data released.

According to authors Charles Berlitz and William L. Moore, the remains of the dissected corpses, together with a group of other discovered, extraterrestrial bodies and relicts, are at present being stored in a CIA warehouse at their headquarters in Langley, Virginia.** Other sources spoke of transparent, vertical »freezer coffins« within a subterranean installation in the supersecret AREA 51 in the Nevada desert.

* An earth clone experiment can only have taken place after 1980, however. Before that time, our genetic engineering know-how was clearly not far enough advanced, not even in secret military research centers. The being does not seem to be a teenager either.
** The Washington Post reported that on June 11, 1995, a UFO was seen floating directly over CIA Headquarters, radiating a bright light. It then drifted northward toward Great Falls, where Ron Pandolphi, the UFO expert of the CIA, lives.

The Technical Remains

In August 1995, I was struck by a photo still in the German news magazine »Focus« showing a metallic six-fingered handprint. But I didn't know what to make of it because there was neither caption nor comment on the picture. Since, oddly enough, RTL didn't show any shots of the wreckage in its TV coverage, I didn't become familiar with it until the video showing the UFO wreckage went on the market. In Santilli's video presentation, the weird-looking remains of the spacecraft are shown first briefly between the introductory interviews, then, in three sequences, as an appendage to the autopsy. An attempted description of technical aspects follows:*

• **Reel Un-numbered – Tagging** (1 min.30 sec.): Three raised panels, each with imprints of the six-fingered left and right hands can be seen. The slightly rounded plates are about 2 in. high, one of them is badly damaged. Right beside them, a bunch of I-beams is lying on a second table. The room seems to be the inner chamber of a military tent, whose canvas briefly wafts in the wind. The close-up of a carrier rack follows, on which eight unknown written symbols are discernible. After a shot of other parts, one can see the two tables, with the whole collection of parts arranged on them.

• **Reel Un-numbered – Tagging** (2 min.): The hand panels are lifted and held up by someone for the camera. They are shown above, as well as beside each other. The picture seems strangely distorted. A gloved hand points to a detail. One of the broken racks can be seen in a side-view close-up, complete with its »hieroglyphics«. Another can be seen from above and in profile. Hand-written archive labels hang from each object.

* see photo stills in second picture section, pp. 91-93.

• **Reel Un-numbered – Tagging** (30 sec.): Similar, somewhat smaller I-beams are briefly shown from different angles. They bear four more unidentifiable signs.

Among the items recovered are two important types of debris: four different large-sized carriers with as yet undeciphered symbols and three 12-fingered instrument panels. The curious, not particularly dynamic looking I-beams were used, according to the cameraman, for securing a small disc to the underside of the larger saucer. According to J. B.'s description, the crash was more a belly landing than a regular crash. The carriers seem to have burst on the rocks during the bounce/flipover/slide. The spot at which one of these racks broke was computer enlarged and analyzed by Italian chemist and computer expert Prof. Dr. Malanga of the University of Pisa. He concluded that they were made of a metal with an especially fine crystal structure.

The so-called boxes which can be seen in the film as a kind of steering console, measuring approximately 12 x 24 x 2 inches, appear to be extremely lightweight. American computer expert and scientist Dennis Murphy calculated them to weigh about 2 lbs. apiece. He made a special examination of the destroyed box, with its electronic possibilities and declared »*that the panels are hollow and comprise three chambers. The buttons in the handprints probably lead to the centers of the chamber, which are filled with a hard, dark substance interlaced with thin, bright-colored cords.*«

Bob Shell, a film expert who has also worked for the CIA in this capacity, asked around insider circles for comments on the Roswell relics. A longtime engineer in the Air Force told him that as far back as 1968 he and other scientists had carried out analyses of the same boxes visible in the film. »*We found out how they store information, but not how to get at the information stored.«* According to Shell's informant, the wreckage parts are presented to specialists every ten years, so with every advance in technological research, further secrets can be unearthed. He himself believes the panels to be a kind of advanced bio-computer.

Further information came from Bill Uhouse, a mechanical design engineer of the top secret AREA 51/S-4 base in Nevada, who has developed special flight simulators on which US pilots have apparently been trained to test-fly recovered UFOs for many years. Uhouse said to UFO researcher Lt. Col. Wendelle C. Stevens that he immediately recognized the navigation panels: *»They're for steering the craft. We copied them, but for five fingers.«*

Many experts assume that the puzzling operation of the vehicle works via biofeedback. A truly remarkable cockpit known to be harbored at the Wright Patterson Air Force Base in Dayton, Ohio bears witness to this theory being not too far-fetched. It is the simulator of a fighter plane, developed by Capt. David Turney and three civilian scientists, which in trials has been piloted with brain waves. The captain has mastered this flying technique so perfectly that he can fly a steep 45° curve in less than a second all via thought-power. Did the UFO technology inspire the military and NASA to develop such ideas?

With regard to the handprint panels I am also reminded of something mentioned three days after the first examination of the alien corpses by the nurse and girlfriend of the Roswell mortician who afterwards disappeared. At her last meeting with Glenn Dennis, she allegedly said that the alien creatures *»had little concavities like suction cups on their fingertips«.* And the cameraman and other eyewitnesses reported that *»the aliens held ›boxes‹ tightly to their chests with both hands«.* Round holes in the hand-operated areas of the control panels are clearly visible. So it seems likely that the distinctive-looking suction cups on the fingertips where caused either by the constant operation of the controls (in the way that guitar players develop calluses on their fingertips) or by the fingertips becoming trapped in the contact holes of the panels after »rigor mortis« set in, thereby creating the ominous »suction cups«. On the autopsy film, unfortunately, the fingers can only be seen from above.

Technical Roswell sequences don't seem to have been included in Santilli's exclusive private showings of the films. At any rate, nothing about them was ever recorded by viewers. Why not? According to leaked information, there are other far more explosive things to be seen in this as yet unreleased footage: one reel allegedly reveals the wreckage in the desert, another even shows President Truman standing in front of the relatively intact UFO wreck, which is being lifted by a crane onto a trailer truck. On the damaged label of a 3-minute film reel can, numbered 52, the word »Truman's (inspection?)« appears. He is alleged to have observed one of the other (unreleased) autopsies from behind the glass window. One of these autopsies is supposed to have taken place in a tent, illuminated by paraffin lamps. In the background, armed men in military camouflage suits briefly appear. This information cannot be positively verified and it is more than likely that it has become somewhat distorted in the telling.

Early information that some film footage is in 10 or 12-minute lengths became a bone of contention after it became known that 3-minute films were the rule at the time. The authenticity crisis involving the Roswell aliens later proved to have been created primarily by misunderstandings of Santilli's various hasty and imprecise statements.

Even Stanton T. Friedman, who performed great services with his excellent researches into UFO matters for many years, impetuously turned against Ray Santilli in an interview, probably out of personal animosity. On the one hand, he accused him of deceit, saying he could *»find no connection between the autopsy film and Roswell«*, but on the other, he concluded his criticism by saying he *»still didn't know what to make of the whole thing himself«*.

On the positive side is the fact that in the video documentary »UFO-Secret«, made in 1993 by New Century Productions, sketches based on the memory-pictures of eyewitnesses of the Roswell wreckage parts showed I-beams covered with strange signs. Even though at that time the autopsy and wreckage films had not yet been made public, the similarity with the now familiar carriers is amazing. The very fact that these metallic I-beams can be seen on both films makes Santilli's film a highly valuable bit of evidence supporting a real incident in Roswell on July 2, 1947.

Santilli, who hoped to strike it rich with his coup, is said to have refused offers of 7 million dollars for the worldwide rights of his films. According to latest news, the first autopsy performed on a second alien (9 minutes of autopsy and 7 minutes showing the creature being stripped of a strong suit of clothing and prepared for transport) has already been sold to a private collector. This turned out to be his own German partner, Volker Spielberg, with whose financial help he brought about the whole deal to begin with. In an attempt to get behind the rumors in this matter, I discovered in a phone call that the man said to be co-owner of the Roswell films had cancelled his Hamburg-based company telephone, moved to Austria, and was unavailable for comment.

The remaining celluloid strips are said to have been deposited in a Swiss bank vault. It remains to be seen whether the 23 or more minutes of footage will simply change vaults or perhaps be presented to the disbelieving public one day after all. Apparently there are also films among them which did not survive their long years spent in a cardboard box. Also not to be forgotten are the *»several hundred film reels«* which the cameraman handed over to the Army in 1947, at least excerpts of which were shown to a bevy of Army specialists and troop personnel for the purpose of psychological testing. On those films, according to unanimous statements, not only do the ufonaut corpses appear, first at the scene of the crash, then at their transport destination; but the complete UFO wreck in every detail is also shown. One of the still unreleased Santilli films is the »Recovery«, titled reel no. 31. A spokesman for the Merlin Group announced that in a new TV documentary planned for worldwide marketing, excerpts of both the second autopsy and the spacesuits will shortly be shown.

However, those people today entrusted with the original three-dimensional Roswell relicts are far more important. Perhaps, in view of increasing public pressure to lift the top secret classification of this matter, some of them will have the courage to step forward into the public light with these items so that the real roots of the Roswell saga can finally be proved.

The Puzzled Public

On Friday, January 13, 1995, after the first rumbles about the existence of authentic Roswell film footage were sparked by the TV appearance of Santilli's friend Reg Presley in a BBC breakfast television programme, and an article in the »Sheffield

Star«, even the middle-of-the-road media began to show an interest in the subject. In Germany where I watched the case unfold, the major weekly news program »Spiegel TV« immediately pronounced the film a forgery without having seen it. The upshot was that for a while only the UFO magazines reported on the matter. When Santilli officially invited journalists and UFO researchers to a sneak preview in May 1995, the scoop went around the world in no time. In a trice, TV representatives arrived, from RAI DUE, FOX, NBC, TELEVISA and PRO 7, to say nothing of film producers such as Columbia Tristar and several others. It seemed within the realm of possibility that the most sensational UFO film of all time was about to be put on view.

Santilli gave the first photo stills to the press in the summer, obviously to attract negotiators for international licensing rights. On July 30, 1995 London's »Sunday Times« on the front page, under the headline *Film that 'proves' aliens visited Earth is a hoax«*, wrote »RELAX. *The little green men have not landed«* and inside »*Little green men are a jolly green giant hoax.«* There followed a critical report by Maurice Chittenden designed to make readers wary of a forthcoming broadcast on the subject on Channel 4. Four days later, Ray Santilli wrote a letter to John Witherow, the paper's editor, parts of which I reproduce below, since the letter illuminates various details and is quite amusing in itself.

Santilli: »*I was most disappointed to read the above inaccurate and unsubstantiated article in last week's Sunday Times. – I have never claimed that the footage is definitely real, merely that I believe it to be so. – Unfortunately the article tries to prove the film a »hoax« by presenting unsubstantiated evidence, various unaccredited sources and irrelevant details regarding my working history and*

environment.« Then Santilli responds to the criticism, point-by-point:

• **Point 1**

The »Sunday Times« article calls into question the validity of the Roswell Alien Autopsy footage by stating »experts called in by Channel 4...have declared it bogus«. They have apparently also had special effect guys look at the film.

Santilli's response: »*John Purdie of Union Pictures, which is making the Channel 4 documentary has categorically stated that with regard to the authenticity of the footage: ›no conclusions have been reached‹«.*

For clarification: In the meantime, physical analysis has limited the date of production and also exposure of the films to the years 1947-49.

• **Point 2**

The »Sunday Times« article claims that the security coding on one film disappeared when its accuracy was challenged.

Santilli's response: »*The sequence of film referred to ...is not part of the autopsy footage. As you state in your article, this coding was applied in the same manner as one would a time-code or copyright notice. Far from denying this fact, I am quoted in the same article as freely informing your journalists that this action had been taken.*

For clarification: Santilli made a film copy for a friend, onto which he copied the film reel can label of the cameraman, in order to be able to pursue any future illegal copying of the film. He left out this code on the official copy for the TV station.

• **Point 3**

The »Sunday Times« article claims that a letter of authentication from Kodak was signed by a salesman.

Santilli's response: »*Upon contacting Kodak's head office in Hollywood we asked for the film verification department. They took our representatives to the relevant* place, and the person working within that department, Laurence Cate, conducted the verification examination. This was part of his function at Kodak. We had no knowledge, and we are not informed of any other job title or job description.

For clarification: In the meantime, both film expert Bob Shell and the London and Copenhagen offices of Kodak have tentatively confirmed the 1947 dating of the film material. However they insist on receiving more original frames for purposes of more precise chemical analysis of the emulsion on the celluloid acetate propionate. Mr. Cate, who after inspecting the material found himself suddenly in the news, has since been nicknamed »Authenty-Cate« by his colleagues.

• Point 4

The »Sunday Times« article states that »President Truman, supposedly visible on film, was not in New Mexico at the time«, according to the records held at the Harry S. Truman Library in Missouri.

Santilli's response: »The fact that the President Truman Library does not confirm that Truman was in New Mexico has no bearing, as there would not be an official record on the trip due to the sensitivity of the subject matter – as your article states ›there was certainly a cover up by the military authorities‹«.

For clarification: Cameraman J. B. asserts he filmed Truman. The name Truman can be seen on the somewhat damaged label of a reel can (see picture no. 20). Santilli now claims he never said he saw the President on the film.

• Point 5

The »Sunday Times« article claims that symbols seen on particles of wreckage are totally different from those remembered by an eyewitness.

Santilli's response: »No one has ever claimed that the debris filmed by the cameraman is the same debris as seen by the eyewitness. It should be noted that the supposed eyewitness has not seen any debris for nearly 50 years«.

For clarification: The eyewitness referred to is the son of Major Jesse Marcel who was 12 years old at the time and was shown some of the pieces his father collected and brought home from the wreckage field (see sketch, picture no. 34).

• Point 6

The »Sunday Times« article claims that doctors performing a supposedly unique autopsy on an alien removed black lenses from the eyes in a matter of seconds as if they knew what to expect.

Santilli's response: »The journalists from the Sunday Times were told quite clearly that I had autopsy footage of another alien identical in appearance to the first; so they knew that the autopsy they saw was not unique as the article suggests. As the doctors had already performed such an autopsy previously, they would have known what to expect.

For clarification: A number of researchers who were present at the very beginning and were able to see the original relevant part of the filmed first autopsy agree that, in the film, the eyes are examined for several minutes before anyone tries to remove the discovered membranes.

• Point 7

The »Sunday Times« article claims that experts have told Channel 4 that the film is a good fake and that »in their opinion, it can't be before the 1950s ...but it could be in the past few years.

Santilli's response: »John Purdie of Union Pictures, which is making the Channel 4 documentary has categorically stated that with regard to the authenticity of the footage: ›no conclusions have been reached‹.«

For clarification: Nobody except the US Air Force, which concealed corpses and wreckage, will be able decisively to prove the existence of footage and its contents.

• Point 8

The »Sunday Times« claims that Ray Santilli has refused to identify the cameraman or the place where the 16 mm film was transferred onto video.

Santilli's response: *»Due to the nature of this footage, this information was and will remain confidential as explained to the Sunday Times reporters.«*

For clarification: Santilli's promise to protect the identity of the cameraman was a part of their purchase agreement. It seems plausible that he doesn't name the video copying place either.

• Point 9

The »Sunday Times« article claims suspicions were aroused because injuries visible on the body of the »ET look-alikes« shown undergoing dissection were not consistent with an air crash.

Santilli's response: *»Firstly, the alleged alien featured in the footage looks nothing like ET from the movie. Secondly, I'm not aware of anyone, no matter what their credentials, who has the experience to know how an alien body would react in a crash. Of course, if the person who made the comments has seen other aliens who have been involved in a similar incident and can therefore make the necessary comparisons, I will be happy to reconsider this.«*

For clarification: Various people have conjectured that coyotes or other predatory animals might have caused the injuries.

• Point 10

The »Sunday Times« claims that Mr. Cate of Kodak said that although the film could be old, it does not mean that the aliens were filmed on it.

Santilli's response: *»The film is invaluable, and cutting useful footage would have been utter madness. By the same token it would be utter madness to attempt a world-wide ›hoax‹ on this level by attempting such an easily discovered forgery.«*

For clarification: The German UFO journalist Michael Hesemann was supposed to have recently received a similar exposed but not yet developed film from about the same time which, however, did not survive the span of time. If, based on this, one were to conclude a mass-media swindle, the implication is that it would have to have been planned many years ago in order to come to light in this decade, which is absurd.

• Point 11

The »Sunday Times« article claims that Ray Santilli is already selling on the Internet stills from the footage.

Santilli's response: *»This is completely untrue. However, mail-order videos are being sold.«*

For clarification: That may have been true at the time. Most stills reproduced in this book were in any case made from slides which this author received from Santilli in return for constructive participation in a television update on Roswell. The head of the team sent to interview me assured me during the shooting that the copyright for such slides would cost £500-1000 each. Any abuse of such rights could hardly be legally pursued, since all the pictures were originally the property of the US Army.

• Point 12

The »Sunday Times« article claims that Ray Santilli is now under attack from scientists and also the UFO community.

Santilli's response: *»Even though this is a controversial subject, I am not now, nor have I ever been ›under attack‹ from scientists. There have been those, however, from the UFO community who have always supported the theory that the footage is not genuine. Interestingly enough nearly all of those people have yet to actually see it.«*

For clarification: Certain professional international know-it-alls are meant here, e.g. the arch-skeptic Phil J. Klass, who considers the crash itself to be a swindle; and IRI initiator Kent Jeffrey: *»This is without doubt a manipulated corpse«*; the crop circle fabricators Lundberg and Dickinson: *»This autopsied corpse is* *clearly a cleverly constructed plastic doll*«. There are also a few shining examples of such skeptics in German speaking areas, e.g. the anti-UFO zealot Werner Walter.

• Point 13

The »Sunday Times« article claims that Paul O'Higgins, a medical anatomist at the University College London states, among other things, that the alien shown was basically humanoid. He then goes on to say that »...*the chances of life evolving to be that similar, even on two identical planets is the same as the odds of buying a lottery ticket every week for a year and winning the jackpot every Saturday night...*«.

Santilli's response: »*At best, this is an opinion and not a fact. I am surprised that an academic felt by the Sunday Times to be a suitably qualified ›expert‹ should have phrased his opinion using such a frivolous and populist analogy. I am confident that Mr. O'Higgins does not know the secrets of the universe anymore than anyone else.*«

For clarification: Contrary to the above-stated opinion, astronomic and genetic knowledge of recent years points to the probability of humanlike lifeforms existing in the cosmos being not as low as previously supposed.

• Point 14

The »Sunday Times« article claims that a nurse who supposedly saw the alien crash victims in 1947 said they had only four digits on each hand as opposed to six as featured in the footage.

Santilli's response: »*Even the Sunday Times themselves state that she only supposedly saw the crash victims. What makes her account any more or less credible than any other account?*«

For clarification: According to mortician Glenn Dennis, his missing girlfriend sketched the aliens' appearance on a napkin in a restaurant as having four claws.

• Point 15

The »Sunday Times« has pointed out that Mr. Santilli has pictures of Sergeant Bilko and the Starship Enterprise on his office walls.

Santilli's response: »*I also have record covers, gold records, music business awards and memorabilia plus various Marilyn Monroe photographs – I dread to think what the Sunday Times would make of these!*«

For clarification: Even though this isn't quite applicable, the reader should know that the Spaceship Enterprise saga was created by Gene Roddenberry only after he had maintained contact with extraterrestrial intelligence for years via a medium.[*]

Santilli's summary. »*As a regular reader of The Sunday Times I had always presumed its journalistic research to be of the highest quality. I can only now presume that other stories within The Sunday Times may well contain the same degree of unsubstantiated fact and insinuation against individuals. Ray Santilli.*«

This is how Santilli picks to pieces the commentaries of the once great »Sunday Times«. His letter was of course never published. The intended effect of the newspaper article succeeded. The British press from then on kept the Santilli affair at arm's length.

While dozens of international newspapers continued to report on the subject, the German press, among others, continued to hold back. Only the giant tabloid »Bild-Zeitung« and Cologne's »Express« (»*This is an Extraterrestrial Dying*«) published the first pictures, with short captions. But at the BUFORA-UFO convention in Sheffield, in mid August 1995, another bombshell was dropped which provoked wider media interest. Press, radio and television from many different countries, including the US, Brazil, Israel, France, Greece, Russia and Germany were there live and both auditoriums holding

---

[*] see Phyllis Schlemmer, »The Only Planet of Choice - Essential Briefings from Deep Space«, Bath 1993, Gateway Books.

almost a thousand viewers were totally sold out when Santilli presented a 28-minute piece of evidence. It was undoubtedly the UFO convention with the biggest media presence in history. The German magazine »Focus« titled its relatively serious, illustrated four-page article »*Jagd auf E. T.*« (»*The Hunt for E. T.*«) and »*Rette sich, wer kann*« (loosely, »*Everyone Into the Lifeboats!*«). The »Spiegel« followed a week later in its well known lampooning, polemical manner. At the end of August the autopsy was broadcast by 32 television stations around the world, e.g. Japan, Great Britain and Italy.

German Station RTL showed excerpts from the film on the first day of its release. Alongside a report on bacteria in ice cream, they announced the »universe premiere« of the autopsy of an extraterrestrial, shot by the American space agency (!). Buried in a report about the Sheffield UFO convention of a few days earlier and a bunch of interviews, only a few segments of the actual autopsy were shown. Santilli, the above-mentioned Munich pathologist, a film critic and technical expert, Ufologists and convention-goers all had their say. To start with, it was carried out with a certain seriousness, but both the sequences and the commentary deteriorated increasingly to the level of personal bias. The commentary wondered aloud several times how in the world the cameraman had managed to smuggle this material out of a high security area blocked off by the US military, even though this was never claimed in any official declaration and Station RTL had all the statements of the cameraman. British convention-goers were then consciously mistranslated. It stooped even lower when Berlin film expert Dr. Rolf Giesen went so far as to put on a rubber mask from the movie »Ghostbusters« with the comment, »*that what matters in the end is what people want to believe*«, as if it were of no importance how information from which opinions are formed is presented to the public. In the end, the majority of the audience was swayed to disbelief by the doubting tenor of the RTL report, giving everyone the feeling of having unmasked a cunning hoax. Santilli countered, »*that subjective opinions don't interest him. After five long months of testing, challenging and examination, he has yet to see one watertight piece of evidence that the film is a forgery*«.

Subsequently, countless newspapers and magazines all over the world published comprehensive reports. The German magazine »Focus« published a cover story titled »*The UFO Phenomenon - Belief in Extraterrestrials Reaches New Dimensions*« and proceeded to blend this article »*Hello, Earthlings*« with abductions, Hollywood and Internet. As the caption to a photo of Ray Santilli, »Focus« posed the question of whether this might be the biggest fraud of the century. »Spiegel« gave its report the curious title »*Elephant in the Garden - The Truth about the Alleged UFO Crash near Roswell in 1947*«. The »*Spiegel*« view became evident after a few lines through its choice of words: »*The hydrocephalic creature... shock scenes... the obscure work... interstellar crash pilot... dream castles of Ufologists... corpses of extraterrestrial fabled...*« Instead of sticking to the truth, »Spiegel« came up with a story which had long been disproved by researchers that there were no wall telephones in 1947. Bad luck for renowned »Spiegel«: in the Telephone Museum of Bell South in Atlanta, visitors can inspect precisely the wall telephone, model 350 from 1946, seen in the film. The spiral cord, also criticized by many, was shown by AT&T investigators to have been on the market since 1938. »Spiegel's« quote by Dr. Eisenmenger very nearly reversed what he actually said on RTL TV. Inquiring about this, I found out that »Spiegel« hadn't even bothered to contact the professor. In the meantime, the Roswell film footage has been shown at a whole array of pertinent lectures and conventions, with and without Santilli's permission. In UFO magazines, the pro-and-con fanatics have been at war with each other ever since. And various activists have been offering a Santilli video (containing only parts of the 22 original films) »exclusively«. (It is now also available through Gateway Books for a special price of £ 11.95.)*

The FOX television network devoted itself assiduously to the theme. In a TV Special of the »Encounters« series, Star Trek actor Jonathan Frakes moderated the material in a show titled »Alien Autopsy – Fact or Fiction«. The whole group of eyewitnesses still living and the main Roswell researchers were interviewed, including BUFORA boss Philip Mantle, who has meanwhile conducted secret talks with the cameraman, too. When Santilli had J.B. phone the station, a telephone tracer was in operation. But the call was too short, the trace didn't work. The TV team even hired a private detective to track down the former Army filmmaker. But the only thing agent William Dear was able to find was a different cameraman, who knew of the films his colleague had made, because J. B. himself had told him. Paolo Cherchi Usai, curator of the Eastman House at Kodak headquarters in Rochester, NY, said in public »that it would make sense to assume that this film was made somewhere between the end of the forties and beginning of the fifties. It isn't possible to simply forge a film. The cost and effort necessary would be so immense that it would swallow up any possible profits.«

Hollywood film director Allen Daviau, however, thought the film was forged, because so many close-ups were blurred. The Marine cameraman Dr. Ro-

derick Ryan, who himself filmed top secret government projects in the forties and fifties, declared: »The fact that the film gets blurry is completely in accord with the equipment used then. The cameras in general use by the military then were hand-held Bell & Howell 16mm cameras. Their lenses couldn't be focused, they had to be changed. That took time and in emergency situations wasn't possible. So if all the scenes had been in sharp focus, one would have to conclude that they were set-up scenes or were taken with more modern equipment. The cameraman moves around, in order to get the best angle. It was always the job of a military cameraman to film an occurrence for protocol, not to produce beautiful pictures. And what is shown here is a reasonable film of an occurrence.«

Film expert and retired Colonel Colman S. von Keviczky, director of the worldwide UFO research group IFUCON, himself an experienced military cameraman who had used the same camera, was of the same opinion. In his 3-page expertise, he declared »This camera could be loaded with 100 ft. of double-perforated silent film or single side-perforated sound film. These Kodak negative films were all developed by the Signal Corps. Camera mechanisms like autofocus and zoom lenses were just a dream in those days. There is no reason whatsoever to criticize the cameraman for some unsharp sequences. No one, in the circumstances at the autopsy, could have supplied better work with this technology.«

The programers then questioned the two prominent pathologists already referred to, Prof. Milroy and Prof. Wecht. The latter claimed »that a potential swindler, in which he didn't believe, should really work in Hollywood with such capabilities, and make fantastic films with Steven Spielberg«. »Encounters« then turned to Stan Winston, special effects guru of Hollywood. The creator of the Jurassic Park dinosaurs and of the horrible »aliens« in the movie of the

* for ordering address/coupon, see appendix pp. 215/216.

same name first thought it might be a doll. »*But when the autopsy got underway and they began to dissect the being - and I know how difficult it is to simulate the cutting open of skin in the world of special effects (SFX) - I said to myself I would be proud if I could create something like that today. Do you see how steadily the blood oozes forth from the body, how uniformly it flows down the sides, and how uniformly moist the inside of the body appears? Nothing looks suspicious. I mean, we never could have managed that. Whoever did that could start working for me immediately.*«

The report concluded that the film was indeed genuine and that that could only mean that we are not alone in the cosmos. The program was an incomparable hit in the ratings watched by 7.6 million households. This meant, according to the usual calculations, that 30 million viewers were actually glued to their screens. Because of this success, the program was shown again a week later, and still later a third time. A further documentary, delving deeper into the subject, came several months later in autumn 1996.

The highly welcome International Roswell Initiative (IRI) is headed by the biggest skeptics of the Santilli film, but is nevertheless trying to force a legal clarification of the Roswell incident. It found the success of the TV program just too much. In an open letter to media mogul Rupert Murdoch, members complained vehemently about the »imbalanced reporting« and sent copies of their letter to all the big networks, with the request that they stop showing any more programs of the Santilli alien autopsies. The subject was also dropped by most of the other networks.

The expanded German version of the FOX documentary was shown six months later by Station PRO 7 and got good ratings. However, in Stern TV (the television version of a major news magazine), Germany's most popular TV moderator, Günther Jauch's obsessive drive for »infotainment« really stole the show. His editors had a lifesize alien made of paper mâché and filled it with freshly slaughtered pig's intestines. In all seriousness, he then tried to foist off a black and white film of this unappetizing doll on UFO researchers at a convention as an additional autopsy. Instead of delving deeper into the objective story, Jauch exploited it for all the drama it was worth. The fact that cuts of this flop were shown in several retrospectives of the series at a later date demonstrates just how proud the »infotainer« was of himself. In the show »*The Making of Stern TV*«, it was asserted that the extremely high ratings of this series were all due to the moderator, »*who doesn't need to stoop to sleight-of-hand tricks*«. Jauch then babbled on about the guardian role television plays in society and how he – without trying to appear like a know-it-all – was trying to get things moving with his type of television journalism. All he really managed to do with his dubious Roswell »report« was convey his own ignorance of the subject to a listening audience.

As an Austrian myself, I can report that the media in my country were above it all...or else simply never caught on. In any case, they didn't find that events concerning Roswell merited discussion. My own random questioning of acquaintances and passers-by in the street while this manuscript was being put together showed that the great majority of those who had seen or heard anything at all through the press, but mainly via RTL-TV, about the »alleged alien autopsy«, whether directly or indirectly, already had a hard and fast prejudice. They were either fascinated, or disgusted; but hardly anyone was willing to admit being at a loss or even slightly perplexed about the matter.

In the meantime theories about the Roswell film, put out by skeptics range from its being a Brazilian science fiction B-movie to the idea that the creature subjected to the autopsy was a victim of secret nuclear testing, genetic engineering, bacteriological weapons testing or was a special effects distraction by US Intelligence against the Russians. Another theory was that Santilli was bankrupt and staged the large-scale fraud for that reason. The only trouble with such insinuations is that all those sophisticated trick possibilities didn't exist in 1947. Even genetic engineering has been around only since the eighties. At the time this book went to press (and also the English translation), not a breath of proof that the film was phony had been presented, despite all the polemic and ridicule the mass media had heaped upon it.

On the contrary, latest deductions permit the only possible conclusion that the film has to be absolutely authentic. Film forgers in those days could not have known that the autopsy would be carried out by Dr. Bronk. His name only became known much later in the MJ-12 documents. Also the roughly coinciding appearance of the sketches of the I-beams which were drawn by various eyewitnesses points to the genuineness of the celluloid film, since they were all made at a time when the world didn't know of the existence of the extraordinary film documents. Furthermore, the astonishing similarity of several historic descriptions of the alien bodies has to be mentioned; this applies especially to the report of the doctor informed by pathologists Dr. Sanford and Dr. Sullivan, which was completed before the film fragments came to light. If, somehow, film footage had become known or had been seen by anyone beforehand – for example, through internal military showings – that would at least prove the historical existence of the film material, particularly at a time when the term »special effects« was not yet born.

President Clinton's »Executive Order No. 12958« will surely add more oil to the flames of the alien and UFO discussion. This order, which came into effect on October 16, 1995 requires all secret documents which are more than 25 years old to be released to the public. Despite immense resistance from intelligence circles, the bureaucratic process of freeing about 100,000 pages of microfilmed documentary material from the US Air Force project »BLUE BOOK« has begun. Nevertheless, there are still several insurmountable obstacles, enabling government officials to keep sensitive subjects from being made public. Article 5/552 of the »United States Code« cites no fewer than 16 grounds for preventing public access to certain files, even after they have been declassified. However, UFO researchers are already getting their first look at this mass of literature.

There are also more and more retired US astronauts who are beginning to come out with their long-held secret experiences, despite being prohibited to do so. This stirs up the waters still further. Neil Armstrong made several veiled references to his having filmed a UFO landing while on the Moon. Astronaut Aldrin filmed two shining objects. All space flights from Apollo 11 to 16 were cloaked in an especially heavy mantle of secrecy. Live television coverage and radio communication were only released after a delay; thus, NASA exercised a quiet selection over what the public was permitted to hear: UFOs were artfully erased from a series of Moon photos before being released to the media. Later, through an indiscretion, some of the phenomenal photos came to light, e.g. Apollo 12/NASA-Photo AS12-51-8553 and AS12-50-7346, on which extraterrestrial spacecraft can definitely be seen. After the Apollo missions, NASA suddenly and inexplicably gave up its »idée fixe« of setting up a permanent Moon base.

Astronaut Gordon Cooper declared that a »Center for Advanced Technologies« (since then disbanded) was working on reconstructing extraterrestrial power units. Astronaut Dr. Brian O'Leary even said that ongoing contact with extraterrestrial cultures exists.

From insider sources it was revealed that the North American Military Space Observation Center NORAD, with its especially powerful radar systems deep in the Cheyenne Mountains, spots and pinpoints an average of 500 (!) »speedsters« , i.e. UFOs, which enter Earth's atmosphere from the depths of space every year. Sgt. Major Robert Dean, former NATO intelligence employee, revealed that informed people in government circles are of the opinion that we are dealing with hundreds of different extraterrestrial civilisations, both intergalactic and interdimensional ones. He succeeded in talking a whole covey of cosmonauts into reporting on their UFO experiences, insofar as their »vows of secrecy« permitted, before a US Congressional Committee.

President Jimmy Carter wanted to ease the UFO information policies, but couldn't get past his own intelligence agencies. The CIA refused him access to the top secret UFO files because he did not have the required clearance. There are evidently certain levels of security even beyond the reach of the White House. A group budgeted with illegal money inside the CIA, NSA and DIA (internal Defense Intelligence Agency) operates independent of presidential knowledge or control. This clique seems to be able to protect and conceal its knowledge about UFOs, thought control, genetic engineering, free energy and anti-gravity propulsion so well that the Watergate affair appears by comparison like a children's game. MJ-12 seems to be somehow still active...

Bill Clinton is also dissatisfied with the information he receives about UFO activities, since it completely contradicts what one of his own scientific advisors has been able to ascertain. The President now in office has apparently given orders to have pilot videos shot for alternative public revelation of the existence of UFOs and extraterrestrials. With the President's approval, Dr. Steven Greer is said to have made contact with leading authorities of various European governments to work toward an understanding about releasing a coordinated global statement on the hard and fast existence of UFOs and extraterrestrials.

To induce Clinton to keep up the pressure in UFO matters, 85-year old philanthropist Laurence Rockefeller has been active in poignant ways. According to an August 24, 1995 article in the »New York Daily News«, he let Clinton know, in the course of Clinton's 49th birthday party at Rockefeller Ranch near the Grand Tetons that he would only be willing to make substantial contributions to the re-election campaign coffers if Clinton made a breakthrough in the UFO question in the present administration. *»The administration has to finally put an end to the negation of this subject which has gone on for 40 years.«* In particular, the Roswell affair should be used as a test case. But what Clinton announced in the course of a speech in Belfast on December 1, 1995 was utterly trivial. He answered a 13-year old boy over the loudspeaker: *»No, as far as I know, no spaceship crashed in Roswell, New Mexico in 1947. If the Air Force really recovered extraterrestrial corpses, they haven't told me about it so far. And that sort of thing I want to know.«*

At least a Rockefeller-sponsored study about UFO activities, which was recently made in cooperation with three astronauts, is supposed to have been sent to all congressional representatives in spring 1996. The Rockefeller Foundation also finances the Committee for the Study of Extraterrestrial Intelligence (CSETI), which tries to make contact with extraterrestrials via laser technology. So let us hope brisk and bustling Mr. Rockefeller enjoys a long and healthy life and is, furthermore, able to put Clinton and his bunch under every possible pressure in the matter of UFOs, in particular with regard to Roswell.

Another piece of the puzzle has been put into place. Through greed and/or good business sense, the J. B./Santilli/US Air Force film footage has been fitted into the larger picture of the overall Roswell scenario. Disapproved of by the media, celebrated by UFO enthusiasts, regarded with suspicion by intelligence circles, the celluloid and video fragments have nonetheless unleashed an ongoing discussion which will not end until the secrecy of the Pentagon and the defensive tactics of successive administrations cease. Along with several other mysteries, the Roswell crash and its aliens can assume a worthy spot in the Hall of Famous Shockers, right along with a) the annual crop circle mysteries, which despite all the phoney man-made circles which have slipped in among them,* continue to keep people scratching their heads; b) the puzzling animal mutilations on American grazing pastures; c) the drastically increasing ET-abduction syndrome and im-

plantation enigma*. The Roswell mystery, its aliens and all the rest of it, has at least shaken up the slumbering masses.

---

* All disbelievers of the crop circles are advised to look a little more closely at the »Mandelbrot«-crop circle which appeared in a wheatfield near Cambridge, England in the night of August 12, 1991. This formation owes its nickname to the chaos theory of fractals and is one of the most complex mathematical forms which can only be calculated by powerful computers. It is highly unlikely that such a form could just be trampled down by nocturnal tricksters.
Just before the first printing of this book, an equally interesting and evidently authentic wheatfield phenomenon occurred in the Lower Austrian village of Flandorf (see picture no. 48). The sign depicts a nearly perfect hexagram in the form of points on a circle around a circle, which suggests through the central circular surface that the structure is meant to be looked at three-dimensionally...which, in turn, has a lot to do with UFO power units.
Perhaps it is also worth mentioning that I was told the name of a special, evenly growing grass seed years ago via a channeling contact with other extraterrestrials, in which even small versions of wheat circles can be formed »paranormally«.

* For some time now, there have been reports about miniature-sized, usually microchip-type implants made of strange materials, which – sometimes following extraterrestrial experiences – have been found under the skin or deeper inside the body. Some »abducted« people discover that a kind of homing transmitter has been implanted in them. I myself in the meantime, have met two people who have personally experienced just such a phenomenon.

Scenario III: The Roswell-Alien Contacts

Signposts Along the Way

People who become obsessed with extraterrestrials have usually had some formative UFO experience.* To give the reader a better understanding of my personal involvement with the subject matter, it is appropriate to grant a brief glimpse into my own, as well as my wife's, development in this subject.

My first sighting was also the most close-up, the loveliest and the most exciting one of all. It happened 17 years ago, but the event made such an indelible impression on me that I feel as though it happened yesterday. Apart from a short radio interview at a UFO convention which came about by chance, I have never related my experiences to a wider circle. My encounter can't be proven and I had no desire to focus attention on myself. In connection with my Roswell psychic-contacts of later date, however, it is imperative to relate these earlier occurrences in the interests of coherency.

As a 29-year old student, I was living in the center of the Austrian industrial city of Linz, in an attic apartment with slanting ceilings and dormer windows. To save space I'd shoved the desk into a niche, with two windows behind me. That is where I sat on that memorable sunny afternoon in spring, studying different angles of a subject which had been nagging at me for months: sunspots. To be exact, I had discovered something I thought significant a few days earlier. In the course of long study, I had found that the sun distributes its energy to the planets in the solar system according to a highly refined space-time formula and that sunspots and sun winds connect causally with Earth's rhythm. At that point I had spent ten years studying the biophysical and bioenergetical research of Wilhelm Reich, whom I considered the first holistic scientist of modern times.*

I was especially interested in the kinetic power of orgon energy, Reich's name for life energy per se. I would go so far as to say that at that time I had mastered the fundamental principle behind the orgon motor, so that I only had to occupy myself with theoretical details of this generator which would ultimately be able to solve all Earth's energy problems. My main aim was to find out where and when our (orgon) blue planet would next be flooded with high doses of cosmic orgon energy, since that knowledge, according to my researches, was essential to starting up bioenergetic perpetual motion and keeping it fully revved up.

On that sunny afternoon on May 7, 1980, I was also trying mathematically to prove – particularly for myself – certain details in reference to this. This was partly because I had got a letter from a highly gifted Belgian channel medium who, together with a half-dozen other top deep-trance mediums, I'd got to know at a PSI-Workshop in France, where I had experienced some truly remarkable things. I had casually mentioned my admiration for Wilhelm Reich's researches a few weeks earlier at this workshop, saying that I would love if possible to be able to ask

---

* None of the authors investigating Roswell, according to their own accounts, has ever seen a UFO.

* Parallel to these studies, I had also been running the Austrian Wilhelm Reich Archives for many years; at that time its responsibility was to make many of Reich's publications which were destroyed during the Nazi period and the McCarthy era again available to interested researchers worldwide.

him a whole string of questions. To my astonishment, a second letter had been included, taken down in dictation by the trance medium and directed to me by Reich himself. It seemed that he wanted to give my researches an assisting nudge. He did this not by conveying finished formulae to me, but in the form of spiritual parables, mathematical puzzles and illuminating geometrical sketches which, after a bit of head-scratching, pointed me in the right direction towards a deeper understanding of the mysteries he had left behind. I have to add here that my studies thus far had not been conducted purely rationally, but had to some extent been arrived at intuitively through certain »coincidences«. Besides that, I was in the habit at that time of reading about a dozen different books more or less simultaneously and leaving them, opened at certain pages containing important passages, lying around my apartment. As I had always approached many subjects from a cross-disciplinary perspective, comparing different points of view, it happened that there were books on a whole host of different subjects lying about: crystal structures, Indian mythology, astronomy, astrology, biophysics, cosmology, as well as lots of Wilhelm Reich's writings. All this promoted a state of euphoria in the few days preceding the sighting, which I shall presently describe.

What then occurred was extraordinary. All the open-paged passages from the books suddenly coalesced into a complete whole with regard to my questions and lit up a whole row of little lights inside my consciousness. Eureka! I had discovered the principle which Reich had quite consciously withheld – or hinted at between the lines – in his books. For several nights I could scarcely sleep, getting up again and again in the wee small hours to re-examine various aspects of these insights. More and more, the most important mandala in Indian mythology, the

Sri Yantra, took on a central importance. I perceived that the mathematical laws of planetary power supply were contained in their entirety in the geometrical proportions of this »meditative image«. Moreover, that these intertwined triangles were but a two-dimensional representation of a mystic crystal, in whose planes of refraction all the laws of the universe were perfectly reflected (see illustration no. 48).

The above digression is necessary, to fill in the background to my approaching sighting and make it comprehensible. So imagine me having sat for hours working and puzzling over these geometric patterns covered with intertwined triangles, and after several sleepless nights in a kind of trance pursuing the various aspects of this problem. While in this meditative state of mind, I suddenly heard an inner voice from my psyche almost commanding: *»Go look out the window.«* Not precisely those specific words were uttered, but an inner psychic energy was suddenly inside my head which I instantly grasped as constituting that order. Like an automaton, without thinking about it, I rose from my chair and walked, not to say floated the few steps over to the window, somehow in these moments being utterly oblivious to gravity and time. I threw open the partially-closed shutters, and stared spellbound up into a huge blue hole which had opened in the cloudy sky. My jaw dropped and my heart nearly stopped beating: right in front of me, about 300-500 yards away, a silvery disc danced in the air.

In any case, it carried out movements a conventional aircraft would never have been able to execute. I saw the object for only a few seconds (it bore a certain similarity to a UFO I've since seen in a trailer of the television series »X-Files«) before it disappeared behind the clouds. However, in my heightened state of consciousness, that was quite sufficient. From the instant the sighting began, something inside me had switched over to a kind of slow-motion perception. Consequently, I could clearly see how the saucer-like disc, which was markedly concave on the upper side, and slightly less so on the lower side, tipped toward the sun quite intentionally so that a reflection of light, almost like a greeting, flashed into my eyes. When I awoke from this strange, brief »hypnosis« (normally I cannot easily be hypnotized against my will) and my reason again took control, it was only seconds before my reactions responded in a determined way. I quickly turned on the radio to listen to the 3:00 pm news, which was on. Hundreds, if not thousands, of people I reasoned had to have seen the vehicle. A UFO right above the Upper Austrian state capital wasn't something one could overlook. It was frustrating that nothing about it was reported on the radio, but I told myself that such things weren't broadcast that quickly. Since I had spent my military service mostly attached to a radar unit, my next move was to call air control at the nearby airport and ask to speak to the radar-control people. My call was put through; but when I asked if they had seen the fast moving, probably extra-terrestrial disc above Linz on their screens, they thought I was a crank and hung up. I then called the editorial offices of the biggest Austrian daily newspaper, where my girlfriend at the time worked as a reporter. I knew they listened in on police bands, but they had heard nothing of a UFO either. By now I was somewhat perplexed, but not yet discouraged. After all, I had sighted the object with a clear mind – or rather, it had intentionally revealed itself to me. I puzzled over it the whole evening. The next day, I bought all the morning papers, but there wasn't any mention of a flying saucer.

From my spontaneously sketched diagram, I was able to calculate that the silvery craft had been flying at about 350 - 500 mph and was no more than 8 - 10 yards in diameter. When in the following days nothing whatever appeared in the papers about the incident, I began slowly to doubt my reason. How could I in broad daylight have made a shockingly unequivocal sighting which no one else in the whole city had seen? Until then I had had little interest in UFOs and ETs, but for no other reason than to re-establish my inner equilibrium, I acquired a few books on the phenomenon. Over the following twelve months, books on the subject filled a whole shelf. This literature contained several references asserting that UFOs materialized and dematerialized, intentionally showing themselves to certain individuals while remaining invisible to others. It was hypothesized that the brain frequency of the observer was somehow changed from afar. Be that as it may, it at least suggested that the phenomenon I experienced was genuine and I could sleep peacefully again. The upshot was that serious interest was awakened in me by this engrossing event, and I proceeded to gobble up everything I could find on the subject. From then on, I found myself gazing much more often at the sky with wide open eyes, during the day and at night.

About two years later, another intensive sighting experience, similar in character, took place in the middle of Linz. It occurred at about 11:00 in the evening as I was strolling alone in the pedestrian zone. It was early autumn, under a full moon, and at first I didn't give a second thought to the Moon being so huge and low, just over the rooftops, until I saw its color changing. I was shaken to the core when I suddenly spotted the real Moon, in another part of the sky, at my back. I began to observe the huge object more closely and noticed it was moving very slowly. So as not to lose sight of it behind the houses, I had to walk fast and then run ahead some distance. The streets were rather crowded and I didn't want to be overly conspicuous, having my earlier experience still in mind. Should I tell other passers by that I was looking at a huge shining object in the sky which they might not be able to see? After all, no one besides me was paying the slightest attention to it. After a few minutes, I lost it from view and to this day cannot explain it.

Since then, I have gazed at the sky still more frequently. It is possible that I made three or four other sightings, but they all occurred at night and the objects were much further away. It is also possible that one or other of these phenomena has a perfectly natural explanation. One of these stories of movable stars merits telling, however.

For a time in 1982, shortly after meeting my wife, I conducted several weeks of seminars on New Age themes high up in the mountains of the Salzburg Lake District, with the gifted PSI medium from France referred to earlier. During one of the workshops – probably due to over exertion in the exercises – I contracted an extremely painful nerve inflammation. My wife-to-be and another friend took me to the emergency ward of the nearest hospital. Leaning back in the car on the way down the highway to the hospital in Salzburg, I looked up at the star-filled sky and had the distinct feeling that one of the largest stars was moving along with us. I asked the woman who was driving to stop at a rest area, where, lo and behold, the light also came to a stop. And started moving again when we did. All three of us could see it. Somehow it created a quieting, calming feeling, as if we were being escorted by protectors.

My other sightings were not so remarkable. But a related experience is worth mentioning. During my in-depth studies of Reich, a question nagged at me all the while I was trying to build a model orgon motor. In this emotionally charged situation I spoke, inwardly, directly to Wilhelm Reich himself. »*Willy, if you can hear me, and I am correct in my present assumption, then please give me a sign.*« No sooner said than done. I had barely finished thinking my message when a glistening sphere of light about a yard in diameter came zooming out of a corner of the room and pierced straight through me. It nearly gave me a heart attack, but at the same time was so »heartwarming« that I continued in the same mental vein. »*If that was your sign, please do it again, but a little more gently, if you don't mind.*« The ball of light appeared out of nowhere again, rushed at me as before, but truly more gently than before. Nonetheless, it again rocked my insides. In all truth, I wouldn't like to experience anything like it again...and in fact never have. The sign I received was double-edged besides, since it related very directly to the orgon motor itself. That is just what it looks like, in fact, when it is working at full throttle, then it disappears in a self-luminescent field of light, like certain unidentified flying objects. Some years later I was able to conduct some deeply moving personal conversations with Wilhelm Reich through my wife Mira's evolving channelling abilities.

I pursued my studies of the orgon motor for many more years, but finally gave them up when I realized that a practicable implementation of these principles would not only require enormous funding, but would also necessarily involve officialdom in some way, which in such a controversial subject was not to be trusted.

My wife also experienced a few very impressive UFO sightings. But unlike mine, due to her different sensitivities, they all occurred while she was more or less in a kind of dream state. While lucid, she was »beamed« to astral UFOs or invited to examine them. She even visited astral aliens on other planets. Later on, when her gifts as a medium, in the course of our trance training together, had fully blossomed, we turned out to be able to conduct – sometimes intentionally, sometimes »coincidentally« – a whole series of verbal dialogs with extraterrestrials. About nine years after my »dormer window sighting«, the creatures whose UFO I had seen, and who signalled to me, communicated directly with me via my wife, explaining their sole intention had been to awake me from the sleep of my present incarnation. They told me that I had once upon a time been one of them in an earlier incarnation, as had a friend of mine. Interestingly, I had received a letter from this person, whom I hadn't yet met at the time, in response to the first book my wife and I wrote together. I intuitively plucked his letter from a whole stack of unopened correspondence, telling my wife I didn't know why, that I would certainly answer this particular letter. It was a letter from the former fighter plane pilot and present-day airline pilot who agreed to a long term sponsorship of our small para-institute.

To prevent any possible misunderstanding, I in no way mean to claim that I am an »extraterrestrial« in the classical sense of the term. Many of us are in a certain sense extraterrestrials in that we are able to choose the planetary base of future embodiments relatively freely after a certain, more conscious level of spiritual evolution has been reached. It is no wonder, given the present day acceleration of consciousness, that in the initial phases of the Age of Aquarius on Earth, increasing numbers of men and women in their process of awakening occasionally recall their own previous lives in other worlds. Apart from that, seen from the point of view of anyone beyond Earth, we are all extraterrestrials, i.e. living outside their home planet.

Perhaps this chapter has helped the reader grasp that without the paranormal experiences related above, the author would certainly not have been able to approach the Roswell theme or direct alien communication with such an unbiased mind.

Synchronizing Hemispheres

Sometime in early August 1995, on a summer vacation with our children on Attersee Lake, I happened upon a copy of the German weekly, »Focus«, in which there were several pages of reporting on the Roswell autopsy film. The largest photo of the ET corpse immediately captivated me. Even though I suspected for several days that it was probably only a newpaper hoax, the photo evidently touched me unconsciously far more deeply than I first admitted to myself. My wife had just returned from an extended consulting tour in Jungian trance dialogs in Switzerland. In passing, and without a word, I showed her the alien photos. Her only response was, »Yes, the time has come«, after which she showed no interest in pursuing the matter further. I tended to agree with her that probably for the first time in modern history, we were being confronted with facts confirming intelligent extraterrestrial life which could no longer be dismissed. Nevertheless, I quietly concluded that we ought to avail ourselves of the paranormal possibilities we had open to us to research the matter further. To transmit this point of view to my wife, that is, to make Mira receptive to the idea, was not easy, since she had often declined any cooperation in channelling whenever it had to do with ETs. This was not unfounded: she had had some precarious experiences with extraterrestrial mental contacts and dream contacts too.

My own pertinent experiences had sometime contained explosive incidents, but I, unlike my wife, have a rather benign attitude toward the crews of light-powered vehicles from outer space.

My wife's reservations are based primarily on an experience about eight years ago with a male channel friend. Through this friend, odd beings passing themselves off as extraterrestrial entities threatened us and our son Manuel, if we didn't cooperate by letting them – via this particular medium – scan certain of my »rare books«. It was all quite absurd, but we were not in a position to evaluate it as such at the time. I solved the problem by asking the medium – who was also our house guest – to leave the premises at once, cutting off all contact on this level with the supposed ETs. It is theoretically possible that these were some of the so-called »grays«, the dark-side of the alien species, as it were. But regardless, we never had anything to do with them again.* This experience remained a rather traumatic one for my wife, sharpening our sense of discrimination in such matters.

About our relevant UFO experiences we have remained silent so far in public in order not to risk clashing with what at that time had been our main concern, namely, embryo communication and contact with »Carl Jung«. We also wanted to avoid giving the impression that we were people who have their fingers in every esoteric pie; besides, we were too involved with the publication of what were to us extremely important transmissions.

I have always had a certain weakness for paranormal phenomena. My wife was no different, even long before we met. However, unlike Mira, I could not point to specific experiences of such things for many years. It was not until I stopped studying architecture, which tied me too inextricably to the purely rational side of life, that my old worldview began to disintegrate, piece by piece. It was triggered off by a year long stay in India and Sri Lanka. That was where the ESP experiences I had longed for began to rain down upon me. Moreover, a clairvoyant jungle guru in Asia predicted astonishingly accurate details about my future wife. At the time I paid it no heed. But after my return home, I had a clairvoyant dream of my own, with a lucid vision of Mira. About one and a half years later, I met her – corporally, that is. Already on the very first day of our »reunion« (a karmic connection from an earlier existence can be assumed) we began living together and the wedding ceremony was only a formality. That she was a specialist in holistic nutrition was fortuitous, since I was organizing at the time the previously mentioned weeklong seminars on the Aquarian Age, for which she enthusiastically took over the kitchen duties. With the help of diverse tests by French psychologist Dr. Gerard Bellebon, himself a gifted medium, the buried abilities and talents of my wife were recognized. Together we were initiated into the techniques of esoteric trance by Dr. Bellebon and over the next six to eight years we attained a certain degree of mastery in their practice.

One of the major requirements for the necessary stable state of trance is to be able to harmonize utterly the wave frequencies of both halves of the brain during the production of alpha, delta and theta waves, an ability which my wife has mastered near to perfection. We were able to demonstrate her ability visibly with electronic meters developed for the purpose of measuring brain waves.*

Our son Emanuel was born in 1983. Through inner speaking, a form of telepathy, he dictated, starting in Mira's fifth month of pregnancy, a whole book of his experiences in the womb. Working on

---

* This experience was a powerful taste of the importance of cultivating a high frequency of one's own, through nutrition, meditation, etc. in order to ward off sinister, tricky beings and their mischief.

* With a prototype of a device called Mind-Mirror, an electronic screen which measures and compares brain waves of the left and right hemi-spheres. The meter is helpful in objectivizing meditative states and via bio-feedback feeling one's way into the consciousness of another person.

88

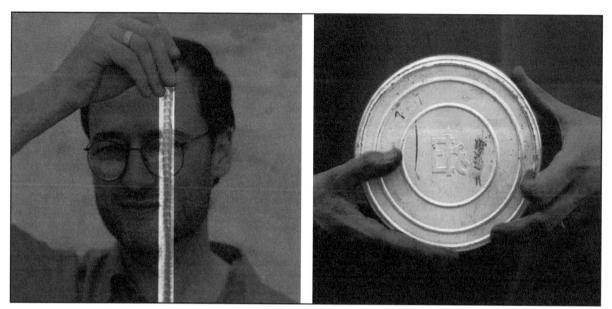

17 *London film dealer Ray Santilli shows original strips and film can of material bought for about $150,000 from a former US Air Force cameraman, and showing autopsies of several aliens.*

18 *Written expertises by Kodak and international film expert Bob Shell, assessing the age of the film fragments which they said they were 95% sure were genuine.*

19 *Two labels from the 3-minute film cans, 22 of them »illegally« purchased and released piece by piece by Ray Santilli. Are about 300 reels still being kept inside the Pentagon?*

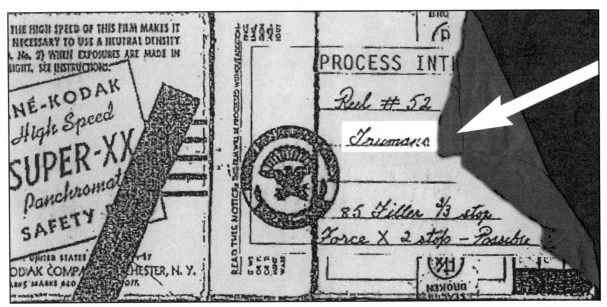

20 *Slightly damaged original label of film can no. 31 with clearly legible lettering »Truman...«. Did President Truman visit the site of the UFO wreck himself?*

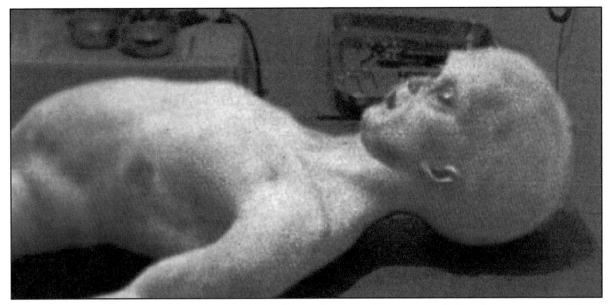

21 *The picture that went around the world: the disputed corpse of an apparently female extraterrestrial being awaiting autopsy by two military doctors at the base in Fort Worth, Texas.*

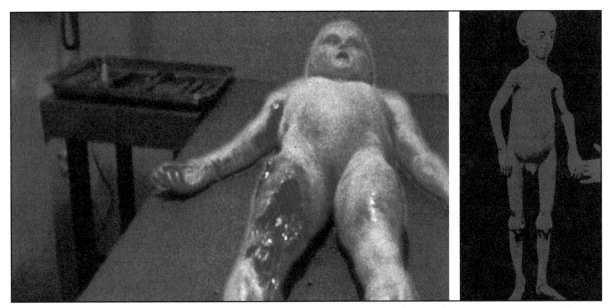

22 *A severely injured, bloated, humanlike alien body without any sign of a navel. For comparison, r., a human being with the rare premature ageing disease, progeria, photographed in 1917.*

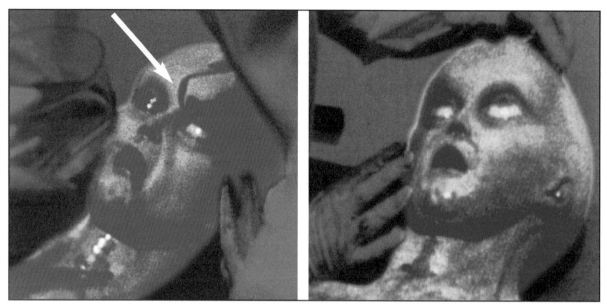

23 *Black membranes are removed from the oversized eyeballs. According to Lilit, they provided protection against harsh radioactive radiation in certain cosmic areas.*

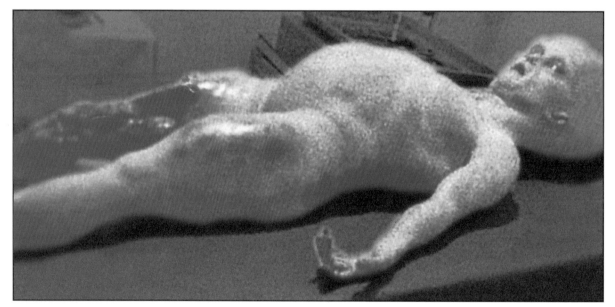

24 *SUE (Santilli Unidentified Entity) or »Lilit«? A large metallic splinter was removed from a thigh wound. The swollen left leg seems to be broken.*

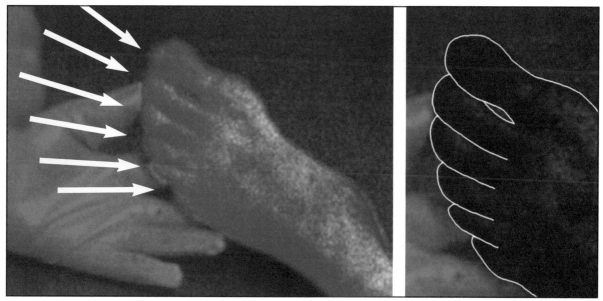

25 *The six-toed foot of Lilit, held by one of the examining pathologists. No genetic illness is recognizable, it appears to be a harmoniously proportioned foot.*

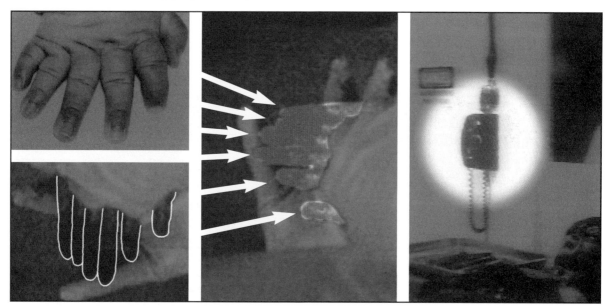

26 *The harmoniously formed six-fingered hand of a crash alien compared to the rare human malformation of a six-fingered hand known as hexadactylism (left above). The Bell wall telephone turned out to be from 1946.*

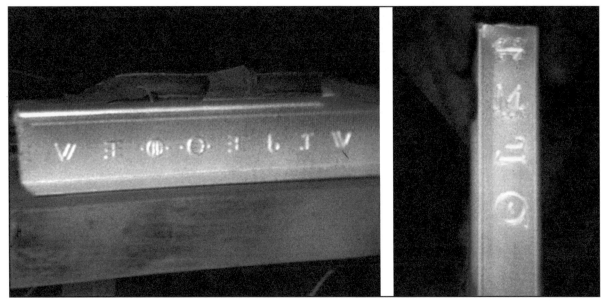

27 *A 1.5 in. thick I-beam broken off from the spaceship, with extraterrestrial code. The original purple-colored symbols are embossed in the material.*

28 *Based on eyewitness accounts, this drawing of a »metallic« I-beam was made nearly ten years before the Santilli film emerged. It bears a startling likeness.*

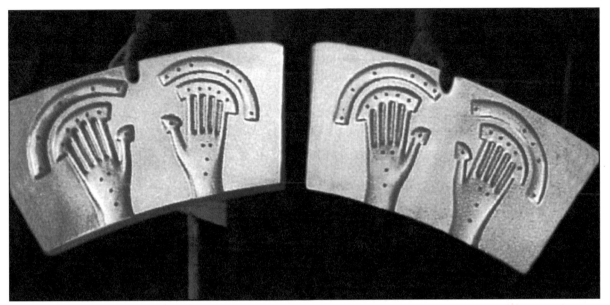

29 *Two of the three recovered biofeedback navigation control panels are held up to the camera in a military tent at the initial »inventory« Note the six-fingered points.*

30 *From the rounded parts of the panels and their logical arrangement, the approximate diameter of the flying saucer can be calculated at about 18 feet.*

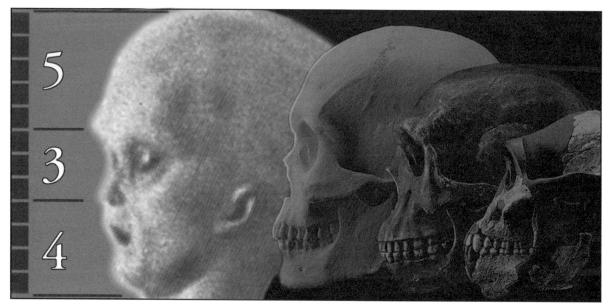

31 *The size of the human brain since the beginning of mankind has tripled to 1400 cm³. Lilit's brain has grown at least up to 2000 cm³. A character analysis of her skull proportions was: Mind 5/12 - Body 4/12 - Soul 3/12.*

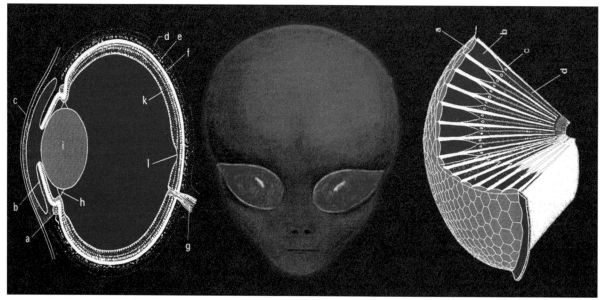

32 *As Lilit reported, the Asastanian alien eye is a genetically manipulated combination of a human eye and a faceted eye capable of multiple functions.*

this book with my wife, which has since been translated into eight languages,* shifted my socio-political orientation totally to spiritual activities. From that point on, during the trance sessions of my wife, I acted as a kind of navigator/ground control and broadcaster to the external world, while Mirabelle projected her own spirit to the cosmic heights of the psyche. With my logistical help she reported back to me what she saw and heard, while I saw to it that what she received was duly recorded on tape cassettes. With time, we learned to feel rather at home in this invisible world, even receiving assistance from beyond when I was at a loss about how to continue.

This form of medial communication is known as »channelling« these days, a term which was unknown in Europe when we first began our work. Through many years of training and practice, my wife is now in the position to act as a funnel for communications from the beyond for as long as 90 minutes at a time, and even longer. Hundreds of spiritual seekers have benefited from this service, sparing some of them the trouble of protracted psychotherapy. Mira is also active as a mediator between children about to reincarnate and their parents-to-be. All the above is referred to by way of defining my wife's primary field of work, in order to illustrate how extraterrestrial contacts are only peripheral to her. This applies especially to the following Roswell contacts, which are really an exceptional departure from her metier.

To put it simply, channelling is the active use of a cosmic intercom, a spiritual channelling of information from higher dimensions that we've closed ourselves off from in our everyday consciousness. To reach these frequencies both the mental condition of a highly meditative state and the synchronous

connection/fusion of the two halves of the brain are essential. The deeper the trance, the higher the spiritual frequencies of the universe's information network can manifest themselves. The quality and purity of the communication depend first of all on the mental frequency attained by the medium, and, of course, on the intelligence linking into that channel. Since like attracts like, the »reality windows« of the two participants, one from this world, one from the other, have to overlap to permit contact capable of dialog.

Channelling thought impulses of disembodied entities presupposes an acceptance of the immortality of consciousness and a »sphere of spiritual residence«; that is, a sphere of vibration aware of its own frequency of energies. For this, it is not absolutely necessary to believe in the beyond, because the unconscious carries out the same functions, as Carl Jung often stated in our dialogs.

Sound and well-founded channelling cannot, despite the claims of certain advertisers, be learned at weekend workshop seminars. It requires years of coming to grips with oneself in comprehensive psychological self-examination, and usually implies a cultivation of the finer faculties over the course of many lives before they have developed adequately. Science has only just begun to get down to the problem of this phenomenon, though it has not yet managed to find a common denominator.

Telepathy is energy transfer. The reception or sending of the mental contents of another person without the »interface« of sense-perceived signals was already known to Heraclitus in dreams. In the 19th century, distant perception beyond the bounds of the five senses became a subject of parapsychological research, for the most part, however, taking spiritual requirements into consideration. To this day it cannot be explained convincingly whether

* Published in English by the same publisher as this book, see appendix.

these extrasensory perceptions are also extra-corporal, that is, out-of-body. This delicate question, which if answered affirmatively would mean that our bodies are nearly superfluous things, is carefully avoided at present. Since for most of us, thought transfer »appears« (at least consciously) only sporadically out of nowhere like a gift from the gods, the difficulties of proof lead us to distance ourselves from this answer. When, for instance, word impulses »float« instantaneously from one consciousness to another, the recipient can recognize these in their spontaneity as well as in the difference from his or her own individual mode of thinking.

But what is the precise nature of mental transfer? The more frequently one experiences it, the more one becomes aware that not just thoughts, but also the state of being correlating to the given consciousness of the sender is transferred and reproduced in the brain of the recipient. And that means – even more for trance and channelling – that an actual energy transfer takes place and that the relation between matter and spirit can only be understood on the basis of an acceptance of the phenomenon of telepathy.

Channelling is also a telepathic contact, usually simultaneously verbalized, to permit a dialog with another person. Formulated a little more pithily (according to William Kautz, American pioneer in channelling) it is »*a mental process in which the individual sets aside his awake consciousness to permit the flow into his mind of an intelligence beyond normal awakeness*«.

The prerequisite of authentic distant contacting is invariably a willing partner on the other end of the astral channel. Failing that, one either hooks into the cosmic storehouse of knowledge, something called »Akasha reading«, or one practises the phenomenon of »Higher Self communication«. But these days there is a lot of dilettantish fooling around in the subconscious or unconscious. Games which are not easily seen through are being played by lower astral energies.

In our case, the medium is fully aware of the process during channelling (there are many different variations of psychic transcommunication). The challenge of being involved in such rarefied levels may be rewarded by better quality material. However, distortions or blockages can happen, particularly if the medium is unfamiliar with the material (or has not assimilated the dialog). Areas in which the medium doesn't feel »at ease« can readily lead to an unsureness of the consciously transmitted communication or to a complete trance break-off.*

After this digression, it is time to return to our summer vacation on Attersee Lake. A few days after coming across the ET pictures in »Focus«, I bought a para-science magazine with a (for the uninitiated) rather repulsive picture of an ET corpse on the cover. I couldn't shake off the subject. I began to wonder if I could talk Mira into granting me a psychometric test** with the larger of the two alien photos in the magazine during one of her next trances. A week later during an internal trance, there remained enough time for an attempt with the alien portrait. Mira felt her way into the extraterrestrial frequency for about ten minutes, attaining a state deep enough to switch over to »receive«. I can usually tell from the subtle changes in her facial expressions whether contact has been established. As the energies stemming from a different consciousness to some extent take over the movements of face muscles, they show themselves, for instance, in an altered laugh or wrinkle formations, sometimes also in dif-

* Especially in such situations it is valuable to be able to check the facts in objective source. What use is it to, say, transmit an important formula with a tiny error, but you don't know where the error lies?
** Mediumistic tactile analysis of aura frequencies emanating from an object or a photo.

ferent gesticulations of the hands. Since temporarily ceding one's body to another mentality or entity represents an inner conscious decision, which sometimes at the start is not strong enough, the verbalization must at times be coaxed along by empathetic support through someone from outside.

I should mention that during such highly sensitive experiences, the personal subconscious of the medium can't always be simply put aside, which is why one has to reckon with a few distortions even under the best of circumstances. Depending on the depth of the trance and how near the communicating being is allowed to approach or enter into the aura, the vocal cords of the »instrument« are modulated to a greater or lesser degree directly by the incoming energy. That means that a practised entity can enter and utilize the vocal cords and gestures of a trained channel in such a way as to alter the voice instrument's timbre, and manifest unusual articulation. While entering the state of trance, Mira requests, through a certain ritual, personal protective beings to be present specifically to keep away any damaging influences during these moments of extreme psychic exposure and to guarantee the requisite trust for a deep trance.

Mira is numbered among the very rare deep-trance mediums in the world who remain fully conscious during the whole session. She steps aside from her own consciousness, but is aware of every word and inner picture as if she were awake. The only difference is that she doesn't respond rationally to it. One can go on questioning her many hours after any trance about the events that took place in her mind; only then does her memory slowly begin to fade. Most contacts we recorded acoustically with a special sensor microphone, occasionally a trance is even video-filmed. Out of this we have assembled a large archive of almost a thousand hours of trance material, a storehouse of experimental scientific, poetic and spiritual/ psychological dialogs and a veritable treasure trove for future readers.

For the ET research, I placed the enlarged side view of the Santilli autopsied alien reproduced from Focus magazine under Mira's left palm to allow her the opportunity to receive the modulations of the SUE* and adjust to the alien frequency. I always try for the duration of the trance to adjust my own mentality to a harmonious modulation level. On the following pages, the transcriptions of all five Roswell sessions can be found. It should be noted that I obtained the related literature only weeks after the trance contacts were made and at first didn't give the slightest thought to publication. If I had, I surely would have structured the questions and answers more firmly. What are printed on these pages are but spontaneous dialogs without much concept behind them. Regardless of my necessary mental inclusion in the dialogs of our subjective paranormal world, I would ask the reader to come to his or her own conclusions about this phenomenon. I also want to remind you that these extraterrestrial impulses were first translated into German by my wife's trance mind and then again by the translator of the English language edition.

To ease readability and aid one's intuitive grasp of the conversations, the trance dialogs have been given a certain typographical order. The transitory visions and remarks of the channel are in »narrow type«; whereas the telepathic responses of the alien female and the other transmissions are in »**heavy type**«. The extraterrestrial messages are also all written totally in small caps, in order to remind one of the exotic nature of the transmitter. My own part in the conversation is in »*italics*«.

---

* »Santilli Unidentified Entity«.

The First Roswell Psychic Contact

Studio Phoenix, 13 August 1995
10:15 - 10:35 pm

Even as she was slipping into deep trance, Mira reported to me that she constantly heard Greek-sounding words deep inside her. I advised her temporarily to ignore the sounds and concentrate purely on adjusting to the vibrations of the being on the photograph. A few minutes later, she began to describe the things she was seeing on her inner screen.

Yes, a picture is now appearing. There is a huge, impressive object out there in space. It has a bottle-like shape, but flatter. On top of it, something is poking out, which is rotating very strangely. On the rear side is – oh, this is hard to describe – something almost like on an airplane. The whole thing looks a little like a spaceship, but oddly, it seems to be standing upright, not the way one usually imagines it. Oh God, what in the world is that?* – Ohhhh, I somehow have the feeling I'm getting beamed or something like that. All this is really weird. – I don't know if I should get into this...

Don't worry, I'll bring you out of the trance the minute something really unpleasant or worrisome happens. And your guardian beings are also present.

The really eerie thing about it is how it rotates. – These holes are apparently some kind of observation portholes.

For the moment, forget the technical aspects and concentrate on the body on the photo, try to get into the specific frequency of the spiritual inhabitant of this body.

I hear a foreign language again, something I cannot understand.

Make an imitation of it.

I can't. But I hear my own voice saying:

»...weren't poisonous...not infected.«**

*This may refer to the vision of a mother ship.
** Possibly an inner translation of the »language« heard at the start.

Who wasn't? Or what wasn't?

The corpses, maybe?

Where does the corpse on the photo come from? Can you find out anything about that?

(short pause, then softly) »plus terra...from plus terra.«

Plus Terra? What does that mean?

I don't know. I have no idea.

For a minute I had the feeling that some kind of contact was being established, but then the feeling disappeared.

Hmmm...Let's make a short call, to try to get a little closer to this being.

I collected myself somewhat and began to speak, like a human radio, in hopes of being picked up by the addressee. Mira transmitted along with me on the same frequency.

This is Psychological Research Station Studio Phoenix on Terra calling. We are attempting to take up contact with the extraterrestrial beings killed near Roswell in 1947. We request direct communication with the consciousness of the ufonauts who crashed. – Come in, Roswell aliens.

It is worth mentioning that such mentally-powered calls into space don't take the form of words, but rather of imagined thought-imprints which make their way into infinity telepathically. They can be received by the addressed consciousness – evidently without any time loss – as long as we transmit outwards on the right frequency. That, in any case, has been our repeated experience over the years.

In precisely the same way, but in the reverse direction, we pick up mental impulses from outside. These are inwardly comprehended in accordance with the spiritual potential of the respective medium – and/or decoded for others, instantaneously translated into the appropriate language and articulated. It can even happen that nearby entities (that is to say, entities that have entered one's own aura during deep trance) which are well-versed in transmitting go so far as to take control of the receiver's voice, right down to its characteristic intonations and facial expressions.

Thus, Mira, after my repeated radio calls into the universe which I kept on repeating inside myself, attempted to go via the photos still deeper into the specific frequency of the aliens. After a few minutes, she reported:

Oh, I think I'm finally getting into it. I am somewhere in space, inside a model, or some kind of miniature something or other that also exists in a larger size. Everything is dark blue outside, it reminds me a little of those spaceship movies. – Now all of a sudden it smells like burnt flesh. *Why?*
(whispering:) »crashed...because of landing error.«
What sort of error?

Mira's voice began to sound more authentic at this point, a bit more mechanical. It seemed to me that she had managed to let the transmitting entity a little closer to her. Shortly thereafter I realized that this faltering, fragmented speech was »Lilit« speaking, as the female ufonaut was later to introduce herself.

»...recapitulate...we wanted to explore this race...barriers...«
What barriers?
»...not an assignment...it was our own desire...«
What? It was your desire to land there?
»...no...through energetic winds...«
What about energetic winds?
»...drifted off...«

The process was too piecemeal for me, the substance too confusing and scanty. It was sufficient as an initial contact, but I was used to trance sessions proceeding more dynamically. Most of our sensitive conversations, albeit with less exotic entities, flowed relatively rapidly and smoothly. Even the whispers coming from Mira's vocal cords were still too soft for me, since it can easily happen that the sensor microphone does not record immediately, so that important sentence parts get lost. So I tried once more, this time through more emphatic calling to the entities to introduce additional dynamic energy into the initial contact:

This is René speaking, from Studio Phoenix on planet Earth. We are attempting to establish communication with the aliens who crashed in Roswell. Please try to establish direct vocal contact.

In order to better understand this session, it is helpful to know that especially with new contacts, the received contents at first tend to get rather topsy-turvy in their sequence and only in the course of deepening dialog do they form an intelligible, coherent flow of speech. Towards the end of a conversation, it usually becomes clear what got distorted or twisted at the beginning.

I see chimpanzees...no, but something like pale chimpanzees. This almost looks like a bear now. ...Oh, they have such animals there. They are unbelievably intelligent and have a near-human consciousness. These aliens have undertaken research and managed to change the animals' brains so that they can live close to the full potential of human beings. But despite that, these animals have none of the mental nimbleness that the entities have.
That's interesting, but better try to concentrate more on the owner of this body laid out on this bier.
I just heard a strange tone. A noise, like »wee-iee-sha«. Oh God, I think I heard the monkey talking. It seems they managed to get animals to talk.

See if you can find out the name of the former owner of this body.
I hear a kind of ringing in my ear.

Unfortunately, by trying to step up the power of the communication I had slowed down the tele-contact rather than speeding it up. But with such subtle undertakings, one often finds out only afterwards how one should have proceeded. What else could I do but try again, before the contact broke off completely?

We request contact with the ufonauts who crashed near Roswell. Dear friends in space, please give us through the channel an acoustic identification of the female entity on the photo we are touching.
(short pause)
I see a hand with an implantation, kind of a microchip. – Now it looks strange: these are artificial viruses, with a certain mission. They don't kill everything, nor do they attack everyone. They have been programmed with a kind of code they have to follow.
Hmm...I repeat, I request direct contact, verbal contact with the Roswell entities.

After attempts to speak accompanied by light grimaces, the same delicate, yet somewhat raw whispered voice from earlier began to speak again:

»**am here**... (what followed was incomprehensible.)«
I greet you and request gentler modulation of the speech organs of the channel .
(again very softly) »...**speaking.**«
Yes, I hear you. Please speak more loudly.
(softly) »...**female.**«
Female? Do I understand you correctly?
(Mira's body nods)
Are you the former inhabitant of the body on this photograph?
(again, a nod)

Is this the first contact you have attempted with human beings on Earth? I mean, since your crash?
(almost gasping) »...**water!**«
Water?...Oh, I'll get some right away.

I ran quickly to the adjoining bathroom to get a glass of water and placed it to my wife's lips for the consciousness which was waiting for it inside her.

Here, drink.

The entity took a few sips via Mira. Evidently it was not possible for the entity to speak with a dry throat. It is important to know that in the course of twelve years of working in trance, we have often discovered that when the entities communicating through my wife begin with their energy to enter the body of the medium they at once experience its physical sensations and its psychic perceptions.

In this particular case, it was also possible that, through the contact, the memories of the last bodily death was evoked, which in the transmitting consciousness could very well have had something to do with dying of thirst.*

Can you hear me?
(slight nod)
On Earth, films have recently come to light which were made by the American Army after your crash. According to reports, shots of your autopsy are allegedly on that film and are soon to be aired publicly on television. I'd like to ask you for clarification of the circumstances leading to your accident. And please send more energy into the voice channel to stabilize the contact.
(softly) »**ilid.**«
Ilid?...Hmmm?
(louder) »**lilit.**«

* Especially when one considers that the dying bodies supposedly lay next to the wreck, which was radiating heat, and were exposed to the merciless desert sun for several days.

103

Lilit? Is that your name?

    (strong nod)

What region of outer space do you come from, Lilit? – Or what do you wish to communicate to us?

    (softly) »asas...tan.«

Please repeat that.

»asastan!«

Oh, from Asastan.

    (renewed nodding)

Is it possible to say how far away that is?

    (partially incomprehensible) »...fifty million.«

Fifty million of what?

    (slowly and softly) »we...are...the...future.«

What...? What did you say?

»we...are the future.«

You are the future?

»we are...your future.«

Do you come from the future?

»with time leap...back...are stranded.«

So, you came back through a time leap from the future?

»...and crashed«

Did I understand correctly in the beginning, that you were thrown off course by an ›energetic wind‹? Did it have anything to do with a storm at the time?

    (Lilit nods)

Was it a bolt of lightning?

    (renewed nodding)

Aren't your spaceships protected against such influences?

»don't have them.«

You don't have lightning? Doesn't it occur in your atmosphere?

    (shakes her head) »no.«

Was that your first visit to Earth?

»yes...are warned now.«

Against what? Against lightning?

    (nods)

Did any of you come back to Earth after that?

»no more.«

What drew you here? Was it a sort of reconnaissance?

»it was the past.«

Whose past? Yours?

»yes...we are your future.«

Do I understand you correctly? You're saying that it was Earthians, so to speak, who came back to visit Earth?

    (no answer)

Do you mean humanity per se?

»yes...future of earthians.«

From how far in the future did you travel here?

»seven...five...million light years.«*

Do you mean in time, or in space?

»both.«**

Do you exist bodily anywhere right now? I mean, is your spirit housed anywhere in condensed matter?

    (nodding) »on asastan.«

I see, and you are communicating with us from there right now. Could you send us a short report of your crash back then?

»...are shocked.«

At what?

»at reality.«

What specific reality do you mean?

»reality of humans.«

At our primitiveness?

»that we found...«

What did you find?

»you.«

So you are shocked by the fact that you found us human beings in your past...or something like that?

»that you still exist.«

Well, didn't you assume that we still existed? Did you travel here just on a hunch?

---

*During a later contact, 750 million light years was spoken of more clearly.

** According to this, they came from a distance of 4 quadrillion, 94 trillion, 362 billion miles to us, for which we, in order to visit them on their home planet, would require about one million human lifetimes lived in sequence, traveling at the speed of light.

»yes...wanted to know whether some of you are really alive.«

I see. Is there in this...

(interrupting) »we didn't know whether there were any of you left.«

Yes...Hmmm.

»it is as if you were to discover dinosaurs.«

I see. How different are your living conditions?

»because we passed through that stage of development, you are the past.«

What is your present stage of development? Can you describe it?

Only a frail sigh escapes Lilit.

Do you experience something like rebirth?

(nodding) »we do.«

How long do you ordinarily live in your bodies, counted in earth time?

»almost 500 hundred years.«

And does your birth take place like ours on Earth?

(hesitatingly) »without...without pain.«

Only in retrospect, after several more contacts, did I come to realize there was a much deeper reason for this hesitation.

Are your new bodies sexually procreated?

»with thought power.«

Do you have something akin to bipolar sex, to our male-female union?

»affinity principle...no pain.«

Hmmm...Why don't you have any hair?

»because we're not animals needing warmth.«

And why do you have six fingers?

»much more practical.«

What else distinguishes you?

»are peaceful in struggle to survive.«

How many are there in your colony?

»six million.«

No more? — What would you call your race?

»humanoid.«

Does your people have a name?

»asastanians.«

Oh, like the planet. Is it actually a planet?

(nods) »asastan.«

And it revolves around a sun?

»yes...many moons.«

Do you have other inhabited planets? How many satellites revolve around your sun?

»seven.«

What's your word for sun? What do you call your sun?

»like me...lilit...sun and moon together.«

What do you mean?

»our sun also took over the moon's function...has combined male and female.«

Hmmm...You said something about »many moons« before. How many do you actually have all together?

»twelve moons.«

Do you have a form of astrology?

»only astronomy...which doesn't refer to humans.«

Why no astrology?

»feel free of it.«

And some kind of religion? Do you cultivate something like that?

»respect life.«

Hmm...When you died and left your bodies, were you able to observe the following developments from outside?

»partially.«

What really happened back then? What did the US Army do with your bodies?

»deep freeze.«

And do they still exist?

»in ice.«

As far as you know, did the US make contact with other extraterrestrials?

(no answer)

Is it true that some extraterrestrial entities are alive, in the care of the US Army?

»not us...perhaps from nearer...from our past.«

Would the opposite also be possible for us, to travel into the future the way you travel into the past?

»no, past is lower evolution...we can only go back...not ahead.«

I see. What is the next step in the evolution of our race on Earth? You must know that.

»you'll find humanlike apes...apes will develop...get bigger and more human...humans will become more intelligent.«

How will this come about?

»through evolution...which is your path in space.«

How much time will have to pass for that to take place?

»three thousand years.«

So...the still undiscovered archaelogical »missing link«* linking apes to pre-human beings will once again somehow arise?

(Lilit nods)

Hmmm...about your method, that you're using to travel through time: what technology is utilized?

»based on quantum physics.«

Is the spaceship whose wreck was found a material object you constructed?

(a further nod)

And what happened to the debris that was collected by the US Army?

»saved.«

Were the Americans able to figure out your technology?

»no.«

According to some reports, small wooden-like sticks with strange purple symbols on them were found. What are they?

»a coding.«

What's it for?

»represents functions.«

Could you explain that further?

»for burning mirror lenses...liquifies things.«

That doesn't tell me much.

»we pave the way for new things.«

Are you those beings who allegedly at the time of early man on Earth carried out genetic and other operations to provoke evolutionary leaps? Were you those human gardeners?

»nature does it better...it is smarter.«

So actually there were no early human gardeners, is that right?

(pause) Then Lilit/Mira shakes her head and answers a little timidly.

»no...is a lie.«*

How old is humanity, seen from our point in time?

»for seventy million years star system like today.«

And how long have there been humanoids?

»three million years.«

How long will our planet still go on?

»five million years.«

Is it endangered?

»they were again and again.«

What, the planets were often in danger?

»every three million years.«

And we are in such a phase now?

»within a quantum leap.«

Yes, but what is the primary threat? What is the thing which brings us close to the brink?

»coming pole jumps.«

And what unleashes those?

»changes in earth's atmosphere...system moves into different energetic space.«

Do you mean what we call the Age of Aquarius?

---

* The discovery of an 18 million-year old skeleton of a hominid primate called »Proconsul« in Kenya is what to date comes closest to the missing link between ape and human being.

* Either these legends are really wrong or created later and projected onto prehistory, or, what is likelier, Mira's unconscious blocked at this point, not wanting to touch this matter. Unfortunately, I posed the question rather too suggestively, but it is possible to read through the lines of the previous response that Nature, in retrospective comparison, does it more intelligently and better.

106

(Lilit nods)

What about our present atomic testing? Do they represent a great danger?*

»they change environment...planet earth will survive.«

What will be the next major step in the forms of energy people use in the world economy?

»solar energy.«

With fusion reactors?

(no answer)**

What is your ›UFO time machine‹ made of, the one you used to travel here? The material couldn't be identified.

»kind of new synthetic...like aluminum.«

What components is the synthetic made of?

»nickel...cobalt...and various earth materials.«

How do you communicate with each other?

»via telepathy.«

On Earth we continually get reports of abductions by extraterrestrials. Do you kidnap people?

»not us.«

Do you know of other aliens who do?

»yes.«

Why do they do it?

»boredom.«

In all seriousness...really out of boredom?

»that's what we think.«

Where do these kidnappers come from?

»out of the past...asastanians conduct no research which causes pain.«

What is your own next evolutionary step that you're preparing for?

»immortality.«

Do you mean immortality in a physical body?

(Lilit nods)

How far advanced are you in this endeavor?

»not very far.«

What is the major problem hindering you?

»harmony with neighbouring universes.«

Is it because of you or the other universes that there is imperfect harmony?

»because of evolution.«

From your perspective, can you see something like the end of evolution? Is that perhaps reached with immortality?

»we don't know.«

Are the other universes surrounding you more advanced than you?

»some more and others less.«

How many of you travelled in your spaceship?

»three.«

Can you tell me something about the others?

»male and female.«

Evidently one of you was still alive when you were found by the military.

»were all dead.«

What were their names?

(softly) »bax.«

Pax?

»bax...and alira.«

Bax and Alira, all right. Are you together with them again?

»in contact.«

Are they reborn into bodies?

»they have bodies.«

Are you also in contact with those of you without bodies?

(the medium nods)

Are you all together in contact with each other, with or without bodies?

(nodding again) »yes.«

Then why do you want to be materialized?

»such is life.«

You mean, coming and going is life?

»without body, there is only consciousness .«

---

* The hopefully last French nuclear tests recently took place on Mururoa island.

** I assume that this initially vague contact did not permit a technically more complicated response at this point, thus resulting in silence.

But no evolution?
»but no life.«
Hmmm. That's an interesting thought.
»must go.«
Already? Can we contact you again, let's say in a few days?
»up to you.«

Mira terminated the reception too, and slowly emerged from her trance. She opened her eyes and clapped her hands as usual to link up with her physical body again. »Must go« usually means that the energy reserves of the medium are no longer sufficient to continue the contact for long. For the sake of the channel, the connection is then interrupted.

She stretched and groaned as if she had shaken off a heavy burden. One could tell from the way she looked that it hadn't been much fun for her. That's why she wasn't very talkative about what had happened. With the words, »that's too much for me, more than I can handle at the moment«, she turned over exhausted and promptly went to sleep.

The Second Roswell Psychic Contact

Studio Phoenix, 18 August 1995
11:30 - 11:40 pm

The first contact was somewhat frustrating for me, not exactly what I had hoped for. Nonetheless, some interesting questions had been raised. So I made notes of the thoughts which coursed through my mind, hoping to talk my wife into another session. And that is just what happened a few days later, with the assistance of our eleven-year old son. As a space age enthusiast, he insisted, despite the late hour, on being present for the next attempt at speaking with »real ETs«. Mira assumed half-lotus position on the couch in the studio. I placed the same photo on her knee that we had used the first time, and began, after some initial meditating, to place my calls on the same frequency into the universe.

This is René and Mira of Studio Phoenix on Earth speaking. It is 1995 and we are calling Lilit on Asastan. We request renewed contact with the Roswell ufonaut Lilit.

After an interval of a few minutes, it suddenly began with a bang.

»some of us would like to incarnate among you in order to assist your progress.«
Do you mean us personally or simply on our planet?
»on earth.«
Nice to hear that. Today I would like a bit more information about the things which happened back then so as to better understand the proceedings. Among other things, I would like to know if you had a chief or captain in your crew.
»had different scope of duties«

How were your functions allotted? For example, what was your job?
»path-finding through the stars.«
So you were the cosmic navigator, so to speak.
»yes, and observer of cruising objects.«
And Alira? What was her task?
»took care of us.«
What did she do for you?
»everything we needed.«
And what did you need? Name something.
»water.«
You mean water in our sense of the term?
    (slight nod)
Did you bring water with you?
»is produced...« (undecipherable on the tape)
So you are able to produce your own water in the spaceship. How do you do that?
»with generator.«
What's the technology behind it?
    (short pause)
Can you explain it in terms we can understand?

Lilit shakes her head slightly, in negative response.

Okay, maybe we can come back to it later. And Bax? Was he the male member of the crew?
»he steered the spaceship.«
So he was the helmsman. Did you also have some kind of ground station on your home planet that you stayed in contact with?
    (nodding) »yes.«
Hmm...maybe this is a stupid question, but how long did the time leap to us actually take?

»forty-five minutes.«

In Earth time?

»yes.«

Do you have the same time as we do? Do you measure in Earth time?

»one can.«

And how else do you do it?

»not at all.«

Hmm, sounds strange. Your ›UFO time machine‹, who built it?

»father lorin.«

Father Lorin? Did he do it specially for you?

(Lilit nods intensely)

Is he part of your ground control?

(nodding) »yes.«

Did your people build other machines like it?

(renewed nodding)

How many such ships do you have?

»five-thousand.«

And with them you zoom around different worlds and times?

(nodding) »yes.«

Was there a special point to travelling specifically to the year 1947?

»we were travelling to the twentieth century.«

And the year 1947 was the year you coincidentally landed in?

»we wanted to conquer* this galaxy...only exists like this in this millennium.«

What do you mean?

»in three thousand years, it doesn't exist any more.«

What happens in three thousand years?

»we can no longer find you in this aspect...not on this map.«

Where will you find us then?

»everything is changed...like earth displacement.«

---

* The term »conquer« is intended here more in the sense of »exploring the terrain«.

I see. – Does the Milky Way enter a different space density?

»not only...changes position and emission...so different constellations will be created.«

What did your UFO look like?

»has round center section...everything very round.«

Is it what we would call a flying saucer?

»roughly speaking, yes.«

Was it arched?

»much more...had something on top and below...looks like double saucer.«

Did the ship have windows to look out of?

»can't call them that...a ring for roundabout viewing.«

Ah, a viewing ring.

»yes, dark glass...not glass, but dark-transparent.«

What material is it made of?

»nothing you know...is unbreakable, transparent material.«

How long did it take you to construct the spaceship?

»five years of your time.«

How many of you worked on it?

»twelve.«

How would you describe the technology that went into it?

»worked much with space wave generators ... with high frequency waves ... sonar waves ... light-breaker codes and crystal structures ... also with solar energy and what you call orgon-light.«*

Also with so-called tachyon energy?**

»that too.«

The spacesuits you wore, what was their purpose?

»for atmospheric balance.«

It allegedly looked just like a second skin. How did you manage to put it on?

»it stretches.«

What is it made of?

---

* Reich's term was seemingly spotted in the vocabulary of the medium.
** Tachyons are imaginable particles in relativity physics which move at speeds beyond that of light; they are supposed to get slower when energy is applied and give off energy when accelerating.

»radiation resistant, but air permeable...maintains constant temperature and changes atmospheric pressure ...helps body adjust to changing pressures.«

Did you also travel to other times?

»not us.«

That means your crew came straight to the twentieth century?

»fascinated us most...very important time.«

Why? How did this century go down in history? If one can phrase it that way?

»upheaval...from destructiveness to constructiveness...we call it a time of hope.«

Sounds good. Are you in telepathic contact with anyone else on Earth at present?

»no...only with own people.«

Have you ever been contacted by other Earth inhabitants?

»nothing serious.«

Are we really the only ones who have seriously tried to speak to you?

I perceived a slightly amused smile.

So it appears. – Tell me something about your bodily-psychic structures. You told me at our first contact that you've achieved the union of male and female. But on the photo of your dead body, the female gender seems clear to me. Does that mean you still have distinct sexual differences in your bodies, but none in your spirits? Can you explain that?

»we live together with our opposite pole.«

With what we call our dual soul?

(profound nod)

Can you describe your psychic structures? Is your psyche vastly different from ours in the twentieth century?

»i think so.«

Do you have emotions, or something like them?

»very little.«

And aggressions?

»no aggression...are peaceful.«

To what degree are you materialized on your planet? Is its matter less dense than ours or just as corporeal?

(Lilit nodded)

Why do you have such big heads compared to ours?

»we have more brain mass.«

What about your ears, they're much smaller.«

»hardly need them...use telepathy.«

Your nose and mouth are also very small. What food do you eat?

»water.«

Only water? Where do you get all the other things your bodies need?

»all added to our water.«

Your eyes are...

I was just about to talk about her strange looking alien eyes but Lilit interrupted me.

»must go...medium cannot sustain further contact.«

Why not? We've just started to talk.

»is getting sick.«

Okay, then we'll wrap up. Thank you for talking with me. I am looking forward to another contact very soon.

»see you later.«

Being told »see you later« by an extraterrestrial may seem rather odd to the reader. However, it merely signifies that the farewell impulse of ETs is appropriately translated into an earthly linguistic form by Mira's inner »translator«. The expression actually made me feel good, since it led me to believe that my distant interlocutor was interested in further communication with me.

I had noticed Mira's ever deepening pallor during the trance, but paid it too little heed, being so involved in the question-and-answer process. It turned out that my wife was quite nauseous after the session, *»as if every cell inside me had been turned inside out«*, which might be attributed to the too close proximity of the unaccustomed frequency she had been working on...or else merely something she had eaten hours earlier. The fact that she described it as a strange kind of nausea in her head such as she had never felt before, makes me tend to discount the latter possibility. Perhaps it was a combination of the two.

Incidentally, our son had left in the middle of the conversation, saying it had become too ominous for him. He later said that the atmosphere in the room had made him very uncomfortable.

A few hours later I got Mira to make a rough sketch of the UFO seen in a vision. It was no artistic masterpiece, but apparently comes close to what she perceived.*

The next day, I typed up my notes of Lilit's terse answers in abbreviated form to serve as a guideline in future conversations. Somehow I still had hopes that Mira would be able to acclimatise herself to the frequency modulations so that further dialogs could be conducted more extensively than the short snippets thus far.

* see picture no. 38 in third picture section.

The Third Roswell Psychic Contact

Studio Phoenix, 20 August 1995
7:00 - 7:50 pm

Since the television broadcast of the alien autopsy was approaching, I was intent on gathering more concrete, first-hand information in order to have a solid basis for comparing methods of determining authenticity. In the past, Mira had often shown herself unwilling to conduct ongoing paranormal experiments unless I was able to clearly prove the reality of the contacting beings, or at very least demonstrate a logical coherence in the communicated contents.*

Mira, who can fluctuate enormously in her moods and frame of mind, seemed to be getting accustomed to the idea of dealing with Lilit, especially after I had a talk with her about the meagre yet constructive and encouraging results we had obtained thus far. My optimism was evidently infectious, for already two days later she was ready to continue with another experiment. Our children were playing in the room next to the studio and we could hear them through the wall, causing Mira's trance entrance to take a bit longer. However, the dialog, once established, proceeded at an astonishing tempo.

Hello!
»we are ready.«
Am I speaking with Lilit?
(nod) »yes.«
Are you the spokesman for all of you?

---

* Our talks with »C. G. Jung«, for example, only became very intense when I, while doing long-term researches in university libraries, confirmed certain statements on the subject of neurophysiology. These could not have come from either Mira or me, finally convinced my wife that some intelligence was communicating them; this was not a hoax of the unconscious.

»today alira nearly wanted to speak.«
Well? Does she still want to?
»uhhhh...she changed her mind.«
Would she rather listen? Today I want to ask you more about the events of so many years ago: if I understood correctly, in your attempt to land on Earth in the twentieth century, you were drawn into an energy storm. How exactly did that happen?
»twentieth century in your solar system has same time as we do...we merely evolved differently.«
Mmhmm. You said it only took forty-five minutes for your spaceship to make the time leap. What happened then?
»we entered earth's atmosphere...reduced our speed, then... could see it coming on horizon...on 35th parallel hit a bad weather front...and then everything started to go haywire.«
Tell me precisely what happened, in the thunderstorm.
»we'd been told nothing could happen, since we had projectors shielding us from electrical jolts...but they hadn't figured on the frequency displacement inside the electrical-magnetic gradient we were in...some equipment started to get hot, overheated and exploded...that sent us into a tailspin...sizzling hot equipment was overturned...we went down and our flesh burned.«
While you were still in the air?
»partially...just before we actually crashed.«
Were parts of the spaceship destroyed?
»yes, but most of it inside...there was a hydrogen explosion...conduits and motor parts broke apart through the overheating.«
According to my records, you were visible to the US Army on radar.

»possible.«

Didn't you make provisions for staying invisible to radar?

»yes, but it stopped functioning through the magnetic displacements of earth...the calculations were no longer correct, because the electromagnetic field in the immediate vicinity was altered by the energy jolt...that came very abruptly.«

Where did you originally want to land?

»in bermuda.«

Why there?

»because there is an intersection there.«

And what did you plan to do there?

»we wanted to look around...just wanted to land and see what would happen.«

How long did you plan to stay?

»a few days, a few weeks, depending on whether we were discovered or not...we wanted to go into a cave.«

In order to escape notice?

»yes...we also could have lived underwater...had the necessary equipment with us...our spaceship can also move underwater.«

About how large was your spaceship?

»about 16 feet in diameter.«

Did you come alone?

»what do you mean?«

I mean, just one spaceship.

»yes, but there were also others of us who landed on earth and nothing happened to them...five to ten spaceships, don't know exact number.«

At another time?

»yes, yes.«

Strange to say, another crash was in fact reported somewhere in the vicinity of Roswell. Various fragments, resembling a kind of aluminum foil, were found strewn over hundreds of meters. But that is supposed to have been miles from the spot where you crashed.

»we don't know anything about that...we weren't in contact with any others...only with our ground station.«

Was your ground station able to react when your situation became critical?

»wasn't possible any more.«

How large was the crew on board?

»there were three of us.«

Certain reports said that there were four or five crew members in the UFO.

»they would have had to come in another ship.«

Did you all die immediately upon crashing?

»we left our bodies when we realised we wouldn't survive.«

And after you left your bodies, what happened then? Did you stay around to observe the scene?

»the man came and found us and the wreckage.«

To what degree was the UFO destroyed?

»pretty much...was no longer capable of flying...there were those explosions.«

And to what extent were your bodies damaged?

»not so bad...we got out soon enough.«

How did you get out of them?

»got out while ship still aloft...before we crashed to earth.«

Yes, but how did you do that?

»with a kind of ejector seat...like on air cushions.«

Mhmm. But it seems you were found right next to the saucer.

»yes...catapult doesn't project one very far...left just before crashdown... would have been torn to shreds otherwise.«

At least one of you was seriously injured. Who?

»me and bax...an extremely hot, metallic object bore a hole into my flesh...it hit bax too.«

Your corpse was strangely bloated on the photo. Is that your normal body shape or was it due to decomposition?

»through change, but we have larger bellies.«

And why is no navel visible?

»we don't bear children like you do.«

Then how do you bear them?

It was a little while before an answer was forthcoming. I thought I could read from Mira's expression that Lilit didn't really want to give an answer.

»we...we breed them.«

How do you do that?

(short pause) »in test tubes.«

Wow. It's a little difficult for me to picture that. – How does it happen?

»none of us have parents.«

But you spoke of Father Lorin!

»yes, yes...but he isn't...«

(interrupting) *You mean he's not a physical father?*

»no...he isn't.«

I see. This is starting to get interesting.

»we...we have birth laboratories.«

Really? Why do you make such a face when you talk about it? Does it make you feel awkward to speak of it?

»we think, you don't like it.«

Well, I try to look at it without making any value judgment. Why did you begin practising this method?

»we found it practical, that frogs don't have any births.«

Mmm, yes that is a point of view worth considering.

»we began to place eggs and ovaries outside...«

(embarrassed silence) *...to transfer them?*

(nodding, softly) »and it worked.«

But what happens then with sexuality?

(nodding) »not like with you...it is primarily energetic.«

Really? How do you go about it?

»we find our counterpart very quickly...quite often in early childhood...we are drawn to each other magnetically and then stay together a lifelong.«

How long does your childhood last?

»thirteen years...after that one is responsible for one's own life.«

To return to the subject of your bodies: I read that you had very unusual black membranes over your eyes. What are they for?

»they protect against radiation.«

Did they grow naturally?

»no, they are implanted whenever we leave...otherwise we could go blind... radiation is extremely aggressive in some

galaxies...we then take them off again.«

What kind of radiation is there?

»radioactivity.«

You mean that as long as you wear those membranes, radioactivity can't harm you? Doesn't it penetrate your spacesuits?

»... we are resistant...just our eyes aren't completely.«

So that's what it is. Do you have teeth? There are none visible in the photo.

»no, no teeth.«

You also seem to be without normal lips.

Lilit giggled a little, clearly at my, from her point of view, strange aesthetic perceptions. I searched through my notes for other substantive questions to ask.

What is the composition of your blood?

»much more oxygen than yours, and much thinner...our abdomens are bigger because we maintain such high water levels in our bodies...we can go for long periods without drinking if we store enough.«

Which makes you something like intergalactic camels!

»yes, yes...we are probably ugly in your eyes?«

Let's just say we are not accustomed to your looks. On the other hand, you also have some very human traits.

»we were created through genetic engineering and an invasion of our planet...we then split away and continued evolution in these monstrous bodies...they are not our idea of ideal beauty.«

What is your idea of beauty?

»you earthians... your bodies.«

Are you built like us inside? Or are your organs differently organized?

»we have no liver and no gall bladder...have a small heart, small lungs and kidneys.«

Do you have intestines?

»yes, well, something like that, but not so much of it.«

Do your dissected bodies still exist anywhere?

»are slowly decomposing, even though kept in ice, because

they are so watery...they are denser matter, heavier, but decompose faster than your bodies.«

Where are those bodies now?

»in storage in army research laboratory.«

Why are these contacts with you, that is, with your bodies, still being kept secret by the US Army or the government? Do you know the real reason?

»because we remain something inexplicable to them...they can't figure out whether we are dangerous or not.«

What would happen if those bodies were shown on TV?

»but that will happen...they show me.«

Yes, those old films. But I meant the somewhat decomposed yet very real body parts now in storage in ice ...what if they were shown publicly and officially on TV?

»will be prevented...there would be uproar, but not much would change subsequently.«

Which of you survived the crash?

»all of us were still alive.«

And then this man arrived on the scene? *

»when he found us, we had already been dead for hours.«

How did he react?

»he was totally shocked...we appeared very odd in his eyes.«

What did he do?

»we didn't observe that closely.«

How old did you become?

»about three hundred fifty years.«

Are you all the same age?

(Lilit nodded) »about.«

And how quickly do you reincarnate?

»that happens right away.«

What? What do you mean by right away?

»you know, new bodies are always waiting for us.«

In a test tube?

I noticed that the extraterrestrial being once again seemed to react strangely at my mention of the subject, since she smiled almost as if she were ashamed.

* This was probably the hydraulic engineer, Grady L. Barnett, who was working in the desert at the time.

»when the embryo begins to glow, it comes out of the test tube into a nutritional pool...then it is fed with this primal fluid...that's where we develop until we've grown enough.«

(interrupting) *How long does that take?*

»just a few weeks...then we're taken out of the fluid.«

That's all? That is incredibly fast.

»compared to your rhythm, it takes seven months.«

Hmm...Let's return to the crash again. How long were you actually dead before you were discovered by that man?

»three days.«

Had you already begun to decompose?

»our bodies don't decompose, they disintegrate...they don't putrefy...they sort of dissolve, since they have such a high water content.«

About how long does this process of disintegration take?

»varies...depends on heat.«

I see. On your UFO there were apparently symbols or signs like hieroglyphics.

»nautical script.«

What does it mean, translated into our language?

»are signs to bring about certain things.«

Yes, and what's that supposed to be?

»don't know which signs you mean.«

I didn't see them myself. I only know from reports that undecipherable signs were found on certain pieces of wreckage. It seemed that such symbols were also visible on the outer surface of the UFO.

»they show where we come from, and all sorts of other things.«

Is that a sort of language?

(Lilit nods half-heartedly)

What is it based on? Are they pictograms or characters of an alphabet?

»nautical characters, yes.«

How many characters does your alphabet system have?

»thirtyfive!«

Hmm...How much did your UFO weigh?

»not heavy, compared to size.«

About how many kilograms?
»close to five-hundred.«
*Up to how many crew members would it accommodate
if they were all your size?*
»to live in for a longer span of time, four or five.«
Do you have diseases in your sphere and if so, what kinds?

Again Lilit made various expressions which seemed
to say that she didn't really want to answer the question.

»nnn...mmm...no...we are very radical with illness.«
What does that mean?
»we immediately exterminate anyone who gets ill...be-
cause we go right into a test tube again.«
That's wild! You just leap into the next waiting body.
»because we know that, it also gives us the feeling that we
don't get ill...therefore we get very old.«
*Is the immortality you strive for of any importance when
you are reincarnated so quickly anyway?*
»yes, because of the unpleasant interval.«
What is unpleasant about it?
»it is as if one were paralyzed, while developing in the test
tube...one can't do anything at all...it's a terrible state for us.«
How long does that phase last?
»several days to a few weeks...when we then land in the
pool, we still can't do anything...but one is quite conscious,
and that is very unpleasant.«
*How many of you are listening in on our ongoing com-
munication?*
»don't know.«
Does anybody on your planet know of it?
»maybe the father.«
Why is he called father?
»because he is the initiator of all these happenings...it is his
karma to be tied to us, at least until we have redeemed ourselves out of this form...he was a major genetic researcher
and perfected our process of artificial conception on another planet a long time ago to such a degree that our women no longer wanted to bear children, they wanted to

spare themselves the risks and the pain...but for that it was
essential to maintain full consciousness from body to
body...not having parents, with time we would have lost
our psyche otherwise...then it wouldn't be possible to enter
a new body, since it would contradict the law of nature...in
that sense it's true that we are immortal, since we take our
consciousness totally along with us and carry it over into
the next body already fully developed...nothing of our individuality is dissolved, it merely changes along with us.«
*So do you have subconscious and more superficial levels of
consciousness? Or has it all melded together inside you?*
»we have restrained and dynamic consciousness...we have
dream or sleep consciousness and an active, creative consciousness.«
How long do you usually sleep?
»one to two of your hours at the most.«
How long is your day?
»24 hours, like yours...but we just sleep any time.«
*It doesn't sound like you keep to any rigid patterns like
we do on Earth?*
»oh yes we do...but everyone has his own rhythm...when i
have discharged my energy, i go to sleep for two hours.«
Don't you have something like day and night?
»no, because we have so many moons and our sun is a moon-
sun...so we have only light variations, but no day and night
time halves, like you do...we also don't have high and low
tide, just slight warm/cold displacements...then clouds gather, so that it can rain.«
What is your most significant recurring rhythm?
»there are periodic floods.«
What causes them?
»they accompany monsoon-like winds which occur whenever our planetary axis changes position...whenever it
moves a degree in one direction or the other...our axis
changes much more often than yours...our planet also
moves much faster than yours through space, what you call
the zodiac...we also have that.«
Is your planet larger or smaller than ours?

»about seven times the size of yours...asastan is huge.«
And what is the terrain like?
»grass, trees and mountains, we have all that.«
What about insects?
»none...we exterminated them all...we also have no poisonous plants.«
What kinds of animals do you have?
»oh, we have lots of white animals...we love them, and all white things...we also have a kind of your lion and zebra...they're not ferocious, they don't kill...they don't eat other animals any more, just plants, and they drink enriched water.«
Hmm, that's amazing. And when you are grown up at age thirteen, about how big are your bodies then?
»quite large...like yours, about three-quarters of full size.«
Since you live solely on fluids, how can you develop such large bodies in such a short time?
»that's no problem...it is not just the minerals, also the richly energized water that contains all vital nutritives necessary for building one up, which are produced in water photosynthetically from algae.«
Do you live in buildings?
»in palatial mansions with a lot of glass...partially also in subterranean structures, but then there are domes.«
Do you have cities?
»we don't need them...we just live where we feel like.«
How do you get around?
»we have these microchip-equipped boards which move us around...we call them air rollers...they float about twenty inches above the ground.«
That's sounds great. I guess the force of gravity is weaker where you live than here on Earth?
»quite a bit weaker...that's also why our brains are slightly larger.«
Would we Earthians be able to live on your planet?
»no...at least not for long.«
Why not? What would happen?
»the pressure would be too high...your bodies would feel like they were bursting.«

But it wouldn't actually happen, would it?
»don't know...we wanted to perhaps take someone with us.«
But surely someone who would come along voluntarily?
(Lilit nods)
»friends of ours have already taken along some animals before...but they didn't tolerate the change, so we had to bring them back rather soon...they had to stay in a pressurized chamber with their oxygen supply.«
That means others of you have already visited us?
»yes, yes, that has happened several times.«
Would we manage to survive psychically on your planet?
»there you would have enormous problems too.«
What would be the biggest stumbling block?
»your senses would be completely unsatisfied.«
Why is that?
»you wouldn't be able to eat or have sex...what else would you do here?«
There are also a few other things. What do you do all day long, then?
»lots. we always have something to do.«
I mean, what does your daily life consist of, if you have such a thing?
»first of all, lots of travelling... ... ...«

I had to change the tape in the recorder at this point, which caused the loss of the rest of Lilit's answer. Unfortunately I can no longer remember what other activities Lilit mentioned. It seems that I had asked a different question before the next answer was taped again.

»... ...we are a transformed race...you know, that bears a heavy karma.«
What is so burdensome about it?
»that we are unhappy about our bodies...even though we know it is just an intermediate phase.«
In between what and what?
»until we look like human beings again.«
How will you manage that?

»we don't yet know that exactly, but believe in it.«

Is that also one of the reasons some of you want to reincarnate here?

»yes, we realized we're not happy with our development.«

Yet that would be quite a step backward into your past.

»no, you don't understand...we departed from the original law which says ›as above, so below; as inside, so outside‹* ...we pushed many things forward through genetic engineering, and our bodies have gone through a great many changes...we tried to create life without pain and become ever more intelligent, yet we now miss being human...we no longer correspond to the divine principle envisioned for being human...yet since we originally stem from the genesis of earth, we would like to correspond to the primal idea of earthly human beings...but that is not the case at the moment.«

When, during the course of evolution, did this radical divergence of your race take place?

»five hundred million years ago, a new satellite began to form, which however never appeared to earthians...much earlier it departed from the system through an explosion.«

*Is that the mysterious planet Mallona? The one whose remaining fragments are allegedly our asteroids?**

»yes...at that time there were already developments there which went in that genetic direction...but human beings haven't been on earth for very long...at that time also other civilizations came into being inside other planetary systems of the milky way...from one of them, these genetic developments visited earth at an early stage...but the forms then disappeared, because they wouldn't have survived here.«

Here? You mean here on Earth?

»yes...at the time mallona went out of kilter, ex-people from earth went through these developments with other

* Just like the fundamental principle of Hermes Trismegistos, handed down on his emerald table.

* In certain highly esoteric scriptures, the name of the erstwhile planet Mallona (sometimes called Phaeton or Marduk) can be found, which is supposed to have exploded because of karmic action of its inhabitants and now exists in the form of an asteroid belt.

beings, our father was one of those people... he also is the only one who still looks like you, he is also the only one who has long hair...but it is his gruesome fate always to have to look upon our bodies...he is our embodied hope.«

(interrupting) *From our point of view, all that lies far in the future, right?*

»if your genetic technology develops in that direction, it is.«

You mean to say that we should leave well enough alone!

»you should learn from us what can happen if you continue this way...we have no mothers and no fathers...you do not know what that means!«

I am trying to find my way into this situation, probably not very successfully. Do you have some sort of message for those who are ruling our world?

»no...it's true, they support this genetic technology, that is the problem...it's not that we don't take the blame for what we did, we have to see through to the end what we started...but one should be aware ahead of time of the path one is taking.«

You said one can...

(interrupting) »there are other civilizations that look more like yours...they also have immense problems, but nowadays they are happy nonetheless...we found out that the price we are paying to be without those problems is very high.«

From your point of view, we are living in the past, is that true?

»seen that way, that's right, yes...you are the original creation from which we developed...what happened is all right, but we are lacking something.«

I see. Were you ever incarnated in or around the 20th century?

»you can't say it that way...we are actually living in the very same time...but the very things which are now developing out of your genetic technology are just beginning to pursue the direction of what we've already become...do you understand?«

Yes, I think so.

»we have nothing but computers that do everything for us...that's not very nice.«

Are you, for example, in a position to...

(interrupting) »we have also had some unbelievable catastrophes...we survived them all...because we have become immune and saw it all coming.«

You mean nuclear catastrophes?

»yes, yes, we also tried all sorts of experiments with atomic power...then we programmed all our cells to resist radioactivity...a genetic imprint, do you understand?...you can't imagine all the things we did...what evolved out of it you can see in the photo: a monstrosity...you know, we suffer no mental anguish, but because of that we forfeit our mental profundity...because our original structures are missing...we now feel like cultivated tomatoes.«

I couldn't help laughing. In spite of all the cosmic tragedy, it seems that this species has still not lost its sense of humor.

Do you see any way we can intensify our contact? So that we can construct, within the framework of our possibilities, a set of technical instruments? I would like to set up a more objective type of communication between us.

»that might be possible...yes, we think it could work.«

I have had ambitions for such a project for a long time. *
Are you actually capable of speaking our language?

»we understand all languages.«

So written messages would present no problem...

(interrupting) »we have a brain center which stores all imaginable speech patterns...we don't have to study them...when we are born, we automatically recognize all speech patterns which have been stored.«

That's a terrific achievement!

»we also bring our mathematical memory with us...we need no schools.«

What kind of cultural life do you have?

---

* I was referring to my »ParaFax« Transcommunication Project. More about that later.

»hardly any at all.«

Don't you have any artists?

»no...look at us, look at us...without suffering, there is no art...we have no spiritual needs because we don't suffer.«

Because you don't suffer? Hmm...Do you know of spiritual figures such as Jesus and Buddha?

»yes...they are the ideal, they are the source.«

But if you have no spiritual consciousness, how can these enlightened beings represent an ideal for you?

»spiritual consciousness is born of suffering...but we can't suffer, making us superficially unhappy...real happiness is only perceivable when one can also be deeply unhappy.«

Yes, I understand. For a person on Earth it nevertheless seems a little absurd at first, that one can only be happy and artistic through suffering.

»and yet, that is just the way it is.«

Could we talk about technical ways of setting up an objective two-way paracommunication sometime? What I mean is primarily non-mental contact via instruments. The communication via mediums is not yet accepted on Earth, we require proof.

Suddenly Lilit, via the hand of my wife, began to touch me from top to bottom clumsily.

Yes, now you are feeling a genuine human body. Maybe not the most sophisticated model, but probably relatively acceptable, in relation to your own.

»you look a lot like us.«

In what way?

»in your shape.«

Does that mean I'm not a genuine Earthian, or what?

»those are the hyper-rational ones, they have a triangular head, an extended abdomen and heavy-set legs...and an aura like a sponge.«

Hmm, I don't know if that is supposed to be flattering. What are your astral bodies like? Do you have something like chakras...those subtle power centers, like at the solar plexus?

»our bodies are walking power centers...we don't divide into subcenters, we also don't have an energetic navel-center.«

Do you have any idea how often you have reincarnated on your own planet?

»perhaps seventy-five times...i can check on it.

(short pause) yes, seventy-five times.«

Where do you go to check on such things?

Lilit pointed to a lower rear region of Mira's brain.

»when we reflect on something, it immediately enters our consciousness, all by itself.«

That's utterly stupendous. I can't do that so easily... Have you always been called Lilit? Also in your last life?

»yes, yes...again and again.«

Why specifically ›Lilit‹?

»i like it...we name ourselves whatever we like...since we have no parents, there isn't anyone else to give one a name.«

Yeah...and how do you actually go about giving yourself a name?

»you emerge from the pool feeling absolutely wretched, yes ...then you are mentally asked what you wish to be called, and you send a name.«

And you mean you already know?

»yes, it just pops into one's mind...«

(groans and adjusts Mira's posture) »...oh, everything is so strenuous here.«

We can improve on that. How many dimensions does your world have, mathematically speaking? I mean how many dimensions do you take into consideration when you calculate your physical world?

»we have just as many as you do.«

I see. And why are your eyes so large?

»we enlarged the retina, and...«

(interrupting) *Do you have pupils like we do?*

»they are multifacet-eyes, like bees have...with them we can see different frequencies, segments and patterns.«

Are you capable of switching to different ways of seeing, like a computer?

»yes, we can also reflect and do other things as well...but we still aren't happy.«

Do you have any concept of God?

»we've none at all...well, there is something like an ideal that transforms itself...we believe that such a god permits everything.«

So it seems. What do you think of fate?

»on asastan, we all share an unfortunate fate.«

Can you see into the future?

»no, only into the past.«

Why doesn't it work in both directions?

»it's too imprecise...we can examine about seventy different futures...but we don't know which version will come about, since the way destiny develops doesn't just depend only on us...in the end, all our wishes point to our origin...that's why we came, because earth, too, is in the process of wanting to find its way back to its origins.«

Do you meditate?

»no...just quiet contemplation.«*

Do you know when the next pole jump will take place on Earth?

»in about seventy years.«

What will it unleash?

»great deluges... continents will be displaced, and where there is now land, there will be water in many places.«

About when did human beings arise on Earth?

»about three million years ago.«

And...how did it come about?

»through development.«

What I mean is, out of what did human beings actually develop? We had a man called Charles Darwin, who thought that evolution brought forth the human being.

(Lilit nods in agreement)

But where human spiritual potential, or, shall we say, the soul, comes from, that he couldn't say.

»i think that was always there.«

---

* meaning a pre-meditative phase.

Maybe. But how and when and why did it enter the human being? Did it simply take over apes, and it's what turned them into humans?

(Lilit nods anew)

And where was it before that?

»perhaps in other animals...consciousness only began to recognize itself through the ape.«

That may be...Hmm...do you have anything like money on your planet, some kind of economic system?

»not the way you know it.«

Do you have to work?

»we are always at work, but that happens from being conscious for the maintenance of our planet and bodies...that acts as motivation...existential power lies behind it.«

Do all of you get whatever you need?

»yes...but it would never occur to anyone to stop working for that reason, since then we wouldn't get what we need anymore.«

Are there some among you who have the say as to what work one or the other of you has to do?

»no...that is obvious.«

But how? Do you have any form of government? Or a council of wise men, a group of elders, or something similar?

»we don't have that, everything is self-sufficient...everyone lives for himself...yes, certain groups do form, but a government we do not have.«

And why does your climate have no thunderstorms?

»because we don't have these greatly differing temperatures.«

I see. During our first attempt at contact, the channel saw in her clairvoyant state something like viruses which you seemingly artificially created. What do you do with them?

»we conduct experiments.«

What kind of experiments?

»all sorts...we explore how they develop, what mischief they create, how one controls them again...they are like living beings.«

Do they also have a kind of mind?

»no, but a special capability to react...similar to elementals.«

Hmm...To return to the crash: an unusual brown paper was also found at the scene of the crash, a kind of parchment. Can you tell me what it is?

»oh, that's used for imprints...we insert it into a machine that has a kind of microscope inside, then with mental power we can record certain impressions reduced in size...the brown paper records the mental pictures.«

Do you have dreams?

»no, we perceive everything consciously...we have no pregnancy as such...thus, no myths or fairy tales, all that we are without...that's why we're in shallow states of mind.«

I understand. Your spaceship has a round central point, you said. What was located in the hub of the vehicle?

»a sun generator...also a large pipe, a kind of suction canal.«

Exactly what does the light breaker you mentioned do?

»it breaks the energy jam that collects on the focal disc ...light and heat are used as moving force...our thoughts change light into power...consciousness is also nothing else but light, can you understand that?«

Slightly. You mentioned that perhaps a period of hope was beginning for us on Earth, a change from destructiveness to constructiveness. What makes you say that?

»because human values are fulfilled more and more...it is a development we never experienced...for human beings things at present are proceeding in a direction that we had hoped to go in ourselves...however, it didn't happen...you have hopes of your own mastery...we don't...we no longer correspond to the original image of the universe...we changed our cellular structure and developed into a form that no longer corresponds to the universe as it was originally.«

Where is this original universe?

»right at the center of all the galaxies...that's where jesus and the other masters live in the pure, original form of the human being.«

How far away is this original center from our Milky Way galaxy?

»not as far as we are...earth is about halfway between our planet and the center.«

Is it possible for you to give me a quantitative measurement of how far apart we are from each other?

»in millions of light years the figure 750 comes to me.«

Is it within your capability to send a miniature UFO to Earth that is remote-controlled or manned by a robot?

»if it is, then only a spider.«

What is that?

»automated space probes for the transporting of unmanned equipment to other planets...we send them out often...just like you sometimes do.«

How big are they?

»about three feet in diameter.«

And you can land them wherever you want?

»that depends on the local conditions...we now have more experience of your energetic wind currents, for example.«

I have an idea: you could devise and construct such an instrument for purposes of objective communication between you and us and send it to us with one of your spider probes. How would that be?

All I heard was a sigh.

Isn't it interesting enough for you to have a more comprehensive exchange with us?

»at the moment, it isn't.«

That's too bad. Why not?

»it doesn't do anything for us...maybe within fifty years, when you have developed a little more.«

But it would do something for us right now.

»we aren't that human yet...we only speak here in order to fulfil our karma.«

What is your karma?

»we have to rediscover our human roots...but we aren't far enough along to involve ourselves actively.«

Might your father Lorin be interested in such contact?

»he is too busy.«

Busy with what?

»with his own bad karma...his trauma is that he was responsible for making our civilization into what it is today ...he was with you, too...he often reincarnated on earth... you see, his genetic researches go back a long way... it was ....* who formed us... that's why he is so depressive ...he was so scientific he didn't perceive what he was doing to us.«

That's a little hard to swallow. Sounds a little like cosmic drama.

»that's all part of it, as he always says.«

That is really hard to accept.

»it is difficult.«

It sure is. Would Alira like to say something?

The motions of her head seemed to signify that she was inquiring.

»no, she doesn't want to now.«

And what about Bax?

»bax isn't here.«

Where is he?

»on an expedition.«

To return to the subject of technical communication with all of you: what would we have to do to set up such a thing?

»i could implant something inside you, then you would have an easier time of it.

Hmm...I'm not sure, but maybe that is worth considering. How would you go about it?

»maybe i should begin by giving you a jolt of energy.«

What for? How does that work?

»i would place my right finger on your brain, right there.«

Lilit showed me the spot, using Mira's finger.

What happens then?

»it is possible that memories will be evoked, until at some point the required knowledge comes out of you by itself.«

* At this point, the name of one of Lorin's earthly incarnations was mentioned, which I prefer to keep to myself for the time being, to insure an unprejudiced appreciation of the text.

What kind of memories?
»well, that you were one of us...why do you think i'm here?«
So that's what it's all about! Well, before I let you give me this energy jolt, I would like a little more information.
»it acts as a constantly operating developer of brain cells ...we do it to ourselves, too...nothing to worry about, it's like an injection.«

I didn't know how to respond at that moment, but I quickly decided that it couldn't do much harm. As I didn't want to miss out on this opportunity, I agreed to let it happen.

Hmm...Okay, let's do it.
»all right...when i say ›now‹ you hold your head still.«

Lilit felt her way to the back of my head - my wife's eyes were closed the whole time - and placed a finger against the lower right section of my skull. After a few seconds of her evidently collecting her spiritual energies, I heard, »now«, and, accompanied by a soft whispering, I received an energy impulse right at that spot.*

I'd like to hear more about my connection with you.
»what should i say...you lived here at one time.«
When? How often?
»a few times...the last time was 350 years ago.«
And...why? How did it happen to be me?
»because you're interested in all this...and because you, too, like to play little tricks on life.«
Hmm...And as what did I materialize?
»oh, nothing special, just one of us.«
Did I simply want to look around, to see how things are up there?
»just to be here and learn something...yes, yes, vipan.«
That sounds dangerous...Oh-oh, the tape is just about over.

* I can't judge yet whether it has had any effect.

124

»i'll withdraw now.«
Okay. Thank you. Goodbye until next time. Maybe we can talk about the techno...

The recorder turned the 60-min. cassette off before I got to the end of my sentence. Not counting the warm-up phase, the conversation had lasted about 40 minutes, quite a bit longer than the previous talks. Mira had descended into her meditative trance much more relaxedly, and thus, went deeper. I didn't notice until later that I had jumped haphazardly from one thing to another in the course of my chatter with Lilit. Each one of her remarks stirred me to new inquiries. Some of her responses amazed me so much that I needed a week to digest it all.

The »ParaFax« machine referred to is a transcommunication project that I've had my heart set on for a long time. In the course of time, clever hints have piled up from diverse paranormal sources, e.g. extraterrestrials, as to how such a technical communications network might best be established. Namely, with something akin to our own earthly fax machine with which both language and graphic work – for example, mathematical formulas and scientific sketches, which are far more difficult to transmit medially with any accuracy – can simply be para-faxed from the other side. That this seems, at least in principle, possible is shown by diverse trials of a group of intrepid researchers from around the world, who manage through radio, video, computer, etc. to receive interesting messages from disembodied beings and those who have never had a body. In order to find sponsors for this rather expensive project, I have already set in motion various activities, but the fact that they have borne insufficient fruit shows that this chance of making a transcommunicative quantum leap is not yet taken seriously on Earth.

The Fourth Roswell Psychic Contact

Studio Phoenix, 27 August 1995
11:45 pm - 12:45 am

Once again, I put together lots of questions as a result of the last talk. Mira entered into trance relatively quickly and began with a rather strange item that seemed to imply that, this time, some kind of telepathy appliance would be operating. It started with a strangely monotone voice:

»we can broadcast.«
Am I speaking to Lilit?
»this is not a personal contact...we are broadcasting.«
Okay, we are reading you. Among other things, I need clarity on your concept of time.
»we use the super helix* as our point of departure, that is central sun time...and we observe the motions of the planets...whenever they change their adjustment, one large unit of time has elapsed.«
What exactly do they change?
»their torque along the planetary path.«
Hmm...You said in our very first contact, ›You are our future‹. I want to understand that better.
»we stem from the selfsame development which you earthlings underwent...and developed to the point where we now are.«
Does that mean that your present is definitely our future?
»no...but it is highly probable it will turn out that way... we once had similar problems to yours...that's why we took the path of total technology...but it didn't make us happy.«
You travelled to Earth using a time leap. How does that work?

* Helix, Latin-Greek, for something spiral, winding, twisting.

»you have to plow through lots of different elements in order to get outside the bounds of your own universe... which, in turn, changes the time frame...don't you comprehend einstein's mathematics of time?«
Only partly. – You said you also use thought as propelling power. How do you transform thoughts into kinetic power?
»that is precisely what we are doing at this very moment.«
How? Can you explain it in greater detail?
»we receive your thoughts and clearly respond to them without being present.«
Okay, if you see it that way. Do you also have an acoustic language?
»well, we do make occasional sounds.«
Could you give me a few examples?

Some very unusual tongue-clicking sounds emitted from the medium's mouth, it sounded almost like a cackle.

What would those sounds translate as?
»they are expressions of mood, like animals make.«
What about love on your planet?
»it exists...for our partners.«
How would ›I love you‹ sound in your language?
»acoustically?...we don't have any acoustic language.«
Or somehow audibly expressed?
»we only have sounds expressing feelings, they are all quite different...our language consists of impulses...we are all telepathically connected to each other...we speak-send your language inside ourselves and comprehend it that way too.«
But you have a written language.
»yes, yes, but it is really more a mathematical script.«

Would it be possible for you to write a little something via the medium's hand?

»i don't know.«

Let's try it. Here is something to write with and something to write it down on.

I handed my wife a pad of paper on a clipboard and a felt-tipped pen and was anxious to see what would happen. After a while, Lilit scribbled something indecipherable to me on the paper.*

What does that mean, approximately?

»it means ›welcome‹, but more than that...also ›union on the energy plane, when we speak‹.«

Very nice. That means you have visual symbols. Which of them is the most important?

»a four-dimensional triangle.«

Hmm. It sounds like you mean a tetrahedron? What does it signify for you?

»it symbolizes our plane of existence, the level on which all matter explains itself.«

*And what do two intertwined tetrahedrons signify?***

»wholeness...the possibilities beyond our universe.«

I suppose that element is also present in your spaceship?

»of course!«

What is its function?

»it works in association with the mentally operated controls and is located within a kind of safety valve...it also serves to harmonize brain waves and is connected in many different ways to the kinetic propulsion power of the craft.«

That's what I thought. ...You have very small noses. What do you breathe?

»we don't need much oxygen...we can live for a long time in water...we have very small lungs because our water is enriched with oxygen...that's why we don't putrefy or decompose for a long time.«

And what is your planet's atmosphere composed of?

»lots of oxygen, then nitrogen, steam, carbon dioxide... among the solid elements, there is more magnesium than calcium, more iron than sodium.«

What do you have in place of teeth? Anything at all?

»a jawbone is there, yes.«

Why don't you have any lips?

»we do have small lips, but nothing bulging anymore, since we don't suckle.«

You said you can reflect with your eyes. What do you mean by that?

»we can reflect back all light which reaches us, or send signals with them...we call them magic eyes, we can also activate energy that way.«

What huge catastrophes did you survive?

»enormous atomic explosions, mainly.«

And how did you manage to program yourselves to be immune to radioactivity?

»with genetic inoculation.«

What does that consist of?

»we took tiny doses of radioactivity and proceeded to increase them by small increments...we do that during early pregnancy in the test tube.«

You mentioned an error in trying to land your spacecraft. What did you do wrong?

»we failed to regulate a blackout in our power propulsion system, since we were used to being cushioned by vacuum-like spaces...but that does not exist in your atmosphere.«

At what speed did you enter our atmosphere?

»about 300,000 miles-per-hour.«*

Braking must have created an absolutely unbelievable pressure.

»we were fully protected against the pressure by our suits ...they're of spiral-shaped fibre cells that equalize pressure and vibrations...they're also bulletproof.«

You also said your spacecraft has projectors protecting you against electrical shocks.

* see picture no. 37.

** The spatial »Seal of Solomon« had long fascinated and inspired me.

* I assume that this entry took place in not-yet-fully-materialized state.

126

»they broke down.«

How do they function when they are operating?

»on the basis of repulsion.«

Which parts of the craft overheated and exploded?

»the hydrogen tank and the heat regulators.«

How did your ground control maintain contact with you, if it did?

»via fully telepathic transmitters...but only as far as earth's atmosphere.«

What instruments did you have on board?

»oh, we had devices for object-finding, magnification appliances, navigation tools, also ›narrow angle focusing‹ modules, with which we can observe spaces from close-up before we actually enter them...we also had sensors, for recognizing any threatening elements within a radius of half a light year long before we would actually bounce against them...also light screens displaying everything going on in the machine room...we can also partially pre-perceive, which enables us to prepare for the precise situation we are approaching.«

You intended to land near, or on Bermuda, because there is an electromagnetic intersection there. What is there exactly?

»a spot where various forces coming from the north and south poles intersect...it is somewhat parallel to the heart in the body.«

And why is it favorable to land there?

»because it provides us with maximum protection...one is most thoroughly invisible there, at such a spot the people are also somewhat confused and less active...all as a result of that power.«

How did you manage to make yourselves invisible to radar? That is to say, when it was working.

»with an electron net...your science hasn't discovered it yet ...we unplug ourselves via magnets.«

What does the planet name Asastan mean?

»it is the name of a very ancient civilization which lived long before christ...in a sense, we stem from the civiliza-tion in the tigris-euphrates valley, that is to say, the first civilization of earth.«

When did you leave Earth?

»you can't really say that, since we disappeared through excarnation...the spirit retains its genetic imprint...our emigration began five million years ago...but our present civilization started to build itself up physically again only 500,000 years ago.«

Before coming to Earth, you were on another planet, is that right?

»yes, on venus...we originally are venusians.«

And genetic research was already conducted there?

»on all planets near to earth...only the martians have closed it down.«*

Why did you settle so incredibly far away from your original planet?

»because we are just as far distant from our origins...with our extreme will power, we wanted to harmonize and beautify everything...and this is where we landed...far from where we wanted to.«

You told us that many of you would like to incarnate here on Earth to accelerate our progress.

»not only your progress, we also want to further the goal of inner harmony.«

Have some of you already incarnated?

»only a few, but many want to...over the next 100 years many such births will occur on earth...and your population will double through the accelerated birth rate**... many things will no longer suffice to prevent births because nature also knows that human beings are in mortal peril...at such times there are always inordinately high birth rates...so that much more can be exterminated afterwards.«

* A few years ago we had contact for over two hours with a Martian, who lectured about Chernobyl and the wrong utilization of Mars energy on Earth. This highly informative talk will hopefully soon be published as part of a collection of our most important ET contacts.
** According to various spiritual sources, our planet can accommodate at least 10 billion people, that is, in harmonious cohabitation.

It sounds like pretty awful times are soon upon us.

»it all serves your development.«

Let's hope so. You also spoke of your central sun/moon stellar body. Please explain how this moon is integrated in the sun?

»the moon is inside...our sun is only hot on the outer surface, inside it is cooled down, the core is a moon – just the opposite of earth – where life is on the inside and on the outside is the sun's fire and heat.«

And your central star is inhabited?

»ours, yes...however our sun is physically inhabited on the inside, not on the outside.«

So a moon is inside the sun and that moon is inhabited.

»yes, yes...by very peculiar creatures...they are earth creatures, they don't look like us.«

Why are they peculiar?

»because they don't walk upright, they are like worms... you know, we don't have to talk about this.«

Just one more question about it: are they at a very early stage of evolution, or what?

»no, it is a question of karma...it is a kind of moon hell ...the dark sides of the moon have to be experienced by these living forms.«

Hmm...You told us you have very little in the way of culture. What does it amount to?

»it gets less and less...it has become very uninteresting.«

Do you have books or music? What about dance and theater? Paintings? Movies? Exhibitions? Anything of that sort?

»all that disappears more and more...we have to go back to our primordial roots.«

You made the odd statement that you're unhappy because you can't suffer. Isn't that a contradiction?

»i meant authentic suffering, not just a shallow lack of happiness.«

But isn't your unhappiness also a form of suffering?

»as long as we are in this form, we can't change it.«

What is the name of your partner-being? Who is the other half of Lilit?

»it is bax.«

Ah, and who is Alira's counterpart?

»that is moran.«

And Lorin's partner?

»he is alone...he is the only one who doesn't live together with his counterpart.«

You said that he has often reincarnated on Earth. Yet at the same time you say he is immortal. How does that fit together?

»he is aware of his immortality, which not all earth creatures are.«

But in order to materialize on Earth he had to die first, didn't he?

»we meant the continuation of the individual, of the individuality.«

I see. Your form of reproduction is conducted via affinity principles, is that right? How does it function?

»in our case it is simply a continuation of an earlier life ...under new circumstances and pre-requisites which develop all by themselves.«

Do you have anything to do with the crop signs?

»they are made by crafts from nearby galaxies.«

Why? What do they do that for?

»to make others aware of their existence...and also to prepare them.«

For what?

»for the unexpected.«

Is a large-scale UFO invasion expected to take place? One often hears about such conjectures.

»i do believe that we will have to come.«

You are coming too?

»not us in particular, though perhaps some of us will...but it will have to be done.«

Why does it have to be done?

»many people will be in danger of their lives, they will have to leave.«

33 *Retired Major Jesse Marcel Sr. broke thirty years of silence by daring in a TV interview to make public at least parts of his Roswell experience.*

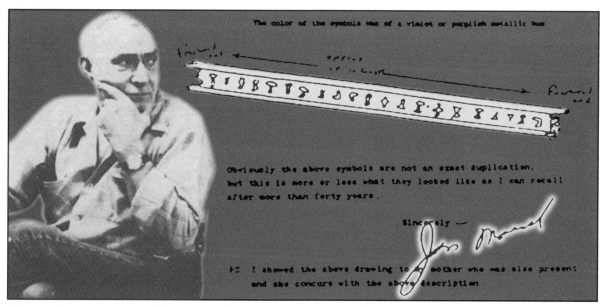

34 *Sketch by eyewitness Jesse Marcel Jr. from 1989: a recovered I-beam bearing astonishing similarity to filmed alleged UFO fragments.*

35 *Author René Coudris and channel medium Mirabelle in a British TV interview on her paranormal Roswell alien contacts with Lilit, Bax, Alira and Lorin.*

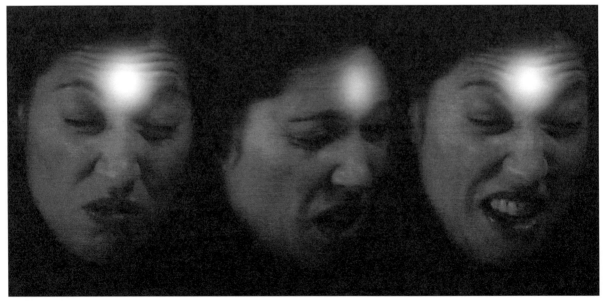

36 *Channel Mirabelle in a trance state: in a darkened hotel room, receiving telepathic messages from Major Marcel in front of a running camera.*

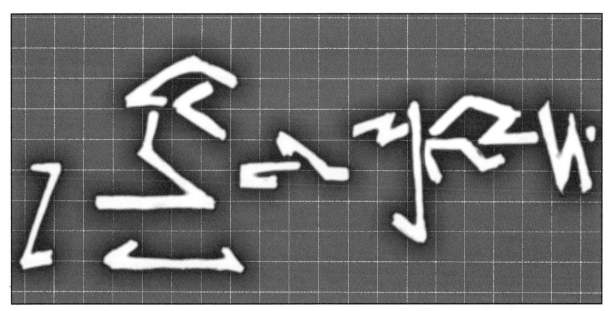

37 *Lilit's attempt at writing through the hand of the medium while in trance. Loosely translated it means »Welcome to the union on the astral energy plane«.*

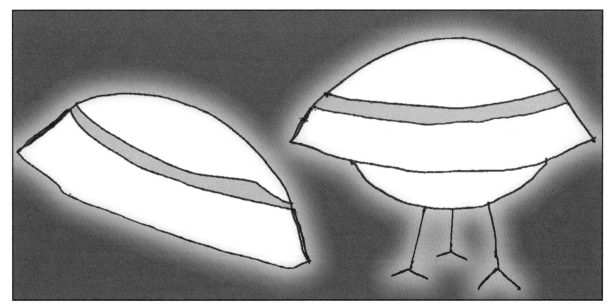

38 *Spontaneous sketches of the outer form and prismatic sight ring of the crashed Asastanian spaceship perceived in trance, and drawn by the medium after the session.*

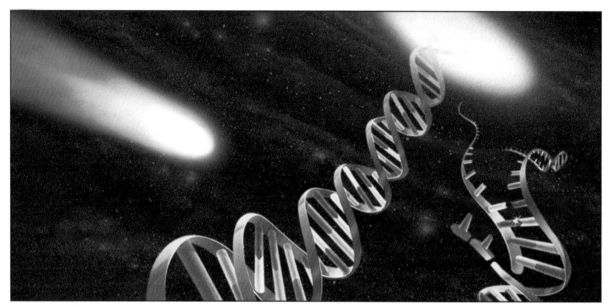

39 *Throughout the vastness of outer space innate forms of life are found ranging from hydrogen to seedlike modules of the DNA spiral. Comets are seemingly distributing life in space.*

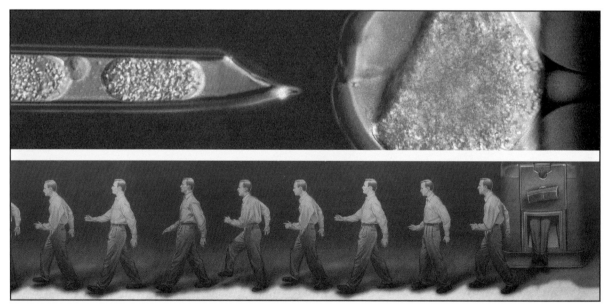

40 *Will the key of life decoded in the test tube lead to a gene-technological horror vision of hybrid mutants? Above, isolated DNA being injected into a cell alien to the species.*

41 *Early Sumerian portrayal of »in vitro«- fertilization and the birth of an Adam. The test tubes and the tree of life on the right suggest our ancestors had knowledge of genetic technology.*

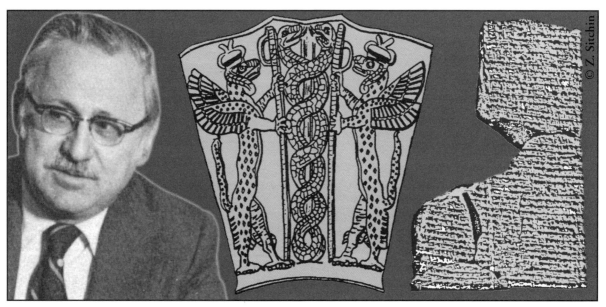

42 *Zecharia Sitchin, recognized decoder of Sumerian cuneiform tablets, played a major role in recent historiography. Center: DNA emblem of a laboratory in the city of Eridu.*

43 *A 4,500 years old Sumerian depiction on a cylinder seal with a complete solar system in which the Sun (not Earth!) is the center, orbited by all the planets we know today. Below: sexagesimal Sumerian number symbols.*

44 *Recently discovered ancient American Indian wall paintings in Canyonland portray petroglyphs of the Anasazi culture: six-toed footprints are seen next to a six-spoked »wheel«.*

45 *Tales of six-fingered star people are told in the Ugha Mongulala legends of the Amazon Indios of Brazil. Right, the white woman who was Chief Tatuncas's mistress for a short time.*

46 *›Carl Jung‹ claimed to have found a reminiscence of six-fingered aliens in the six-armed gods of India and shed light on the mythological background of historical »Lilith« (right: Terracotta 2000 BC).*

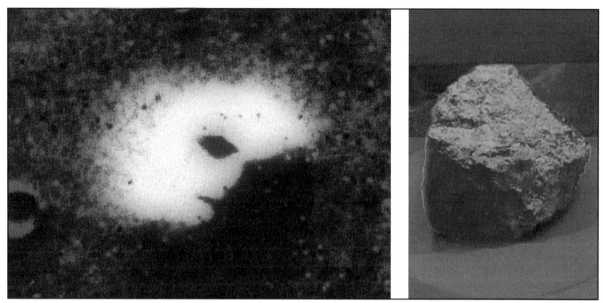

47 *The Mars face is located in the Cydonia region of the Red Planet. Strange artificial structures are also found on the Moon and other planets of our solar system. Right: Meteorite ALH84001 suggests life on Mars.*

48 *Hidden within the Sri Yantra and the double tetrahedron, the 3D-»Seal of Solomon« - captured here in a cornfield in Flandorf, Austria - lies the encoded know-how of UFO spaceship power.*

What will put them into such peril?

»epidemics and nuclear wars...it will get very bad.«

When will it take place?

»in about fifteen years.«

What will unleash the nuclear wars?

»your superpowers...but fifty years from now, the worst will be over.«

I suppose that means that there won't be any more disarmament?

»we don't believe in that.«

Hmm. That leads me to another subject. You are specialists in prolonging and preserving life. What concrete steps would you recommend we take in this matter?

»none at all.«

Why not?

»because in your circumstances it is senseless...what would be the point of it, if you just go into a nuclear war anyway?«

Yeah, I'm sorry to say that you have a point there. But I would be interested to hear your answer anyway

»it will only be of interest in about fifty years, if you manage to survive.«

I will then be ninety-five years old.

»people won't believe it, but it is going to be worse than anything human beings ever dreamed of.«

What will be the major cause of this kind of nuclear war?

»despair...absolute insanity.«

Wow. — Well, could you tell me briefly how you spend your days, the things you do regularly? Are work and leisure separated?

»there are no hard and fast rules.«

Does that mean you just do what you please?

»we do what we have to do...which is also what we want to do...we don't get into any conflicts with our desires... we accept our duties.«

Do you also have larger spacecraft? It seems to me that Mira saw something like a huge mother ship in her early vision.

»we have a colony, connected to the network of our planets.«

Mira gives me a signal to stop talking. She rolls her eyeballs beneath her lids, indicating she has internal optical perceptions. At another sign from her, I can continue my questioning.

You mentioned a spider that you can send off unmanned. Would it be possible to send such a probe to us here on Earth?

»i don't know...they often don't land where they are sent.«

Why not?

»they are very unstable, often get displaced and are then destroyed, or they simply fall into the water...they are not sufficiently powered so as to enable them to operate independently and land just at the point which was planned... it is usually more a matter of hit-or-miss.«

Could you possibly give us another definitive, objective piece of evidence as proof of your existence? We would need some unequivocal physical manifestation of some sort. Can you »beam yourself down« to us?

»not at the moment...we can't simply materialize.«

Would Father Lorin be willing to communicate with us directly?

»the medium is almost at the end of her strength.«

Okay. What we need, in principle, is objective certainty. But that doesn't mean it has to happen today.

»i don't know...we must go now.«

Well, then, thank you for today. With whom have I been speaking?

»with lilit.«

My last question was provoked by Lilit's farewell remark in the plural. Mira emerged slowly from her trance. I gave her a little while to recover, then inquired, as I usually do, about any inner-acoustic or inner visual perceptions she might have made during the conversation which she wasn't able to tell me about immediately.

Nothing acoustical...yes, at the end I saw a large planet and beneath it was a formation of seven connected shapes that looked like spacecraft...it's quite possible they were separable from one another, perhaps a sort of space station...I don't like this whole business, I don't feel good about any of it.

Why not? Because of the wild statements we're getting? They make me uneasy...and I can't feel these things properly. Somehow, the whole thing is a little weird. Sometimes my heart is pounding fiercely. It is all taking place on a frequency that I don't particularly like.

End of tape. Mira stuck to her ambivalent attitude. She rather disliked the whole subject, with the result that she had to transcend herself in order to keep up with it, which, in the end, she did only for my sake. I could only hope that the TV documentary about aliens which was about to be shown would change her attitude somewhat.

The Fifth Roswell Psychic Contact

Studio Phoenix, 6 September 1995
8:45 - 9:05 pm

A week before the following contact, the scenes of the autopsy were finally shown exclusively on a TV program called »RTL-Extra« on German channel RTL. We were glued to the screen in utter astonishment. The impression made on us as we gazed upon the being which Mira had come into such intimate contact with, and with whose consciousness I had already conversed several times, was, from the perspective of a moving camera, simply overwhelming. Oddly enough, the technical objects discovered at the time of the crash were neither shown, nor even mentioned in the documentary.

Since Mira wasn't at all sure whether she wished to get involved in another ET-dialog under my guidance, I suggested an experiment. Having succeeded in interviewing »Carl Jung« a few days earlier on the subject of the aliens, and listening to his fascinating, typically Jungian statement* I conceived the idea of inviting »Jung« to another short conversation in a trance session and asking him to remain listening in the background to one of our alien contact sessions. It was my hope that he would comment on the event. Once Mira herself became interested in »Carl's« attitude toward our project, I was able to talk her into my plan. I explained my proposal to »Jung« and received the answer, »**If it is absolutely imperative**«. Then, in his reassuring presence, the next and to date final contact took place.

Hello Asastan. Hello Lilit.
    (pause of several minutes)

* see p. 121 ff.

We are calling Lilit again, to talk to her some more about her crash.

    A few more minutes of meditation.

»yes...i am here.«

Are you simply beaming your voice to us, or are you astrally present?

»**neither the one nor the other...am waiting.**«*

Fine. A few days ago, we watched a black and white film about your autopsy. I have a few questions on my mind with regard to it. For example, what color are your bodies originally?

»**a brownish copper hue.**«

Are there different races on Asastan?

    (shaking her head) »**not at all.**«

If you are reproduced outside a mother's body, where do the eggs and sperm come from? Exactly how do you do it?

»**they reproduce themselves...there are always enough stored.**«

How so?

»**we have incubators for them.**«

Do your male members still have testicles, even if they are no longer needed?

»**the rudiments of them.**«

Since you are all reproduced through genetic engineering, do you all have the same level of intelligence?

»**no, it isn't possible for us to reproduce everyone fully equal...we do have a program of diversity, although a controlled one...we can introduce a plan into the embryo; with-**

* This signified distant telepathy. There is a major distinction between being in the immediate frequency vicinity of the channel and, as above, remaining in one's own body which exists endless millions of light years away.

in this framework it is supposed to reabsorb something. Everything else is then eliminated or nipped in the bud... but we have no control over the intensity of brain activity or brain cell production, nor what subtle shape and what code the being adopts...we can eliminate traits which we do not like or work deliberately to retain other traits, such as mathematical memory or linguistic ability...we cannot change any individual pattern, but retain or eliminate certain specific qualities.«

Do you have something like fear?

»yes, but not individual fear.«

What other kind of fear is there?

»we are afraid we could one day lose control over all these mechanisms.«

Since you can always enter new bodies, are there also beings among you who are disembodied?

»those exist everywhere...what do you mean?«

I mean, if you are all intent on immediately entering a new body as soon as you lose your old one, does it come about at once, in a kind of instant reincarnation?

»no, not like that...we also go to other places, to other universes, to other bodies.« *

You spoke of twelve moons circling your planet. Then is it always bright as day – or, rather, bright as a moonlit night – where you are?

»that varies, but it is never completely dark...we don't have night, as you do...it is merely shady, and less shady.«

What kinds of scientists do you have?

»we have the gene keepers and lots of others who watch over all these structures we have created.«

And what are most of the members of your population?

»a third of them are researchers, a third guardians, the others are attendants...we all live the project which we ourselves created.«

Does that mean there is a clear social order?

»everything is divided on the basis of function.«

Who does that?

»it is self-evident from birth...depending on what qualities you are born with, you are allotted to a given function ...you recognize it very quickly...after all, we are reincarnated according to various test tube categories.«

So there is a kind of caste system?

»yes...when an embryo in a test tube lights up in a certain way, we know a scientist is about to be born...he then retains this function.«

And if it lights up differently?

»then he belongs to another category...embryos are bred with certain genes according to the function desired, as scientists or whatever...all of them are in the same room... whether they slip into one body or another, they all go automatically into their appropriate category... do you understand?«

I'm trying. Do you also have what we here call the daily news?

»oh, we have an information system...anyone can use it... everyone has implants to call up any information at any time.«

What is the latest news or information of the moment?

»let's see...new craft from foreign planets have just been sighted.«

Do you have much contact with other UFOs or IFOs, as we should probably call them?*

»yes, with many.«

In the Army film about you which was released, there seems to be a rather strange plate with imprints or impressions of your six-fingered hands. At least, a picture of it was printed in the newspaper.

»that was of a computer we built.«

What is it for?

»for various things...that one was for flight control.«

So you placed your hands on it...and what happened then?

»via energy transfer, certain functions were set into operation.«

---

* This refers to their ability to occupy other bodies, the so-called walk-ins.

* Identified Flying Object.

What sort of functions?

»to steer and navigate the spacecraft...one can do lots of different things with it...it works just like with your computers.«

I see. Were you in a dematerialized state while you were engaged in your time leap?

»yes, in a way, but not the way you think...we enter a different wave length...it's not that we aren't extant...but our vibrations are raised and then slowed down.«

Can you mathematically limit the higher wave length for the time leap somehow?

»yes, we can...between seven hundred just before the time leap and five hundred megahertz afterward«*

That means afterwards you vibrate more slowly?

»yes, after the leap, we are on a lower wave length than before.«

Well, maybe that's logical...What is your average body temperature?

»it is higher than yours.«

How high, in degrees Centigrade?

»about 48 degrees.«

Why so high?

»i don't know, probably through the different climate... it is never cold where we are...we are also never cold, either ...the climate remains constant.«

How high are the air temperatures?

»about the same as our body temperature.«

I see. How did you get your six fingers and six toes?

»through genetic engineering.«

You mean you did it intentionally?

»it proved fruitful, yes...it is extremely practical...because of the extra finger, we don't ever drop anything...we also hardly ever injure ourselves since...it's like having a second thumb.«

You described our era as a time of hope, but then you predicted rather dramatic and potentially catastrophic events for the near future which hardly give one cause for hope.

* 700,000,000,000 - 500,000,000,000 Hertz.

»it isn't predetermined...the hope that everything can still be turned in a new direction is what we were talking about...through the great changes, there are also great chances of insights and realizations.«

Do you want to tell me more about your crash?

»don't know what might still be of interest.«

Well, you exited from the craft just before it crashed.

(a nod)

What actually transpired?

»with a kind of air cushion we are catapulted out.«

But the air has to be enclosed in something.

»yes, in the same material as our spacesuits, just a little thinner and smoother...it fills instantaneously with a gas, all by itself, independent of any equipment.«

And it then ejects you from the craft?

»yes, one ties it around one like a dress, it is attached here.«

(she points to Mira's back side) »...after ejecting it causes us to fly through the air slowly...it only prevents the crash from being fatal, but it is not a parachute.«

I wonder what all those silvery foil-like strips were that were found scattered all over the terrain quite a few miles from the spacecraft. When these foil strips were crushed, they immediately jumped back to their original form. Where does the stuff come from?

»that's material from the air cushions...they also prevented the craft from being destroyed completely.«*

That's what I just thought...Can you say any more about your philosophy? We don't really know much about it.

»you yourselves say ›master the earth‹...we took the suggestion literally...we see it as a new experience, as the chance to realize new possibilities, although it did not make us happy.«

Do you have spiritual beings you look up to?

»we tend to look beyond...yes, in a way we do honor the masters who live in the central universe...because they are

* In a a recently televised animated film about the future NASA Mars landings, I was astounded to see that a kind of »landing airbag« was shown to be in use, the only difference being that these didn't burst.

not even dependent on genes...they live utterly from their consciousness.«

What form does your homage take?

»we look upon them as a higher form of development than we ourselves have attained.«

What masters do you think of in particular?

»most of all, of the nazarene...also of buddha...and a few other big ones.«

What is your relationship to us on Earth?

»something akin to sympathy or compassion...and a feeling of responsibility to inform you about the possibilities of development, should you take the same steps as our ancestors did.«

Do you have some form of psychologically structured consciousness?

»we are extremely rational about it...when you are born as a scientist, you have a scientific psyche...it works kind of like a mathematical cycle.«

Where are you directing your own future evolution?

»precisely that is what we don't know.«

Don't you even have an idea?

»we are too far removed from our primordial roots to be able to say...we hope the law which brings forth all that lives and grants us our freedom is a good one...that is really our only philosophy, we don't know any other...we have become empty in terms of philosophizing, having thrown all our energy into research and especially gene manipulation...we no longer speculate, we simply devise our intentions and act upon them.«

Could you act in such a way as to give us an objective sign of your existence? I don't know what possibilities are open to you.

»we all crashed on earth anyway. What more do you want?«

Yes, but you were unfortunately all locked away, removed from public scrutiny. ...Do all of you know of our planet?

»most of them don't really care...for them it is merely... the words which come to mind are, ›old hat‹.«

What things matter to the bulk of your people?

»the future, the work on new projects.«

What kinds of projects?

»oh, new buildings and restructuring the landscape...we go about transforming and engineering the terrain on the largest imaginable scale.«

How do you do that?

»by changing the conditions of growth for plants we can restructure the surface of the terrain...we also grow mountains and create lakes, and many other things.«

How do you do all this? With technical equipment?

»through working with the reflexes of the ground tissue the planet is made of...we place a living organism on it, which creates new structures through cell transformations ...we merely attempt to turn our imagination into reality...we had the idea that nature had no laws of its own and we should issue its orders.«

You mentioned that you're living in a four-dimensional world. I don't know whether you mean our Earth's four dimensions.

»the fourth dimension is will power, through which and together with which everything happens...by implementing one's own will without limits, one gets to the spot where we are now evolutionarily stranded.«

Hmm...is there anything which you yourselves wish to communicate to us?

(shaking her head) »no.«

In that case, many thanks for today. And goodbye.

(short pause)

»sugar does not dissolve only in water.«

Hmm?...What does it do, then?

»also in milk! goodbye.«

I had to laugh at this last remark, even though I do not to this day know what it is supposed to mean. Perhaps a kind of irrational riddle reminiscent of a Zen koan or a droll indication of our own narrow-minded way of thinking.

One reader of the first German edition suggested it could mean that heavenly souls (symbolically labelled »sugar«) not only reincarnate within earthly humans (symbolized by »water«) but also within other planetary races (symbolized by »milk«). Another reader associated mother milk and milk sugar and pointed out that these final words of the aliens probably unconsciously indicate their longing for a mother culture.

If you come up with a better explanation, please drop me a line.

The Telepathic Roswell Commentaries

The Reflections of »Carl Jung«

The famous Swiss cultural psychologist C. G. Jung had a life long interest in the phenomenon of UFOs, albeit with certain reservations in the end. In *»Modern Myth of Things Seen in the Sky«*, he tried in 1958 to interpret the appearance of spacecraft in a purely psychological way. In an article for the Zurich newspaper »Weltwoche« Jung had already several years earlier provided more concrete observations on the subject, saying with regard to flying saucers, *»that it is not a matter of mere rumor; ›something‹ is actually seen, although one does not know what.«* Further on in the article, referring to the critical world political situation of the time, he remarks, *»In such times as these, people raise their eyes to the heavens in search of help and there appear wondrous portents from above, either threatening or consoling in nature.«*

In 1946, a year before Kenneth Arnold's famous sighting, Jung, at the age of 71, turned his attention to the phenomenon of UFOs. He wrote to a friend at the time, *»The phenomenon of saucers could be both ›rumor and manifest object‹. It is almost impossible to come up with a proper notion of these things, since they do not act like physical bodies, instead appearing as weightless as thoughts«*. From the very beginning, Jung felt that the obviously very complex phenomenon might possess, besides a possible physical reality, a significant psychic component. He even considered a third facet: UFOs could be synchronicities, that is, a meaningful coincidence of things which move separately through space and/or time, signifying correlations between consciousness and matter which until then had gone unnoticed.

Jung was not able to give posterity a solution to the puzzle of the source of flying saucers. However, he did succeed in raising the discussion to a higher level. He even considered the possibility that UFOs might be a kind of materialized psyche, that is, a manifestation of archetypes, the most profound patterns of the inner psyche, formed in a physical or paraphysical way by the collective unconscious.

If one were to go so far as to postulate a fluid border between mind and body and between organic and inorganic matter, connected by holographic links, we approach the field of active human mental creative power. Perhaps what we are doing here is staging, as a kind of unconscious production, something which we ourselves first give mental shape to deep down in our individual and/or collective psyche, then unconsciously yet intentionally solidify. We then spot something apparently approaching from the outside in order eventually to make a huge enigma of it with our rational levels of consciousness. Jung himself made the following proviso: *»I still don't know what these ›flying saucers‹ are all about. The reports are so odd that one feels tempted to compare them with parapsychological occurrences, insofar as they are truly genuine phenomena.«* His thoughts then turned to ball lightning and other electrical phenomena, with the final summary, *»Should it turn out that despite this still unclarified possibility, such phenomena stem from extraterrestrial causes, it would be proof of intelligent interplanetary connections. It is impossible to even postulate the implications for humanity of such thing. However, we would doubtless be* *thrust into the highly delicate position of those present-day primitive societies who clash with the superior culture of the white race: the rudder would be taken out of our hands; and we would have – as an old medicine man once told me with tears in his eyes – ›no more dreams‹. That means our soaring flight of intellect would be hopelessly pre-empted and, thus, paralyzed... First off, our science and technology would be relegated to a corner and doomed to just collect dust. What such an overwhelming catastrophe would mean in moral terms can be gleaned somewhat from the wretched decline of primitive cultures going on right in front of our eyes.«*

In the hundreds of para-conversations I have conducted over the past eleven years via channelled transcommunication with the departed »Jung«, – that is, with that essential core of universal consciousness which, according to his own statement, also experienced an incarnation as Carl Gustav Jung, among others – he became ever more concrete in his statements on the subject, even though his thought continued to emphasize the psychic components.*

That's why, within two days of seeing the Santilli Aliens film fragment, and having the four talks with Lilit, I was aching to talk to this old friend from the beyond about the Roswell case. After all, he had been happy to make constructive and illuminating contributions to almost every subject all along. Besides, this time I didn't have to convince my wife of the logic of my intentions.

* Due to legalistic squabbles with the C.G. Jung Heritage Society, I make the distinction between the departed »Jung« and the historic one by putting the first one in quotes or as in this book in horizontal quotation marks.
** I am reserving the statements made by »Jung« on the subject of UFOs in various para-dialogs to me over the course of the last few years for a future publication, since the processing and cataloguing of all the collected materials will require years of work. If you have long-term interest in the English published transmissions of »Jung« please drop me a note.

Studio Phoenix, 1 September 1995

Mr. »Jung«, we have occupied ourselves thoroughly over the last few weeks with the so-called Roswell ET. Apparently historical films of an autopsy have recently come to light which...

(interrupting) »...are doubtful?«
Yes, there is a lot of doubt surrounding them. What do you say to them? Are the films authentic?
»The films, yes.«
And their contents? I have here a picture of the corpus delicti.

I gave Mira, which is to say, »Jung«, the photo of the autopsy published in the magazine Focus, a far from simple procedure, since Mira keeps her eyes closed while in trance and »Jung« does not perceive primarily the physical picture, but rather its aura.

»Such discoveries were made already in prehistoric times, one also found such things in ancient Egypt.«
You mean this type body?
»Yes, also in age-old cave drawings, this form is found, at least in part. And what one has read in certain utopian or science fiction novels also comes from these body experiences.«
And where do the bodies themselves come from?
»My answer to that is that one is aware of such discoveries and that they correspond to the archetypal image human beings have of extraterrestrials. People whose genes have suffered damage can also look like that, although not appearing with the same regularity.«
The remarkable thing is that the film from which this still was taken is evidently really from the year 1947. Beyond that, the voices which claim in all seriousness that an alien UFO crashed and was recovered by the US Army will simply not be stilled. In recent weeks we have made several psychometric-telepathic experiments in this matter with this very picture and a creature by

the name of Lilit, from the planet Asastan, got in touch with us. The things reported are of great interest and, as far as I can evaluate them, do not contradict themselves. Since more than anything else, the name of my contact amazes me, I'd like to ask you about the mythological significance of the name Lilith.* Can you tell me anything about that?

»There is a figure by the name of Twelvehead, with twelve faces, in an ancient Indian epic. The anima of Twelvehead had something to do with the hidden feminine principle, that is, with the dark side of the moon. She represents the multiplicity of the creative force, including, by the way, the goddess Kali. who helps to account for polygamy, both guiding and balancing it. She holds that only to the extent that a human being is polygamous is it possible to preserve the gender. That, by the way, in no way contradicts the profound desires and drives of human beings toward wholeness, origins and melting into one another. This conflict of oneness and diversity has its cultural origins in the so-called Black Moon.

That's why the deities of sexuality and fertility are portrayed as multi-faceted beings in ancient Indian mythology. If human beings close themselves off to this multi-dimensionality, they are doomed to suffer at the hands of the goddess Kali. This aspect of self-recognition in multiplicity is a horrifying thought for people, who as a rule strive for stability, continuity and personality, as it contains the danger of despair that one cannot cope with the balan-

* The figure of Lilith - from the Sumerian »lil«, for wind - symbolizes, according to the dictionary, an image or aspect of the great goddess. The origins of this mother cult lie buried in the long twilight of pre-history. In the Babylonian-Sumerian empire she was revered as the godhead Lilitu, Ishtar and Lamashtu (see picture no. 47). In Nordic cultures she was the goddess of storms. In Hebrew mythology she is already repressed into darkness as the evil demon of the night, who pursues men, kills children and couples with Satan. In astrology, she is called Black Moon, that is, the Moon's second aspect, which depicts our relations with the absolute, with sacrifice and with letting go. Lilith is calculated via the second burning point which the elliptical moon path takes around the Earth. In order to distinguish the medial Lilit from the mythological one, I have spelled »our« Lilit without the »h« used in phonetic writing.

cing aspects of the dark side of the moon. This finds expression in the negative forces of self-destruction. For that reason all forms of being possessed are attributed to the Black Moon, which is called Lilith and has something demonic about it.«

I found in the dictionary that she is called the Nordic goddess of storms.

»Yes, yes. – In any case, Lilith is the diametric opposite of normal life and our conventional desire for social stability because she leads those tendencies to their ultimate absurdity and wants to lead them to multi-dimensionality on a higher plane. Thus, the more a human being fancies himself close to oneness, the more he is plagued by jealousy and feelings of anxiety.«

Let's return to this creature. I'm not sure why it calls itself Lilit, but...

(interrupting) »The unconscious definitely had this form in mind. I think it was the black membranes which inspired the unconscious to give the creature that name. When one speaks in trance, the unconscious expresses itself, evoking these impressions of deeper reality.

We also know the symbol of Kali with many hands from India. Some Kali figures had six, yes, six hands and feet. The six fingers and six toes of this body are for me also a symbol for darkness. I can't confirm that it is an extraterrestrial, nor that it isn't one. That lies beyond my ability to judge.«

I would like to make the suggestion that during our next get-together...

(interrupting) »I am warning you, you have to be very careful with these things.«

For that very reason, I want to suggest that you hover in the wings at one of these encounters so that you can tell me what you think of it all afterward.

»There is a lot of potential in such encounters. Remain suspicious as long as the whole thing is not proven beyond doubt, leave it rather in the unconscious. Don't make any irrevocable statements. Not even we who dwell permanently in the unconscious, can afford to do that. Even we cannot verify beyond all doubt things which go back so far in time and come to light in such ways.«

I realize that. But in my gut I still have the feeling that there is really something to it all, and that these bodies are locked up somewhere even today. The same goes for the UFO, whose technology was apparently at least in part deciphered...the insights of which were then evidently used in wartime technology already. *

»I tend to place the greatest weight on recognizing the negative sides of this matter. That's why I intend to keep away from this problem you have just raised and concentrate instead on viewing its psychological aspects.

Isn't that reducing the subject?

I don't want to lead you astray, even though that is a constant danger when one works with the unconscious. Look at the value that this affair has for humanity in being able to think much more carefully about the extraterrestrial possibilities.«

And what is the probability of these being real extraterrestrials?

»Insofar as my soul here is capable of saying anything about such a subject, I would like to say that we should not force a judgment. But there could be machinations behind it.«

What do you mean by that?

»I can't exclude the possibility that extraterrestrial material is here being used for negative purposes. Regardless of what you do, others, during this stage of human development, will invariably see the negative side of it – even if it is quite authentic. For that reason, I don't want to make any further statements on the matter.

Just think what happened and continues to happen with anything and everything new and unusual, whether astrology, metaphysics, holistic healing or whatever. At the mo-

ment, most of the extraterrestrial subjects are being misused, whether they are positive or negative.«

The media are very skeptical at the moment, but at the same time extremely attentive to the UFO story. It is bound to go on like that.

»Let things take their normal course and try to stay independent of them. The material also has a use when one merely says one has received communication of and from extraterrestrial intelligence out of the unconscious.«

That is just the way I would like to present it. But the central question remains: Are the powers-that-be in the US concealing highly important events from humanity, and, if so, why?

»The problem is that the US Army itself doesn't know how to cope with the matter or even what to think of it. Believe me, there aren't just bad people in government and behind it.«

Yes, yes, I know that, but don't you think that it is a bit too much to...

(interrupting) »These people know that there is espionage going on from space, but they're not in a position to evaluate it all. They don't even know whether it might be their own earthly forces which are manifesting themselves from out there. Or whether it might be the Russians who are sending these things through the atmosphere, since it was already done by Hitler.«*

Did the Nazis really do that?

* According to the literature available to me, initial work on German saucer Hanebu I-III was begun in 1941; it was manufactured in Prague in 1944 and production in series was foreseen. The circular craft allegedly had a diameter of up to 86 feet, maximum velocity of 3750 miles-per-hour (13,125 miles-per-hour were calculated as possible), were fully deployable in outer space, even having the ability to make sharp 90° turns like a rabbit. Incidentally, in the spring and summer of 1946, 987 sightings of »ghost rockets« were made over Scandinavia (the term UFO was not yet in use).

Since the Germans linked up with the South American Ugha Mongulala tribe in 1941, whose chronicles maintained that they had had contact with extraterrestrials and keep watch over one of their vehicles in subterranean caverns this has led to speculation that this was how the Nazis obtained the necessary know-how for their saucers. More about these Indios will follow later in this book.

* Certain high-tech innovations of the Stealth bomber, e.g. its radar and infrared invisibility through copying the alien craft exterior, parts of the now common night vision technology and the newest secret project TR-3A are said to have been derived from the captured UFO technology.

»Yes, Hitler had such spacecraft built in order to have it land here and there. That's the kind of stuff he practiced.«

Was German technology so far advanced at that time?

»Only in a very limited fashion, it appeared more advanced than it was. All that is very easily faked. Human beings are indeed children.«

Humph, you're not making it easy for me.

»I don't dispute that there is such a thing as extraterrestrial intelligence. Wait another fifty years.«

Hmm...this being was also of the opinion that it is going to get really interesting just fifty years from now.

»Then you will be able to form an educated opinion. It is still too early to do that.«

I would suggest that we plan another, final sitting on this subject, as agreed upon. Otherwise I won't be able to get it out of my mind.

The bell rings at the studio door.

Now I have to close, in any case, since our guests are just arriving. Or should we simply draw the clients into the session?

»Why not? As long as I can have a sip of water first.«

That is easily possible.

This was one of the few cases where an arranged meeting/consultation with Cee Gee* – in connection with my dialog – began right on the doorstep, for Mira was already deep in trance.

A week later, we were ready to dare the experiment of the »stereo-contact«. »Jung's« commentary on my fifth talk with Lilit, at which he was present as a quiet listener in the background, follows.

Studio Phoenix, 6 September 1995

Thinking about the strange comment of Lilit which had closed our last conversation, »that sugar doesn't dissolve only in water«, I almost forgot that

we had asked Cee Gee to listen in on our dialog in the background and then tell us his views. Since he didn't report on his own, I called him.

I request Mr. »Jung« to come into the foreground.

I think he got lost somewhere, I don't receive him now.

But I need him right away.

All right, I'll try again. He is so far away, I don't think it's going to work.

He told me he would stay here, so he must be around.

After I had said goodbye to Lilit, it took quite a longish while before our friend was ready to talk again. This may have been due to Mira's very sluggish re-adaptation from the alien frequency to the old, tried and tested wave length of our mentor in all aspects of life.

After Mira's almost aborted readiness to receive messages, »Carl Gustav« at long last reported in and proceeded in his inimitable fashion to launch into a discussion on our extraterrestrial experiences.

Mr. »Jung«, what did you notice? Just exactly what happened before?

»Yes, there was a telepathic connection with a planetary system which in fact exists. Whether or not this contact was really with the soul of this being which was here, I can't confirm. I would tend to think that the medium was, shall we say, inspired by this picture. This identity which both introduced and portrayed itself was quite possibly more an aid for the vision of this other reality. More than that I can't say.«

And the palpable facts which were mentioned?

»Yes, they are interesting and valuable.«

In your opinion, do these previous contacts have anything to do with the Roswell crash and this ufonaut corpse?

»In part, yes, not necessarily in every point. But yes, it is a good supplement to the story.«

But you think the communication was actually inspired by, rather than a direct result of contact with the ET soul?

---

* We occasionally refer to »Jung« by these phonetic initials when publishing his remarks in order to avoid any misuse of his personal rights.

»I don't know whether a soul of this creature even exists.«*
Is it possible, then, that it was a soulless body?
»I can't visualize that, it simply lies beyond my ken. I am basically fulfilling a protective role here. That's why you cannot count on my full objectivity.«**
How would you advise I go about obtaining more clarity in the matter?
»First you have to form a clear opinion of what you yourself believe; second, I would advise you to let things rest as they are for awhile. Simply look at the information as interesting possibilities of another star.«
Yes, of course I could do that. But that will be a rather unsatisfying experience to a reader, in case we publish it, since it is just half of the research.
»You could just tell the reader the truth.«
One could also delve a little deeper into the affair.
»For that you have to turn to UFO specialists. They will, of course, be delighted. There isn't one in my group here. As you know, we work scientifically on psychological and other holistic planes. So we have to look at it as an integrative phenomenon.«
Could you perhaps recommend someone from over there to me, with whom I could conduct some fruitful talks?
»No, I can't do that. I don't want to help you any further in this, in fact I would like to withdraw, for I feel that it is all becoming too much for Mira at present. It goes beyond the limits of what she can endure. You just have to accept where her limits are. Unfortunately, I can't tell you anymore.«
Were you able to make any perceptions in the course of your observation of our conversation?
»In the physical surroundings of the medium I noticed a significant ambivalence. That was sufficient reason for me to slip into my primary protective role. I thank you for your candor. Goodbye.«
And I thank you. See you soon.

After the terse ending of the sitting, I discussed the matter some more with Mira, but found no way to pacify the dichotomy in her attitude to the subject. The trauma of a contact with another ET six years earlier who had threatened to abduct our son was still lodged too deeply inside her.

I made some attempts to pursue »Jung's« declarations about archaic traditions and excavation findings and succeeded in uncovering a good number of references. Unknown flying objects and space people have apparently been sighted in various forms since the beginnings of human history. Rock drawings and cave paintings all the way back to Egyptian rock reliefs provide evidence of this. Mythological and historical records are to be found in the annals of different peoples all around the globe. Many descriptions and archaeological artifacts point to technically equipped, humanoid »gods« from space, pre-astronauts, to use Erich von Däniken's term. The unusual experiences were per force described using the cultural conventions of each respective era, in the terms and metaphors of each given culture.

These begin with the Nordic-Germanic traditions from »*the God of Thunder's wagon flying through the clouds*«, of the Celts, and extend to Roman »*flying shields*«, the »*winged shoes*« of Greek god Hermes all the way to Egyptian »*fireballs*« in the epoch of Thutmosis III. Yet one also has to include the ancient cave carvings of South American Indios in Varzelandia, the Aztec depiction of Quetzalkoatl, who, according to legend, »*came to Earth on a feathered snake*«, sky-ships on Sumerian cylinder seals and the Kachina dolls of Hopi Indians, as well as the Vimanas and Shiva's flying objects in ancient Sanscrit texts of

---

* In a client dialog in January, 1996, »Jung« defined the soul as »**an ambassador of light: it is everything which helps a person to see himself with God's eyes.**«

** This was not the first time C. G. referred to his primary duty as a protector of my wife. Whenever in the course of her medial unfolding the contents channeled to her threatened to overwhelm her, it was »Jung« who slowed things down.

India: all bear witness to encounters with beings and aircraft from space. In the engravings of Persepolis there is a Persian god named Ahura Mazda in a winged wheel, in old Tibetan sagas one tells of »floating eggs which radiate white light«, and in the Chinese myth Schang hai ching, the giant whale Kun is described, »as rising from the water to the sky, where he then appears as the great bird P'eng«. The »glory of the Lord« in the Old Testament, as well as the »ascension of Elijah« and »Ezekiel's vision« may also be roundabout descriptions of divine ships and encounters of the first, second or third kind with, evolutionarily speaking, far superior visitors from the stars. UFOs have been observed in all eras and in all regions of Earth. And were it not for the enormous destruction of great amounts of written testimony in more recent history,[*] we would have much more evidence today which would support the generally ridiculed pre-astronaut theses.

But even today there are witnesses of such mythological occurrences. The North American »spirit dancer« Robert Morningsky, half Hopi and half Apache, whose ancestors, as the legend has it, were sought out by »star elders« thousands of years ago, according to his grandfather, professes to be in contact with six-fingered star creatures even today. He related to Wendelle C. Stevens and Magazin 2000 the following essentials: »In August 1947, I believe it was on the 13th, my grandfather was on a ritualistic vision quest with friends when they saw a light falling from the sky. They then in fact found a wreck and an injured survivor before the soldiers arrived on the scene. They took him into their care and brought him back to health. One day, their guest took out a small green crystal with which he was able to project pictures showing where he came from. He spoke of wars between the stars as well. After a time, he began to relate the history of mankind to my grandfather. He lived in the Indian camp for five years before he disappeared...and this star elder looked exactly like the creature in the Santilli film, including his six fingers and six toes.«

Morningsky was born in 1947. He was five years old when his grandfather allegedly initiated him into the profound mystery. In the meantime he professes to having had a dozen more encounters with the Santilli film lookalike who crashed to Earth, the most recent one being in summer 1994: »Reality is much greater and more wondrous than anything taught in books or school. That is what the star elder was trying to tell us. He also said mankind is not a natural creation, but was specially developed by them in order to work for the distant system of the star creatures. Human beings were created as slaves to serve these gods. They were animals genetically ennobled for special purposes. The star elder admired us human beings for breaking through our chains and trying to live our own lives in freedom, even though we were born as slaves. There is no religion on their star, their way of life is their religion. Their lifespan is endless: a man of 100,000 years is considered young. Everything is oriented toward an extremely long lifespan there, whereas here everything is oriented toward an extremely short one. The star elder said the human body was intentionally designed to decay quickly. Yet even though earthlings' physical structure is programmed for self-destruction, with proper nutrition it could nevertheless live to be 3000 years old.«

Ritual dancer Morningsky communicated in his encounters with star creatures not only via his reason, but also »from mind to mind. That is a holistic-sensuous experience, much more powerful than telepathy.«

He describes the aliens' ordinary clothing as a kind of one-piece suit, »glowing almost like mother-of-pearl. I saw neither zippers nor sign of buttons. He was

---

[*] Foremost, the burning of 500,000 papyrus rolls in the great library of Alexandria by pre-Christian zealots and the monstrous murder of Hypatia, the woman who served as its director at the same time.

about 4.5 feet tall and his body was very trim and fit. His skin color varied from light pink to the skin color of a swarthy white man.« When he was together with this creature, he always felt endless wisdom, reported the Indian in the interview. According to him, rumors of still other such creatures and crashes circulate in different reservations. *»They often survived the crash, but not the military recovery team. They were creatures from the stars, closer to God than anyone else, and the soldiers shot them down or beat them. We Indians alone know of three crashes in the summer of 1947. The first happened at the beginning of June, near Socorro, New Mexico. Roswell wasn't until July. And the third crash was in mid-August in the area of Four Corners, where my grandfather saved the star elder.«*

The recently uncovered petroglyphs in Canyonland, Utah demonstrate in his opinion the history of those ancient wise men who once lived on Earth until they decided to emigrate, leaving tracks of their vehicle and six-toed footprints behind.*

Signs of contact with such cosmic forefathers are also found in the mythology of the Brazilian Ugha Mongulala Indios: *»...But the decisive feature that distinguished the old fathers from human beings was their six fingers and six toes, signs of their divine heritage.«* In the »Chronicles of Akakor«, handed down by the white Indian Tatunca Nara, plans of earlier cave dwellings of the astronaut gods are related, guarded and well-concealed, laid out in the form of their twelve-planet sun system »Schwerta«, from which they are descended. They are supposed to stretch for miles beneath the jungles of Brazil.

The UFO researcher Jorge Martin uncovered interesting facts in his studies in Puerto Rico about an apparently extraterrestrial mummy which manifests many structural affinities with the filmed Roswell alien. A larger-than-human, bald head with enlarged almond-shaped eye cavities extending to the temples, with auditory apertures only where the ears should have been. Instead of a nose, a slight elevation of two apertures could be seen. Neither lips nor teeth were discernible. The long-armed, small being was evidently clubbed to death by a panic-stricken young chemist who was looking for old Indian treasures in the mountains between Salinas and Cayey and was surprised by several of these gnomes as they emerged from a nearby cave. They are supposed to have been a mere 14 inches tall, their hands had only four fingers with claw-like nails and in between, something resembling webs. There are only a few official photographs of this extraterrestrial being in existence today, since the evidence, which had been placed in formaldehyde, was taken from the owner under duress by unknown men contracted to do so by higher agencies of the government. Various scientists conducting comprehensive investigations on the basis of the photos all came unanimously to the conclusion that this was neither an abnormal human fetus nor any known species of animal.

The Statement of »Major Marcel«

Following our interview by a British camera team for Hongkong TV briefly referred to above, the crew talked Mira, who did not wish any further contact with Lilit, into at least trying to make trance contact in front of a running camera with one of the dead human eyewitnesses of the Roswell recovery. Because of the interest evinced by a publisher I began at that time to think about putting our Lilit experiences into book form. A dialog with eyewitnesses of the incident who had since died would be a fitting and fascinating component of such a book, a point with which Mira agreed, in the end. The talk took place

* see picture no. 44 in third picture section.

one evening in a quiet hotel suite with a splendid view of wonderful Lake Traunsee in our home town resort.

We had a sheaf of photos of all those who were in some way connected with the Roswell incident. Among them was a shot of a US Army major named Jesse Marcel, who seemed a good candidate. His likeable mien made Mira select him for her attempt. But first we had to cope with formidable technical obstacles which the experienced camera team had never had to deal with before. First, one electrical unit or another would constantly start to whiz or hum; then subtle malfunctions couldn't be identified. They changed cables and equipment around for over an hour before everything was fixed up enough to operate more or less adequately. In sessions with mediums, it happens again and again – as was recently demonstrated in another dialog with »C. G. Jung« for a Swiss TV interview – that electronic units start to go haywire in the immediate vicinity of gifted mediums. This, by the way, seems to indicate that technical interaction with the beyond via sensitive esoteric-electronic equipment ought to be within the realm of the possible. This has already proven to be rather successful, in a rudimentary fashion, in the various experiments attempted thus far, and, to be sure, purely spontaneously.

We had our own difficulties with the trance we were attempting for three additional reasons: the harsh camera lights proved extremely disturbing to Mira as she tried to enter trance; they ultimately had to be dimmed. Secondly, the person we were trying to contact had never before been our guest; thus, the initial adaptation to the frequency was somewhat problematic, especially since in this case the being contacted had no experience whatsoever with communications with our plane. And to top it all, there was the necessity of creating a channelling session for an English-speaking audience, which forces the transmitter into a limited store of vocabulary of a language not his own, unless the trance is extraordinarily deep. Despite these limitations, the contact was relatively successful. I reproduce it here in full.

Hotel Schwan, 1 September 1995

> For copyright reasons I have to mention that the following texts in bold type are all paranormal transmissions from a spiritual source, which identified with the consciousness of former Major Jesse Marcel, Sr. in the course of a medial trance session. *The author*

I called my summons into the ether, as usual. I could do this silently, but it is a help to Mira if I do it aloud, as it assists her (she is already in trance) in adjusting herself to the person being addressed. It also permitted the television audience to get an idea of what was happening.

We call Jesse Marcel Sr., former major in the US Army, for a trance contact. We cordially invite you to converse with us via the vocal cords of the medium. Major Marcel, please take advantage of this opportunity and permit us the honor of communicating with you.

We all waited in silence, without moving a muscle, so as not to impede the contact in any way. After about ten minutes, a somewhat scratchy, croaking voice could be heard.

»I am here...give me a little more time.«
Of course. Take your time. Thank you for coming.
(after a few more minutes, flustered)
»**Too many things are happening at once.**«

This meant that the method of transcommunication was still unfamiliar to him. Specifically, he had severe difficulties in ordering the contents of his communication impulses into an Earth time-oriented framework – this has been corrected in the transcript.

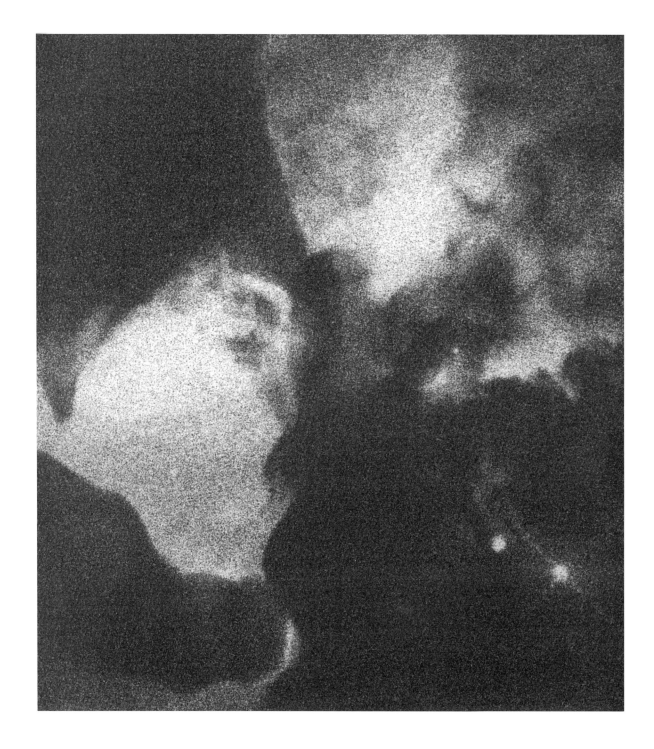

»Externally, I tried just to keep a cool head.«

Who was with you?

»Two others.«

This farmer, Mac Brazel, and...

(interrupting) »Not at that time, not when I first arrived. They called me and two other Army men. But they weren't on duty anymore.«

What did you do then?

»Let me see. I remember the dead bodies. We were heavily armed, which was in itself unusual, but we didn't need any weapons. To begin with, we didn't have any idea what to do. But then I called up to make a report of what I saw.«

Did you touch the bodies?

» No.«

How close did you get to them?

»Very close. But I was very unsure how to react to it all and what I should do. My orders were to remain calm and keep my mouth shut; later on I was told to leave the site. They called in other people to clean up the whole area.«

But later on, you were more involved.

»Yes, in an absolutely inexplicable way, which I couldn't comprehend.«

How?

»I wasn't supposed to say anything – well, they gave me a mental health test. I didn't have a good feeling about that at all. They ordered me to forget everything I had seen.«

Was that a day later, or when?

»That wasn't until weeks later.«

Was hypnosis used, or anything like it?

»Who knows? They said, if you can't promise us to remain absolutely silent about everything you saw, then we will conduct tests. They didn't tell me what or why or give me any information about what actually happened. I inquired several times, but got no answers. That's why that's all I can really remember – after my death I guess I forgot a great deal – well, I have to say that I was much less involved in the matter than you think.«

Do you know where the ET bodies were taken?

»No. I was only able to observe a lot of activity, which was all carried out in secrecy. The interest in it was... »

(sentence left incomplete)

Your boss was Colonel Blanchard, who also has died since then. Have you by any chance bumped into him in the beyond?

»No.«

Are you interested in meeting him?

(shaking his head)

»He was the one who didn't allow me to ask any questions.«

Maybe he has changed his mind since then.

»I wouldn't know.«

Who do you think could give us more information about the alien bodies? Where could we find the right person?

»In the government.«

I am referring specifically to those who were sworn to silence at the time and have died since. My question is whether there is, to your knowledge, anyone among them who might be able to give us information?

»I understand. I am trying to find names, but I am not at all sure of my ability to do so.«

(short pause)

»I am trying to help, but I can't find any names.«

Okay. Please concentrate again on the strange bodies at the site of the crash and their removal. Maybe that will lead you to the spot where they're now being stored. Or rather, to segments of the cut-up bodies.

(no answer)

Do you know who did the autopsy?

»There was a big fight over whether the bodies should be kept by the military or taken to the scientists. In the beginning it also wasn't clear who had the authority to make the decision.«

Who should actually be given authority over them, you mean?

»Yes, also who...oh, this isn't at all easy to communicate.«

Try it in the native tongue of the medium.

(in German) »That doesn't work any better.«

(then in English) »...They had to intimidate a lot of scientists beforehand, to keep them from talking about what they were going to see and would be asked to do... both with the material and the aliens.«

What exactly did the army authorities do to keep these people quiet?

»That was simple psycho-terror.«

What would have happened to someone who talked?

»They said they would do awful things to them and their families. That's why those people avoided saying anything in public. Most of them didn't even share their experience with their own families. They were isolated in their work, too.«

Do you know the man who filmed the extraterrestrial autopsy? Who made the so-called Roswell footage?

»Oh...the problem is, I don't know much more today than I did then. I only came because I heard my name called – there are a few things I would like to know myself.«

What would you like to know?

»Not so much who made the film, but what really happened back then, and why the government even killed people because of it, that interests me.«

The government killed people because of this affair?

»Yes, yes, they killed some people.«

Who? And why?

»A few who were involved and talked. First they locked them up and did horrible things to them.«

And they died from it?

»I often thought about why the government was so terrified of this whole business.«

And why was it terrified?

»I don't know.«

And to this day you have no answer to your question?

»No. – Some of my friends here think that it's a kind of anxiety. But about what? There must be some hidden motive for scaring people the way they did.«

Do you have any idea who was at the top of the chain of command at the time?

»We found out that the orders actually went round and round. One important person would intimidate another, it was like a cycle of suppression. One after another, they all got scared of losing face and having their authority challenged or scoffed at. That's why I also stayed quiet for a long time.«*

You saw the UFO from very close up. What was your impression of its level of technology?

»It appeared to me to be extremely sophisticated.«

Can you remember any details?

»Everything I saw made a deep impression on me. I knew it had to be a »flying saucer«. Even today, I can't imagine it being anything else. Technically I am not very well educated, but I had never before seen anything like it. I didn't touch anything and they sent me away from the site rather quickly.** That's why I can't tell you as much as you'd like to hear.«

That's all right. – Harry Truman was President at the time. Do you think he was informed of these events?

»I don't know about that, but I expect he was. There are still many secrets. I can only tell you that I saw with my own eyes the things shown in the film. I saw the dead bodies and I saw that spaceship. Anyway, I call it a spaceship, because I can't imagine what else it could have been.«

What was your attitude toward President Truman at the time?

(amused) »He wasn't a close friend of mine. What can I say? I did my work.«

---

* Not until 1978, 31 years later, was Major Marcel found in the course of investigative research by Stanton Friedman and interviewed for his book.
** It seems clear from his answer that he was not only present on the field where the foil strips were found, but also at the site of the wreck itself, where he was not permitted to touch or remove anything.

He has also died. What do you think of the idea of asking him about it?

»I don't know, I only know I'm definitely not on his wave length...I have to leave you now. I'm sorry I couldn't help you more.«

Thank you very much nevertheless. It was a good contact and you at least familiarized yourself a bit with a new form of communication. Maybe you would like to use it again sometime.

»I'm not much more now than I was then. Goodbye.«
Goodbye.

Marcel's grave contention that talkative Roswell initiates had been murdered by the Army is corroborated by several previously mentioned details. At the time of this reading, however, neither Mira nor I knew of them. If we had, it would have meant that my wife would never have entered into such investigations.

In a widely-known interview on the US television program »Unsolved Mysteries«, Jesse Marcel spoke in 1979, three years before he died, about his knowledge and his collecting efforts in the foil-covered field of the Foster Ranch: *»This was nothing that crashed to Earth or exploded on ground. It must have been something which exploded above the field, perhaps it shot across it at an accelerated speed. In any case it was something I had never seen the likes of before, even though I was familiar with all the air activities. All that material was so light it weighed practically nothing. Just these scraps lay strewn around, and a whole row of undamaged slats with these geometrical figures embossed onto them. It landed on Earth. But it didn't come from Earth.«*

These slats are described as being much smaller than the ones shown in the Santilli film. It seems there was a second type, scattered under the foil strips and with many more symbols on them than one

knew from the film. Marcel Sr.: *»Indeed, beneath all that stuff were these little slats, about 1 square inch across and in many different lengths, but none longer than one yard, with all these hieroglyphics on them that no one could decipher. They looked like balsa, were about as light, but they were clearly not of wood. They were very hard, yet flexible and utterly non-flammable.«*

The son of Major Marcel also remembers the metallic, violet-purple colored signs quite well. The sketch of one of these slats with more than 20 symbols on it (see back cover) was also corroborated by his mother. Marcel Jr.: *»I remember one of the symbols quite well, I'm absolutely sure that it was on the slat, namely of a small pyramid with the apex cut off and in its place a circle. The rest was a variation of different geometrical designs.«* The son of Major Marcel, a pilot/medical doctor, concedes today that some of the stuff uncovered in the field by Mac Brazel could be interpreted as fragments of a MOGUL or weather balloon. But at the same time, there were many disparities which made the explanations of the Air Force seem more like an Air Farce, as Stanton Friedman pointedly remarked.

According to the statements of Marcel Sr. in the trance, it is at least possible that in his belated confession he came out with only half the truth, and consciously concealed his brief presence at the actual site of the crash even though the military press information reporting on the first hours of the recovery of the saucer mentioned the assistance of Major Marcel. Perhaps he wanted to test the waters by taking a tiny irreversible step in hesitantly going public, and then see what happened. That would also explain why he was never harassed by the military after his statements in 1979, since his half-hearted confession contributed more to the confusion than to a solution of the mystery. However, Marcel Sr. was the one who after 31 years of silence brought the case into the media again.

The Memories of »John F. Kennedy«

The following excerpt of my (second) conversation with President »Kennedy« stems from our most recent book published in German, »Beyond Famous Lives and Lies«, in which the Roswell events were also incidentally talked about. At that time – long before the Santilli film was known to the public – I didn't know that I would be closely involved with precisely those ETs, to say nothing of actually talking with them. In this dialog with Mr. President, we spoke German.

Studio Phoenix, 20 June 1994

John, there's one question that comes up again and again in discussions with New Age people: it is said that US presidents have always known more about UFOs than they admitted to the public. What UFO secrets were known to you during your administration?

»These accidents, these crashes, all happened before I was in office.«

Are you referring to the Roswell crash?

»Yes, that too. To my mind, those really were extraterrestrials.«

Did you see any of them?

(almost awestruck) »Yes, mummified ones. At first they were supposed to be left that way, but that didn't work out, since they began to decompose. That very much shook up my world view, yet in a very positive sense. I never felt any enmity toward these beings, they were benevolent creatures, even though they did look pretty strange. It was somehow also tragic. Through them my feeling that we're all stupid, narrow minded people increased even more, that's the reason things like this aren't dealt with openly and naturally.«

Who gave the orders back then for the whole incident to be kept secret?

»It happened this way: in a vehicle, it was a relatively small UFO - much smaller than our usual conception of such a thing - only a few yards in diameter, there was something like a pictograph that one tried to decode. There was also a somewhat threatening aspect to this, the scientists were in accord about that possibility. These ETs were obviously on a reconnaissance flight, it was not completely clear what their intentions were. Then there was a radar-like unit, something with distant angles or something, seemingly with a reach of thousands of light years, which for us is an unimaginable distance.

In view of the super-dimensioned technology which utterly baffled the technicians investigating it, a number of odd things occurred. Although the crew members seemed to be dead, they appeared to light up somehow. We got a little scared, since it appeared that other beings continued to try to contact them. Everybody was totally insecure and uncertain about to what extent one could burden the general public with such things. There were also influences to be felt from the Church: they wanted to upset the whole applecart.

The pharmaceutical people had their own problems. They thought an alien virus had possibly been transmitted to our race. Even today we don't know which of these hypotheses were true and which weren't. The investigative teams made every effort to keep everything clean, as sterile as possible. But there were hundreds, if not thousands of people occupied with this affair, sworn to silence in the matter. Then suddenly it would happen that a piece of something or other would dematerialize.

Other such things also happened, which threw our scientists into a panic. Some of them suffered strange symptoms: one of them actually died of a mysterious fever. There was probably highly radioactive material or something similar on board the UFO, against which these beings were immune. For safety reasons one was naturally bound to silence.«

Were the Russians informed?

»Yes, but not in detail. I think they are also holding back related information. I really don't concern myself with this kind of thing at the moment, not even with extraterrestrials.«

I simply wanted to take the opportunity to get at information which otherwise is quite unobtainable, at least through earthly means. It would be interesting to know whether there ever was any form of direct communication between the extraterrestrials and the government.

»Only indirectly. The extraterrestrials evidently tried to make contact with us, but our people weren't able to cope with it. There were Morse Code-type impulses we couldn't decipher. There was a kind of desperate attempt on our part to communicate with them, but in the end it failed.«

As of this point, the dialog with JFK turned to other subjects. As mentioned above, there is one, tiny historically documented piece of evidence that Kennedy himself visited and inspected at least one UFO wreck and all its preserved crew members, in '62 in a hangar on Groom Lake, 120 miles north of Las Vegas in an isolated part of Nevada. There exists a briefing map for this act on which the one and only reference to the secret testing zone AREA 51 can be found.

Then there was the subtle attempt at blackmail by Dr. Donald Menzel, Harvard astronomer, alleged member of MJ 12, author of three intentionally provocative anti-UFO books, even though this top secret group definitely knew that at least some of the many sightings reported were genuine. He indicated in a letter written to JFK that he would reveal all his secret knowledge in return for a good job. In 1960 he maintained to JFK that he had collaborated with the top

secret NSA as well as with the US Navy Agency, for longer than anyone else in the administration. Also, Menzel's relationship with Dr. Vannevar Bush, also a member of MJ-12 and chairman of several military research agencies, went back as far as 1934. Dr. Menzel worked on secret projects for 30 different concerns and according to official records made a series of trips in '47 between Washington and New Mexico for purposes of government research. He was a cryptologist for the Navy and was considered because of his experience, the best qualified member of the MJ-12 group to produce sophisticated disinformation with regard to Roswell.

All these facts clearly indicate that President Kennedy was at least partially privy to the details surrounding the Roswell events.

»Marilyn Monroe's« Phone Call

In a preliminary talk with the British TV people before our interview, they said they knew of a CIA document which asserts that Marilyn Monroe knew about the Roswell affair through John F. Kennedy. Two years earlier I had had highly amusing and, incidentally, also extremely instructive talks with »Marilyn« about her »suicide« and all the things surrounding it in the course of our parapsychological researches into celebrities' experiences of death and the beyond. Since »President Kennedy« had corroborated the concealment of the UFO story in my conversations with him, it seemed logical to ask »Marilyn« about it directly. Mira was already familiar with »Marilyn's« frequency, so after the inordinately short talk with »Major Marcel«, and while still in the same trance, I called on »Marilyn« and requested a short chat while the cameras were still running. Our small talk was conducted in English.

Hotel Schwan, 1 September 1995

Hello, »Marilyn Monroe«, can you hear me? We've already had a few nice conversations. I would like to talk to you again. Hello, »Marilyn«, René is on the line again. Please try to come in for a little chat.

After a few minutes:
»There is no room for me.«
Why not?
»The Army doesn't like me.«
Oh, I doubt that. There were lots of people in the Army who loved you.
»Not in the end.«
It's great to talk to you again.
»I'm not... (unfinished sentence) ...give me a little time.«
Sure, take your time.

(short pause) »Marilyn» seemed to try to acclimatize herself first to the strange frequency in the room, made more difficult by all the technical equipment in operation.

»It's a funny situation.«
It's always fun with you. I have to tell you that we're involved right now in researches into that mysterious UFO crash in Roswell.
»I'm so sorry I wasn't there.«
Me, too.
»They would have been wild pictures. (giggling) Maybe I could have exposed myself even more to the world.«
We have some information about an extraordinary CIA bugging operation that has to do with you.* It seems they listened in on your telephone calls.
»Which ones?«

* see fax reproduction, picture no. 49.

This document is specifically about one of your very last calls, where you allegedly indicate having knowledge about UFOs from Kennedy. That's what I want to ask you about. What did you know about UFOs back then?

(downright indignant) »I knew about them, but I didn't make phone calls about it.«
You never said anything about them on the phone?
»I can't remember. You know how crazy people are.«
Did any of the Kennedys ever talk to you about this matter? You were very close to them, and they certainly knew about these events.
»Yes, but why should I talk about that stuff on the phone?«
Possibly you just mentioned it on the side to someone.

One of the TV crew gave me a signal that he wanted to ask her a question himself.

»Marilyn«, there's someone else here who wants to talk to you.
»Sure, all right.«
(cameraman:) *Did you have a friend who was a reporter? Do you remember his name?*
»Yes, I had reporter friends, which one do you mean?«
(cameraman:) *I'm trying to remember his name. I think it begins with »W«. Can you recall?*
(short pause)
»No, I can't remember.«
(cameraman:) *Wingfield, or something like that.**

The atmosphere switched to an unpleasant authenticity interrogation from which »Marilyn« promptly withdrew.

»Listen, René, I didn't make any phone calls about things I heard from John. But of course there were people who were afraid I might do just that. Of course I wasn't allowed

* The name the cameraman used to check up on Marilyn's authenticity was cited incorrectly, he got it mixed up with the UFO researcher George Wingfield. He probably meant to say William Woodfield, the name of a photo reporter, a distant friend of Marilyn's.

to talk about those things, even though I hate that way of suppressing things. I can't remember having said a single thing to anyone. At most if I was drunk, but I don't know anything about that. I also can't remember the names of all these people.«

You mean it might have happened that once while you were drunk, you said something about it?

»Maybe. And if I did, then I just forgot. But I can tell you that we knew about the »flying saucers«. I think I have contributed enough to this evening. Goodbye.«

Thanks, Marilyn. Bye.

I remained quiet for a minute so as not to disturb Marilyn's overly quick exit, then, before Mira emerged from her trance, I spontaneously asked into the surrounding space:

Is there anyone in the vicinity who'd like to say something about the Roswell crash, who has information they would like to impart to us? Is there anyone who can contribute anything further to solving the mystery?

No answer. I tried again.

We would be very happy if after almost 50 years we could finally get a little more clarity about the Roswell crash. Is anyone there who would like to help us?

Again, I got no answer. Mira shook her head and emerged from the trance. The TV crew suggested trance contact with a deceased doctor who had probably taken part in the autopsy. But Mira was tired and not willing to make any more attempts. She was rather piqued at the notion of it, in fact. The tense atmosphere in which the experiment was conducted was anything but pleasant for her.

If President Truman had been a more amenable contemporary partner, I would have attempted at some point in the following days to contact him in the quiet atmosphere of our home. But as he was a hardliner and the man who gave the order for the nuclear bombing of Hiroshima and Nagasaki, I find it very difficult to like him, making the idea of attempting contact with him appear pointless from the start.

I later found out a few things about the CIA bugging report referred to above. The American investigative reporter Milo Speriglio writes in his book, that Mafia boss Sam Giancana murdered Marilyn Monroe with the agreement of JFK's father, Joseph Kennedy, who was worried about developments surrounding his son. According to the bugging report, Marilyn also wanted to reveal the truth about the UFOs to the public; the scandal would have unleashed chaos in the US and have brought about the downfall of the President. JFK is supposed to have told his mistress about his secret visit to a top secret Air Force base where he was shown the bodies of the dead extraterrestrials who had crashed near Roswell in 1947.

According to the highly confidential CIA memorandum from August 3, 1962, Marilyn said quite directly to Bobby Kennedy, »*she was planning a press conference at which she intended to tell everything she knew*«. These revelations to the public were scheduled for August 5th, but she died the day before. The concrete reference of the code word »MOONDUST« in the document, which in fact is used by the Air Force for crashed spacecraft, makes one prick up one's ears. Since there can be no doubt of the authenticity of the CIA document in which reference is even made to »a crashed spaceship and dead bodies toward the end of the '40s«, it provides further evidence about the factual events surrounding Roswell about which the Kennedy brothers were fully in-the-know.

The Roswell Contacts – Condensed Scenarios

The Motive/The Crash

From the accumulated information in Acts I to III – the historical eyewitness accounts of the crash and its cover-up; the ramifications of the purchase of the film footage; and Lilit's channelled messages from Asastan – a condensed picture, though with blurry outlines, can be extrapolated of the entire earth-cosmic scenario. In the following five chapters I shall attempt to summarize the statements transmitted from Asastan with the most probable explanation of what happened at Roswell in the early days of July, 1947.

In a galaxy 750 million light years distant from Earth, in a bizarre solar system by the name of Asastan with a strange sun-moon unit as its central star, a humanoid species whose genetic-archaic roots are closely related to our earthly geneological tree seems to have its home. This »sister race«, which appears in many ways to be far more advanced than our own, has lost many of its earthly/human characteristics over the course of thousands of centuries, but at least a few »eggheads« from this exotic, dispersed-in-space species are apparently still aware of their roots, or, at any rate, are rediscovering them.

The same sort of motive that makes every human being need to find out where he or she came from, also seems to have been the catalyst for their actions. A small group of about a dozen like-minded extraterrestrial free spirits, caught in a genetic dilemma, decided about fifty years ago to follow an inner urge and go out together in search of their molecular-biological sisters and brothers, that is, archaic cell-nucleus ancestors.

To accomplish this intergalactic journey into their own genetic past, they worked together in constructing over the course of five (Earth) years a miniature spacecraft about 15 feet in diameter. Taking advantage of their superior scientific-technical standards of transportation, they sort of »beamed« themselves on that memorable day at about (if I haven't miscalculated) 6.5 trillion times the speed of light toward our solar system in Orion's arm of the Milky Way. That is to say, they rematerialized themselves (probably gradually) first in a local ethereal sphere, then later at a somewhat lower frequency than on Asastan in order to equalize the differing gravitational conditions. For purposes of better orientation, they raced to various fixed points in stellar constellations (perhaps Avior and Canopus) and along the specific positions of planets existing in the beginning of July, 1947 (see picture no. 1) and flew into the solar aura of our planetary system. Because I failed to probe deeply enough in my queries about the »energetic winds« said to be the specific cause of the crash, I can only visualize two different possible scenarios of the events:

• **Version A**

Their still half-astral light ship and its astronauts, according to Lilit, struck Earth's atmosphere head on at about 300,000 mph (1.5 times the speed of light). The crew members were kept safe by their specially constructed pressurized suits. Utilizing Earth's full moon as a marker on this entry path, they navigated their way full of confidence toward the midday point of the blue planet. Coincidentally, the

Moon on that day had just reached its fullest point and was at about 60° longitude in an almost exact vertical line above Bermuda, the destination originally singled out by the ufonauts. However, there were unexpected energetic obstacles to the flight approach of the Bermuda Triangle, an area known for decades for its manifold paranormal events.*

Suddenly, way up in the ionosphere, the Asastanian extraterrestrials were roughly and unexpectedly thrown off course and veered off with no control over their flight. The Asastanians were used to »*being caught in vacuum-like spaces*« from other planets, but Earth's atmosphere couldn't provide this in usual measure. Just at that moment above Bermuda, they encountered one of those bizarre energetic cyclones, against which their type of UFO did not have sufficient protection. The alien spacecraft builders had indeed built in projectors against electric shocks but hadn't counted on »*a complete frequency displacement through radical potential gradients*« in which the half-materialized spacecraft happened to be at that very moment. In the course of their hasty attempts to regain control of their reeling ship, they steered willy-nilly and inexorably toward the American mainland, over which night was just falling...

• **Version B**

In the alternative scenario, I see the Asastanian space tourists slipping slyly and well-camouflaged out of the darkness of the interstellar night into the darkness of Earth's night time hemisphere. Their aim was to orientate themselves so as to approach their objective slowly and at high altitude in the late afternoon heat. Perhaps at first they even considered making an intermediate landing, then visiting Bermuda in Earth's approaching dusk. Then they saw the storm raging alongside their flight path, reported by Brazel and others, at 36° latitude. This spectacle of thunder and lightning, which they had perhaps never seen before, may have aroused their curiosity. It is also quite possible that they intentionally – at what was ostensibly a safe distance – flew right above the thunderstorm to observe the lightning from close up. Right in the middle of their goggle-eyed astonishment, while they were taking measurements, the raging storm may have thrown them roughly off course, confronting them with a totally new situation. Their navigation controls suddenly went haywire or simply stopped functioning altogether. And so the lightmobile tumbled unmastered toward catastrophe, which after several fruitless attempts to regain control of the craft, took the dramatic course with which we are familiar.

Whether in this storm they were hit by one of the upward bolts of lightning called »sprites«,* above New Mexico or a completely different spontaneous energetic phenomenon – as yet unknown to us – took place above the Bermuda region, it appears the UFO crew had to attempt a manual, or mental-inductive, navigation to counteract the spiralling vortex, caused by the failure of their automatic navigation. To avoid an undesirable landing spot »just anywhere«, head navigator Bax, or all three of them in conjunction, tried to restabilize their course through the bio-feedback panels. Their efforts to regain control of the falling disc which was floating westerly (from Bermuda) or northerly (from the southern hemisphere) like a leaf in the wind towards Earth seem to have borne little fruit, since »*they were not*

---

* In the maritime area between Cuba, Florida and Bermuda, an impressive number of ships and aircraft have disappeared, i.e. presumably having been transformed into another dimension. Also, UFO sightings are more frequent in this area.

* red sprites and blue jets are visually observable, quick discharges travelling at 60 miles per second and reaching as far as 60 miles into the outer atmosphere which occur during thunderstorms and have only in recent years, through space shuttles, been proven to exist.

able to correct certain things«. The craft was still racing in uncontrollable descent in the ever-thicker air toward the ramparts of the Rockies, in the course of which, through being jolted by massive turbulences, it was held back by the atmosphere, but at the same time overheated. This, in turn caused more technical equipment to cease operating. *»Part of the lines exploded, so ground control could no longer react.«* Since through extraordinary bolts of lightning the balance of electromagnetic charges was suddenly upset, the automatic calculations no longer corresponded. *»Their radar invisibility also stopped functioning due to the magnetic displacements.«* They began to sink, completely out of control. Red hot metal parts flew around the flight cabin and *»burned their flesh«.* Handicapped by severe injuries, in the end Lilit and Bax *»were utterly unable to regulate the blackout of the motor power«.* After a couple of vain attempts to maneuver, it became obvious they were going to crash any second. The crew, expecting the worst and probably experiencing the event without fear or emotion, took hectic steps for a crash landing with possible emergency ejection during a period of flatter gliding flight.

The light-darkness border lying right over New Mexico came rapidly closer through their sight ring. They were approaching it at breakneck speed when the disc was caught up in yet another storm gust and jack-knifed once again. The rocky desert flats with their occasional settlements right beneath them did not look very inviting. Madly racing, the vehicle suddenly exploded with a bang – the propulsion system or something else had finally burst – and all hope of even the slightest control was gone. Because of its shallow landing angle, after an involuntary touchdown which was somewhat cushioned by its ionic field, it skidded along the desert floor. This brief touchdown caused the desert sands to melt instantaneously into a glaze.* At that moment, an attachment anchored to the underside of the craft for reconnaissance probes must have burst. One of the mounting-racks, broken off through the crash, screechingly drove a furrow 150 yds. long in the pebbly earth, before the silver disc, glowing in garish light, lifted itself like a flat stone skipping across the surface of water. Alternatively it may have been catapulted upward by the terrain and the flight dynamics of the landing angle.

Knowing that the final crash was no more than a few seconds off, the crew – *»in order not to be torn to shreds«* – activated the emergency ejector and alighted by means of *»a kind of air cushion«,* in the final moment clasping their navigational panels tightly in their arms, from the craft. The second they shot out from the cockpit into the thunderstorm, the air cushions inflated, while the flaming disc, (possibly also equipped with a sort of *»crash airbag«)* embedded itself with a tremendous din in a rocky cliff. These *»airbag«* emergency balloons (whose deployment NASA is also presently considering) probably only worked partially, possibly because they were already damaged or overheated by the exploding innards of the craft, and because of that, their function was impaired. One can't help but conjecture whether the thin, metallic-silvery foil fragments found a few miles away from the crash site were the ragged, burst skins of this emergency system – probably comprising several layers, judging from the heaps of foil found on the Foster field – whirled into the air by the sidewinds of the thunderstorm raging northwards, then scattered far away over the Foster ranch. Finally hundreds of shreds of foil, pressed down by the rain, settled in the shrubs of the gullies and fields of Brazel's sheep pasture.

* Sand melts at 1300° C.

This course of events is at least plausible, based on the information we now have available to us. The theory is also supported by the sequence of the discovery sites – first contact point, furrow, crash site, shredded foil drifts – as well as by the corpses found near the wreck. Perhaps the aliens went down a few hundred yards from the spot where the craft crashed (The MAJIC document even speaks of a spot two miles east of the wreck). Maybe they deliberately »neutralized« their ejector foil airbags – then, or shortly before the crash landing – with a built-in self destruction mechanism and, as night fell, dragged their injured bodies toward the smashed craft, clutching in their hands the navigation panels, as their only remaining connection to their cosmic home. After this spectacular foundering just a few miles from the military base of Roswell in the wastes of New Mexico, the crashed victims were physically in no condition to do more than merely observe events as they developed, perhaps communicating with each other through telepathy and trying with the panels to call home.

Since, according to Lilit's remarks, their species had succeeded somewhere in the course of their evolution in mentally or genetically »unplugging« pain messages from their body, it can be assumed that they did not suffer unduly from their injuries (at least one female pilot sustained grave injuries in the thigh, as is obvious in the film) despite the remarks of the cameraman that he heard them still screaming several days after the crash.

The creatures who had been so astonished at the unfamiliar spectacles of a passing nocturnal thunderstorm were able to follow this phenomenon of nature by virtue of the membranes covering their eyes for night vision and radiation protection. According to Lilit, they lay, or crouched, for three days in the sparse vegetation of the desert floor. The sum-

mer nights in New Mexico were surely cold to these creatures accustomed to Asastan's climate, while by contrast, the searing midday heat must have been more than pleasant. Intermittently, they were no doubt visited by coyotes and other curious local animals. After all this time, they recognized (Lilit as the very last one to do so) that their plight was hopeless. Finally perceiving their inevitable end to be near, their consciousness left their bodies and submitted to their fate.

A short while later, the first human being appeared, but »*their bodies had already been dead for several hours.*« The witness first saw only the shimmering wreckage, which from a distance looked more like a crashed plane – the disc was »*pretty well destroyed, except for a few interior parts*«. As the horrified man (according to latest accounts, a shepherd friend of Mac Brazel's or construction engineer G. Barnett) got nearer to the crashed saucer, he noticed the strange corpses covered with skin-tight silvery overalls, took fright and left the area at once. That was the point at which the astrally still-present entities must have decided to totally withdraw their components of consciousness back to their home planet in order to immediately avail themselves of the waiting reserve bodies for a new cycle of bodily life. More or less in this way, the three 350-year old middle-aged Asastanian lives ended prematurely in the lonely wastes of a galactical alien desert on a planet with which they had long, long before been genetically connected, and continued existence in their own Asastanian birth laboratories in brand new cloned bodies. For the three UFO crew members – »*Lilit, Alira and Bax, two female and one male*«, insofar as any earthly classification of gender is applicable here – this was »*the first visit to Earth and the first journey their race had undertaken in the 20th century*«. In this epoch, they perceived »*an important time of change from destruc-*

tiveness to constructiveness, which could turn into a time of hope«. »But now they had been warned and would not return to this part of time/space.« According to their statement, »they had no mission here, but came of their own free will in order to study the earthian species, to which they were archaically related«. To begin with, they merely wanted to find out whether Earthians still existed, based on obvious suppositions. When they ultimately found us, that is, were found by us, they were deeply shocked, just as we were by them, »that our human reality actually still existed«. They experienced this as we ourselves might »if we were to stumble over a living dinosaur«. Actually, they came to Earth because Earth is still engaged in a process through which the Asastanians might be able to find a way back to their correct evolutionary path. »We have to get back to our roots. As long as we are stuck in this form, we can't change our misfortune.« This last point seems to refer to the intergalactically applicable laws of close psychosomatic body-mind interaction. To avoid their quandary and/or to gather new insights with which to solve it, a few of them are supposed to have reincarnated much earlier on Earth. Some of their foremost pioneers are striving toward an earth life »in inner harmony«, with the additional intention of »also furthering our progress on Earth«.

On Bermuda, they only intended to have a look around and »perhaps enter an earth cave, to escape notice«. They felt the spot to be favorable (presumably through a form of remote diagnosis) because it provided greater protection than elsewhere. The power in this part of Earth caused by the »intersecting north-south poled energies, similar to those of the heart...is what best makes them invisible«, since human beings are confused by this power and have less drive themselves. Besides, the aliens could also have lived underwater there, since they said that their spacecraft was also equipped for that.

Their Physicalness/Their Evolution

All three crew members incarnated on Asastan soon after their crash. There they bred themselves in their birth laboratories, so to speak, as a supply stock, so that they could slip into a waiting cell culture in a test tube in an emergency or when their bodies began to decline after about 500 years.* After a time »the growing brood begins to glow** and is placed into a basin filled with a nutritional solution«. There the test tube babies continue to mature, just as human babies do in the mother's uterus during the first seven months (although this process only requires a few weeks on Asastan) until the alien babies are physically ready for birth.***

More and more Asastanian women made the decision not to have children in the way human woman do because they no longer wished to expose themselves to the dangers of pregnancy and the pain connected with child-bearing. Their bio-engineers in early experiments first moved the eggs and then even the ovaries outside the body...and it worked. After perfecting serial artificial insemination and incubation, their women, in time, ceased having children in the customary way altogether and, in the course of evolution, dispensed with their no longer necessary organs with the help of genetic engineering. It proved much more convenient and comfortable to allow reproduction to take place through the affinity

* Even our own earthly bodies will, according to already possible genetic interventions, soon be able to attain a life expectancy of at least 150 years. Thus, with more advanced genetic technology, a life expectancy of 500 years is quite realistic.
** This glowing probably occurs during the actual uniting of the physical with the mental, something also observable in people with clairvoyant abilities.
*** Genetically engineered high-velocity growth, for example with fish, is also being practiced on Earth. For example, the Canadian »turbo-salmon« grows eleven times faster than its natural brother.

principle in breeding factories. Eggs and sperm in the required nuances are stocked and reproduce and multiply by computer program all by themselves. In a kind of assembly line production, in accord with the intentions of the respective Asastanian, consciousness implants itself in the glass tubes. It is simply a continuation of an older life under rejuvenated physical conditions which de facto arise automatically. If, for instance, a science-tube with an embryon of a certain genetic structure has been selected and begins to glow, the gene-guardians know at once that a scientist has begun a new life cycle. The genome structures with the entire incorporated body of knowledge of the Asastanians is then available in one fell swoop to this »new« being through the materials specially implanted in that incubator. Learning from books and data banks is no longer necessary, as it can be instantly, mentally called up from inside, subsequently kept up-to-date and/or extended through specific implantations. However, since not everything goes as perfectly as it is supposed to, especially because the phase between the re-entry into a zygote and the artificial »rebirth« is evidently highly unpleasant, the Asastanians go even further and strive for complete and utter physical immortality. Their stay in a test tube is so awful for them because the Asastanians are used to being very actively involved in their various projects and are consigned, during the three to four weeks the rebirth process requires, to doing absolutely nothing. *»It's like being paralyzed, even later you can't do much in this basin, but one is nonetheless always quite conscious.«*

But since they have no real parents, apart from the laboratory aliens, it is crucial to them to maintain their full consciousness during the processes of being reborn into a new body. Otherwise they would not be able to build up the psyche so necessary to physical life, which in our terrestrial birth process develops during pregnancy in the protective aura of the mother. Were they not to maintain their active awakeness during the self-cloning, their method of survival wouldn't work. What they do contradicts fundamental natural laws, but they have learned to play a trick on nature. Insofar as their last lived individuality or psychic structure of consciousness is immediately transferred to their new body, they are, in a sense, already physically immortal. Nonetheless, when they emerge from the physical tortures of the nutritional basin, they feel pretty awful. They are then (telepathically) asked what they would like to be named. *»Since there are no parents anywhere to give you a name, one names oneself whatever one pleases.«*

Asastanian women have no uterus, and the men have mere suggestions of testicles. That is why they experience *»a more energy-oriented sexuality with their counterpart«*, with whom they live together. The partners who find their way to each other do so very quickly, usually already in childhood, which lasts only 13 years. By then they have attained 3/4 of their final height and are fully responsible for their own lives as of that moment.

Their body structure is attained via energized water, both in the incubator and afterwards. To this oxygen-rich nutritive solution, minerals and life-giving substances of all types are added, some of which are made from special algae through photosynthesis. Their blood is also oxygen-enriched and much thinner than human blood. That perhaps explains the way in which the blood flowed out of the body cuts which so irritated the pathologists. According to Lilit, the main elements of their body chemistry are magnesium, then calcium and iron, then sodium. Due to the other ways in which they are given oxygen, they require very small lungs, yet can still stay underwater for a long time. Their small noses are also a result of the minimal inhalation of air.

49 *Investigative journalist Milo Speriglio recently presented the minutes of a CIA bugging, revealing that President J. F. Kennedy confided UFO secrets to Marilyn Monroe.*

50 *Both President Eisenhower and his successor President Kennedy secretly visited Muroc- (now Edwards-) Air Base to see the UFO wreck and the alien bodies (photo-montage).*

51 *Model of the first recovered Roswell disc at Wright-Patterson Air Force Base. According to recent revelations of his assistent Albert Einstein there had a secret look at the spacecraft and the alien corpses.*

52 *Albert Einstein's theory proves that time is not an absolute but depends on the curvatures of space. Only after his mathematical findings Earth based space flights became reality.*

53 *According to latest research findings and Stephen Hawking, time travel at speeds beyond light is no longer incompatible with causality. Spaceship Enterprise is possible.*

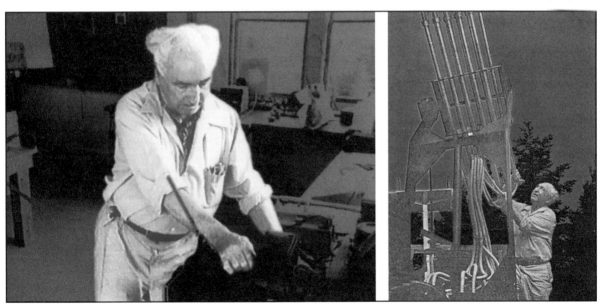

54 *Wilhelm Reich, the first holistic scientist of the modern age, made contact with extraterrestrial lightships through his brilliant »orgon«-energy weather experiments.*

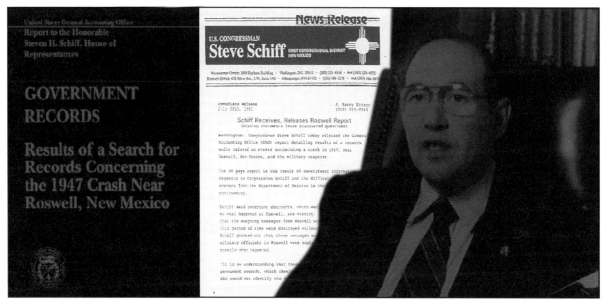

55 *New Mexico Congressman Steve Schiff demanded an investigation of the Roswell incident by the General Accounting Office, but the resulting search shed very little light on the subject.*

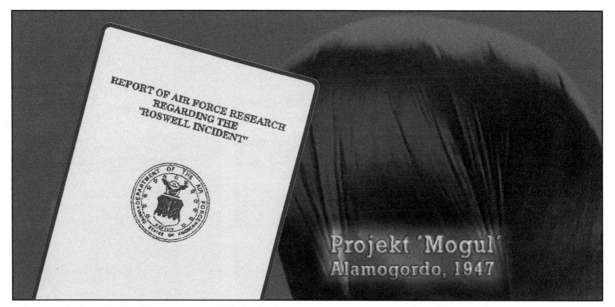

56 *Even before the GAO report was published, the US Air Force countered with a mendacious report claiming that it was not a weather balloon after all, but an espionage balloon used against Russia.*

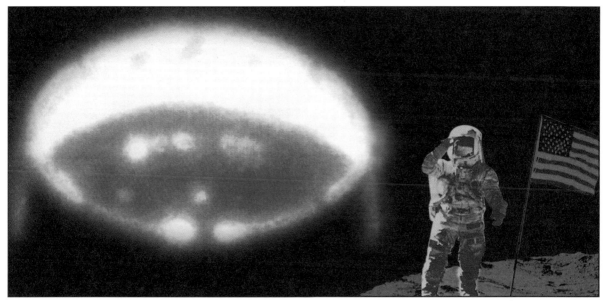

57 *Almost all Apollo Mission crews have allegedly been confronted with UFOs. Despite astronauts' oaths of silence, information has leaked out. (montage of real photographs)*

58 *President Clinton ordered his scientific advisor to investigate the Santilli-Roswell incident. Right, UFO demonstration by US activist group, »Operation Right-to-know«, in front of the White House..*

59 *The mysterious »missing link« in the evolution from apelike hominids to modern human being can now be explained by a genetic-evolutionary leap unleashed by aliens.*

60 *Evidence of early high cultures can be found all over the Earth. Did extraterrestrial masters introduce us to the secrets of astronomy and mathematics?*

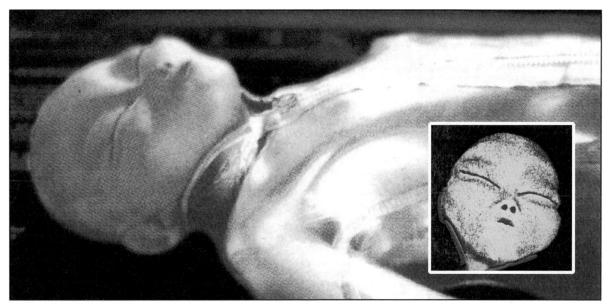

61　*A wax model of an extraterrestrial creature in a diving suit, presented at an exhibition in Montreal in 1983. Was Roswell information leaked at the time?*

62　*If physiological human evolution were to continue along the same path it has already embarked upon, scientific studies posit bald pates and narrow jaws for us in the distant future.*

63 *Through the slowly dawning awareness of multi-dimensional connections, human evolution should be accelerated and Homo Sapiens enabled to awake from its childlike state.*

64 *The ominous message of the Roswell-beings to us on Earth: »If you continue along the same genetic technological path, you will end up as we have. Turn back, the price is too high!«*

Asastanians have no teeth, »*only a jawbone is palpable*«. They have narrow lips without any fleshiness – for which they would have no use, since they do not suckle at a mother's breast. The small, slit-like mouth resulted from their habit of consuming only liquid power-drinks.

Their seemingly magical eyes are overdimensionally large because their retinas are composed of facets, as in the eyes of bees. They have no pupils in the normal sense of the term, even if the coarse-grained Santilli film may give that impression. They can see into various »dimensions«, adjust to panorama view or focus on close-ups, perceive certain structural patterns and even reflect light. That probably means they can actually send back light, in order to give signals or operate various things. It is likely that they also have visual perception of infra-red and X-rays. Their implanted eye membranes serve as protection against some especially harsh radiation. Without them they would go blind. These dark membranes can be removed like contact lenses, as the autopsy demonstrated. According to Lilit, they are used for reconnaisance »*in galaxies where there is very aggressive radioactive radiation*«.

Their twelve fingers and twelve toes were developed through the interventions of genetic engineering. This change has proven to be highly beneficial and practical, since »*through the additional finger, things are hardly ever dropped and we injure ourselves much less frequently. The extra finger acts like a second thumb*«.

The skin color of the Asastanians is copper brown at their normal body temperature of 48° C/118° F. This high degree of body heat accords with the external climate on their home planet. »*It is never cold on our planet and we are never cold.*« Since they are »*no longer animals in need of protection against cold*«, they have also lost their body hair in the course of evolution. An interesting aspect of the constant high level of air temperature and body temperature is that the borderline between inner and outer worlds is only marginally experienced, giving them a completely different feeling of being connected with their environment.* This also seems to depend on the differently structured dolphin-like skin visible in the autopsy scenes.

Their bodies are about as dense as ours. The larger skull with nearly 1/3 more brain mass than that of humans could have resulted not only from genetic manipulation, but from the lesser gravitational force on Asastan as well. Their rudimentary ears are of little use, thanks to their widespread use of telepathy and other far-ranging sensory ablities. They probably simply atrophied due to lack of use in the course of evolution.

Lilit called her species hyper-rational, distinguished by conical-shaped heads, a protruding belly (also prevalent among living creatures), sturdy legs and an aura like a sponge. »*Our whole body is one single energy center.*« For that reason, they don't require a solar plexus or any other energy center. Their large bellies act as a kind of water storage tank, permitting them to endure long stretches without drink. They possess neither liver nor gall bladder, a very small heart, small lungs and kidneys, and only limited intestines.

In place of that, as the autopsy demonstrated, they have a whole series of other organs unknown to us. »*We split off from the path of normal evolution and continued to develop in these monstrous bodies.*« Lilit concludes that we probably find her and her alien siblings ugly, judged by our own aesthetic

* John C. Lilly took advantage of this set of conditions in developing his Isolation Tank, a sealed off container of salt water in which one floats in 37° C/98.6° F water in complete darkness and deprived of other sensory stimuli, one can separate one's consciousness from one's body.

standards. But even they themselves do not fulfil their own ideal of beauty, she said. We Earthians approach that more closely.

Their greatest shortcoming is that they no longer correspond to the original image of the universe. They have changed their genetic cellular make-up so drastically that they don't correspond to the natural, universal evolution of the primordial universe anymore. Their psyche is also structured so very differently that they don't know any kind of aggression and, according to Lilit, are fundamentally peaceable.

They invaded and occupied their present (previously uninhabited) planet Asastan and evidently totally manipulated it through genetic engineering. That is probably how the hyper-fauna seen by Mira was created, without the age-old law of the jungle – eat or be eaten – yet also without bothersome insects and other animal pests.* Asastan's flora was presumably also genetically engineered along similar lines.

The most radical attitude of this species is its approach to illness. For that reason, they have neither epidemics nor contagious diseases. At the very first sign of illness, the victim is eliminated, but only in body. This extermination is performed in a state of collective consciousness with regard to the framework of ongoing new embodiment. *»One immediately goes into a new test tube.«* Although this, to us, murderous attitude has to be seen in relation to the whole culture and purposes of the Asastanians, the process clearly reminds one – even if the aliens perform it in a completely different context – of the selection process of the Nazi era. Fascinatingly, Lilit said that the knowledge alone of this process of eliminating all infirmities creates an amazingly resistent and resilient collective psyche. The upshot of it is that hardly anyone gets ill to begin with. The mere knowledge of this radical prophylactic cure permits one to become very old.

»Father« Lorin, boss of the alien UFO-construction team and of the station monitoring the flight crew, is said to be the initiator of all these events. He was the pioneer genetic scientist who began in earlier incarnations on other planets to build up this brave new world. It is his karma to remain bound to the misery of the Asastanians for as long as it takes to liberate them from this evolutionary thrall of deformity. Unlike all other Asastanians, Lorin lives alone and – apparently also due to his karma – is more aware than any of the others of the continuing existence of his individuality and of his immortality.

His »gene culture« has already survived a number of different major catastrophes, since he was able to foresee them and take precautionary measures in good time. *»Of course we also experimented a lot with nuclear energy, which resulted in our programming our cells against radioactivity and did a lot of other things to our bodies.«** What emerged from all these genetic manipulations were monstrous beings who didn't like themselves anymore. Without emotional anguish, and thus, without emotional depth, they feel like cultivated tomatoes, who have lost contact with their source. Lilit thought she had incarnated about 75 times on Asastan before her crash on Earth. If one assumes that she was embodied rather soon after each death, without much of an intermission on some spiritual plane, that would mean she has lived an impressive 37,500 physical earth-years on Asastan, based on an average of 500 years per lifetime.

---

* On Earth there are about 1.7 million species of animals, including 600,000 different insects.

* With the highly significant ORANUR experiment in 1951, Wilhelm Reich confirmed that finely regulated doses of orgonomically activated radioactive radiation can actually raise one's resistance to radioactivity and build up a certain degree of immunity, which can be firther increased in small increments by repeating the process with ever higher doses.

Lilit confirmed that the bodies which she and her friends left behind«after the crash to earth were deep frozen after the dissection and, at least in part, still exist. Asastanian bodies do not decompose, being high in water content. Instead, their bodies tend to simply disintegrate, but that also depends on the temperature of the immediate environment. »We do not rot, we simply dissolve, because we have so much water in us.« Their remains, salvaged and kept under strict lock and key by the military authorities, she imagines to be in some highly restricted national research laboratory, since they are inexplicable organisms to the human experts. »They can't determine whether we are dangerous or not.« The Asastanians have played around a great deal with viruses in their evolution, trying out all sorts of things with them, seeing what they could do with them – what happened when their capabilities of response were given free rein – but they have always managed to gain the upper hand in the end. »They are living beings, like astral elemental forces.«

Mira was able to smell the burning flesh from the crash while she was in trance. She was told that the bodies were neither poisonous nor infected. The masked army pathologists, of course, did not share her confidence. Lilit also gave us to understand that their lost dead bodies had indeed become bloated through chemical processes, yet they had proportionately larger bellies than we do even in their normal state.

The Asastanic evolution seems to be entirely genetically engineered, from A to Z. They have prescribed a genome programme for themselves called »controlled diversity« into which they program limits as they see fit. They eliminate certain functions, or slough off factors. It is as yet not possible for them to breed all beings in the absolutely same mold, not even in form and color, but it is probably just a matter of time before they learn to do this as well. »We have no power over the degree of brain activity or intensity of brain cell production. However, things we don't like we can eliminate or purposefully work on, keeping and maintaining other things,« ...such as mathematical memory or linguistic cognitive abilities. They still possess slight variations in intelligence quotients, since they cannot as yet determine the test tube code which every being receives as the shell of his own individuality pattern and carries with him. Most of their regulating consists of coaxing along certain qualities or deploying them in certain cell zones, within which they are especially well »re-absorbed«.* Lilit, in an aside, sensitively remarked that we Earthians probably didn't like this sort of intervention.

By means of a brain center for the purpose of storing all possible codes – remember, these aliens come into the world already programmed with knowledge of all known language patterns – they communicate in a plethora of different languages. They also bring along a completely functional mathematical memory, without ever having learned mathematics. »We have no schools.« This last point in particular would gain them a lot of bonus points from our young. They have no phonetic language, but they emit sounds resembling a clicking of the tongue and chattering as we know it from some animals. »Those are the sounds we use to accompany our moods.«

»While asleep we have a reduced consciousness, otherwise a very dynamic, active and creative one.« They regenerate occasionally, anytime they like. »When I have discharged my energy, I go to sleep for two hours. Everyone has his own rhythm.«

They survived near-Armageddons of huge nuclear explosions. They are protected via innoculation

* This word is a sign that Lilit's information didn't simply pour out of Mira's unconscious, since it was a word utterly unknown to Mira.

against radioactivity. This was already successfully implemented during the »test tube pregnancy«. »*The dosage was increased a little at a time.*«

In spite of all these truly remarkable developments, they don't know where their evolutionary path ultimately leads. They have moved too far away from their source to be able to perceive the goal. »*We threw all our powers into research and manipulation...we don't speculate, we act.*« Perhaps the central problem of this species lies buried in Lilit's last sentence.

»*The next step of our evolution is physical immortality, but we have not progressed very far in this yet.*« This, I would venture to say, is an understatement, but also a question of one's point of view. Apart from that, one can question the meaningfulness of physical permanence.

I would like to add to Lilit's statements a suggestive analytical physiognomy of her body, even though using such a study is a bit problematic when applied to extraterrestrials. This is especially true because one also has to take note of the various deviations »within« a given species, which is hardly possible with clones who are all lookalikes. But since the resemblance to human beings cannot be overlooked, I would like to, purely hypothetically, try out the resources of human physiognomy on them. The obvious choice for this task is the ancient Chinese face-reading tradition known as Siang Mien; and the ancient Egyptian science of human characteristics.

Lilit's form is most easily categorized as the Chinese »fire-face«, – broad forehead, high cheekbones and receding jaw region – to which are attributed intelligence, sensitivity and quick comprehension. Her high, arched forehead is of course a much more decisive sign of extraordinary intelligence. The large »dragon eyes« show their owner to be innovative,

easily approachable and brave. Her smallish nose is related to decreasing happiness in middle age (we find both in her crash at the age of 350, I permit myself to mention in jest). Extremely thin lips are, according to the Chinese, a sign of emotional frigidity; small ears are an indication of a hard worker. Minimal or lack of ear lobes is seen as a sign of instable relations with one's parents and lack of libido, something which is doubly true in Lilit's case.

The ancient Egyptians perceived before all else the creative power of Osiris/Isis/Horus in the human face, that is, the mental, emotional and physical (forehead, nasal area and bridge of the nose to chin). The predominant principle, in Lilit's case the brow, prevails over the given (human) being. The straighter, steeper and wider a forehead is, the greater is the power of imagination that person possesses. A pronounced bulge above the eyes suggests highly practical thinking. In the embryonic form of the ear the fundamental emotional state with which the person is born is manifest. If the ear is set as deeply as in Lilit's case, it suggests lack of interest in spiritual matters. Her weak nasal area suggests the same. Lilit's priorities are, in the following order, mental, material, emotional; in other words, a highly intellectual specimen who masters matter ingeniously and permits emotional issues to atrophy.

To categorize this alien form in an overall constitutional and personality typology is hardly possible, due to the mixture of individual factors.

The Spacecraft/The Technology

The inclusion of decisive technical descriptions via channeling is of limited use, since the internal capacity for translation of an inadequately educated medium is not usually sufficient to meet the requirements of the telepathically received impulses. Nevertheless, there were a number of statements which conveyed a certain impression of the level of technological development of the Asastan people. Because of the complex nature of the material, the information received is necessarily presented in a re-interpreted form.

Their silvery disc looks like two saucers placed together with a round center, the upper concavity being more pronounced than the lower one. Its crew consisted of three aliens; there was room for a maximum of five crew members for longer journeys. At the disc's center is a »sun generator«, with a pipe like core. Surrounding the pilot's cockpit is an uninterrupted optical sighting ring made of a kind of unbreakable glass, outfitted with night-sight tech-nology which amplified all available light (seem-ing-ly copied by the US Air Force). The aluminum-like outer surface is supposed to be a new kind of synthetic, composed of nickel, cobalt and some other earth materials (ceramic?). The alien hieroglyphics applied to the outer surface of the UFO – a kind of nautical-mathematical symbol language – record the part of the universe from which the craft comes. On the underbelly of the ship, a small reconnaissance probe called a »spider« is mounted.*

The Asastanian spacecraft is a physically constructed mass of dense material, weighing about 1100 lbs. It took a dozen aliens about five years (Earth time) to build, under the guidance of »Father« Lorin. There are on Asastan at present a total of about 5000 such miniature discs, with which they whiz out to many different worlds and times. All the craft operate on the principles of quantum mechanics with time machine technology. They also have, in the vicinity of their own planet, a colony of mother ships which is somehow connected to the entire planetary network serving as a kind of traffic junction for interplanetary routes. While in trance Mira saw seven such constructions, lined up next to each other which probably belonged to one of these stationary fleets.

The technology of the Asastanian reconnaissance disc is based primarily on space generators, high frequency wave generators and various crystal structures. »Lightbreaker codes« and ultrasonic waves also play a part. Evidently this results in the interaction of solar, orgon and tachyon energies. In addition, the light technology is modulated via thought power, *»since our consciousness is also light«.* In her vision of a UFO in motion, Mira heard a strange high-frequency humming.

The lightbreakers located at the core of the spacecraft utilize the »heat« which is created in a «combustion disc« as kinetic power. The markings on the small slats discovered on the Brazel ranch are all part of this combustion lens *»with which ›solid things‹ are made liquid«.*

On light displays the aliens can always see everything going on in the »machine room«. A double tetrahedron located at its center* serves to couple the thought part of the navigation to the motorized disc, harmonizing brain waves with the kinetic energy of the vehicle. Another such »crystal« is lodged in the »safety valve«. Aside from these, there are also sighting, steering and enlargement apparatuses in the control center. Through *»sonar angular lenses, we can see spaces we want to penetrate close up, which we had previously been able to study«.* Sensors call the crew's attention to dangerous elements in the programmed

* Although the symbol code visible in the Santilli film does not come from the outer surface of the vehicle, but from the mounts (most likely the special fittings from the underside of the craft which broke off), it can be supposed that these symbols, too, indicate the home port of the aliens.

* This is a special Platonic object in the form of two intertwined, regular tetrahedrons, that is to say, a spatially perceived hexagram, i.e. Solomon's seal in crystal form (see picture no. 48.)

flight path quite a long time before there is any risk of crashing into them.

From Lilit's remarks, it was evident that (under-powered) projectors protecting against electrical jolts, operating on principles of bouncing off the jolts, as well as some sort of heat regulators were also installed in the craft. Hydrogen was either taken along or manufactured on board. Moreover, »utterly telepathic equipment« was mounted on the explorer discs. With these they can zoom in on clairvoyant perceptions in order to literally pre-view the conditions awaiting them.

Their ordinarily effective uncoupling of radar visibility is based on principles of the »electric net«, an electromagnetic function still unknown to our sciences, according to Lilit. With it, they can »also transfer electric current«.

According to Lilit, the individual tasks of the exploratory mission were distributed in the following manner:

BAX (male): »craft commander«,
sat at the bioenergetic steering wheel of the disc and maintained contact with the ground control station.
LILIT (female): »navigator«,
responsible for pathfinding through the dimensions as well as the jungle of stars, also as an observer of any possible alien objects.
ALIRA (female): »stewardess«,
responsible for taking care of all the needs of the crew members during and after the flight.
LORIN (male): »mission commander«,
in his capacity as chief of ground control he was the top-ranking authority of the project, who carried the full responsibility for the fate of the expedition until contact was broken off.

The navigational stick and the navigation panels were chock-full of all manner of unusual instruments. »We have computers inside them which do just about everything.« These slightly rounded metal panels with indented handprints, stem from their flight control tableau with which the disc is mentally-inductively steered. »We hold our hands on it and in this way set various things in motion through (mental) energy transference. Then one steers the vehicle almost the way you do.« For specific maneuvering, e.g. lift-off, landing, dimension leaping, the crew seems to have fed their full bio-energies into at least three existing panels.*

The basis for their special, vitalizing liquid nourishment was presumably prepared on board by Alira from scratch, as it were, by means of the water generator. In any case, there were no foodstuffs or victuals found at the crash site.

Their skintight spacesuits stretched when put on. The material used »breathes«, adapts to varying air and water pressure, resists radiation and maintains constant temperature. It is made of spirally shaped pressure and frequency-equalizing fibers which, besides everything else, are also bulletproof.**

The unmanned »spider« probes, one of which was attached to the underside of Lilit's vehicle,*** don't usually land on precise target. Since they are unstable, they are often thrown out of their programmed orbits, fall into the water or swerve off their target path altogether and perish. Since they are imperfectly powered, compared to the disc itself, they often don't have the requisite power to fulfil their missions. If they do manage to arrive at a set target, it is usually through hit-or-miss.

---

* I was able to roughly calculate the size of the vehicle, based on the radius of the presumably semi-circular arrangement of the instrument panel and body size of the aliens and concluded that it must have been about 15 - 20 feet diameter, which would accord with Lilit's information.
** Recently earth scientists invented a similar innovative sort of carbon fiber.
*** These mini-disc probes, whose mounted holders evidently broke off at the first jolt of touch down and completely broke apart as the craft shattered against the rocks, may have been responsible for rumors of a second ship crashing at the same spot at the same time.

Their ejector seats for emergency exits are »air cushions one sits on«. However, they only cause one to fly more slowly through the air in an emergency, and mostly prevent crash landings from being fatal. They are tied to one's backside in critical situations and eject in similar fashion to those of jet fighters, literally catapulting one out of the craft. These emergency landing balloons are made of the same material as the spacesuits, merely slightly thinner and smoother. Like airbags, these balloons fill instantaneously with gas. In an FBI telex from Major Curtan of Dallas to J. Edgar Hoover in Cincinatti, dated July 8, 1947 (the day the wreck was salvaged) there is a special note that the saucer went down »with a cable hanging onto a balloon about 6 yards in diameter«. It is quite possible that this balloon also exploded into thousands of shreds upon crashing to Earth, since the impact was braked only slightly by it, or was already in the air when struck by lightning and then scattered in the wind, causing the silver foil decor on Brazel's sheep-grazing meadow.

The brown type of parchment discovered on Brazel's ranch land served the Asastanians as »imprints«. It was used to store data-compressed pictures and other things by being projected through a spectroscope via mental power.*

For time jump travel, »you have to work your way through lots of elements, otherwise you'll never get out of your own universe«. For that reason, they entered another frequency during their own time leap to Earth and »in a certain sense, dematerialized for a short time«. First they raised the frequency, later on they lowered it, from about 700 Gigahertz before, to about 500 Gigahertz afterward, with which they »wanted to be received into vacuum-like space«. Thus, after the time

leap into our Earth atmosphere, they modulated more slowly than at home. But they waited in vain for a soft landing in »vacuum-like space«. The leap to a different dimension to us took all of 45 minutes, measured in Earth time. »That causes a time change in itself«, just as we know occurs in Einstein's theory of relativity.

They came because they wanted to »conquer«, i.e. explore and scientifically analyze this galaxy. »Your galaxy only exists as it does in this millennium, in 3000 years it will not exist in this form anymore. Seen from that perspective, it won't be found on our map.« Everything is supposed to go through this change because of an »earth displacement«. The planet will transfer to another space density, thus transforming radically its position and aura. An entirely new stellar constellation will thereby be created.*

»On Asastan itself, we usually move about with the help of microchips.« They float along on so-called »air-rollers« about 20 inches above the ground. I can imagine this to be close to a kind of anti-gravitational snowboard.

Their most important symbol is a four-surface, four dimensional triangle. With this tetrahedron - »it is the symbol of our plane of existence« - emphasized Lilit, all matter in their dimension could be explained. The harmonious interpenetration of two such tetrahedrons symbolized wholeness: »the possibilities beyond a local universe«.

Asastanians use many diverse kinds of intercommunication. Besides telepathy and nearly »conven-

---

* The thought photography experiments of American Ted Serios, who was able to develop hundreds of polaroid photos psychokinetically, also work in this direction.

* During the so-called Age of Aquarius, our entire solar system, together with other systems, will move more and more into a different part of space in a kind of galactocentric astrology/astronomy over the next 2000 years. This will presumably create completely new conditions of space/time, which, in turn, will no doubt have their effect on the brain cells of the creatures living on the respective planetary bodies. In addition to that, whole clusters of galaxies will move in tandem with each other into cosmic space of a superior order, which will proceed to modify all the lower orders of movements and conditions still further. Beyond that there are surely further, still more superior cosmic movements.

tional« methods, by dint of which ground control remained in contact with the explorers until the »energetic winds« caused the failure of the on-board technology, they apparently have an instrumental kind of para-communication available to them with which they can receive thoughts and respond to them without being present. To facilitate communication with foreign cultures, all known language patterns are transcoded into adequate telepathic impulses and sent out by *»power-modulating their thoughts«*.

As already mentioned, I operate on the supposition – based on a whole variety of personal experiences – that we on Earth will soon be in a position to engage in a full exchange of permanently objective trans-communicative information of the highest quality with beings of superior intelligence, which, in turn, will have great influence on our own evolution. A cosmic hotline of this kind would already be a great service at some of the flashpoints here on Earth. The crisis management teams of this planet would thus be well advised to make every effort to break through this »sound barrier« as soon as possible.

If one can extrapolate from the tidbits of information which have leaked out of its own records, the US Army has so far succeeded in decoding the Asa-stanian hyper-technology discovered in the wreckage only in minimal ways. The cause is, in fact, rather ordinary: without at least rudiments of spiritual awareness, this technology cannot be grasped; and anyone with sufficient spiritual awareness does not work for the Army. These are mutually exclusive opposites. This applies equally to the personnel of all secret services.

Solar System Asastan/Planet Earth

Readers who have difficulty in accepting such things, are advised at least hypothetically to look upon the contents of this book as a kind of science fiction. Only after a period of familiarizing themselves with the overall context, should they form a personal opinion of it all.

Asastan is, according to Lilit, the name of a very old civilization, which reigned and developed here on Earth eons before Christ. The Asastanians are de-scended from the cradle of civilization in Mesopo-tamia, from the peoples who lived between Tigris and Euphrates, and left our Earth five million years ago. To be more precise, they emigrated into more and more distant spacial incarnations, disappear-ing little by little from our planet. But their spirit took along the energy/gene imprint of Earth to their new bodies and their new destinations. About 500,000 years ago, the species then began to physi-cally build up their present civilization on Asastan. Previously, they also lived for a time on Venus: *»In our present stage of development, we actually come from Ve-nus.«* Research into gene technology was actively pursued at that time on all planets close to Earth, *»only the Martians had already stopped«*. That implies that all the planets in our vicinity were inhabited, and perhaps still are.

With their genetic arts, they wanted to couch everything in harmony and beauty, but in striving to-ward omnipotence, they landed somewhere comple-tely different. *»We are so far distant from Earth because we are so far distant from our origins.«* Via Mira, they gave as their home address, significantly, »Terra Plus«, translating the label only much later to »Asastan«. Located 750 million light years away from us, this planet surrounded by a dozen moons is supposed to orbit around a rather bizarre central stellar body, also named Lilit, which represents a kind of holis-tic sun-moon complex. Seven other planets, inha-bited by other alien populations, allegedly revolve around the same central body.

184

»Our sun-moon central star shelters a moon inside it.« The sun-core of the luminescent star »Lilit« has cooled. Thus, life isn't found on its surface, but in its interior, whereas its exterior glows with blazing heat. This »inner moon« is evidently inhabited by curious Earthians, who move along in wormlike manner. My interlocutor didn't want to say anything more about this, merely that it has to do with a karmic story *»like a moon hell«.* The »dark sides« of the moon, it would appear, regardless where they are, always have to be lived through.

Daylight varies slightly on Asastan, but it never gets completely dark, *»just more or less shady«,* the Asastanians have nothing like our day/night sequence. The great number of orbiting moons makes it impossible. Their sun-moon central star also permits no tides on their planet, only slight warm/cold changes are registered. Clouds, rain, regular inundations with monsoon-like storms occur only occasionally, when Asastan's planetary axis shifts by more than one degree. They have no such thing as thunderstorms, since they lack the extreme, sudden temperature changes we have on Earth.

Their planet is seven times larger than Earth, which is a scanty 56,000 miles in diameter (if the information was meant visually, a circumference seven times bigger would amount to 174,000 miles and seven times greater would make the surface 1.5 billion square miles). The satellite moves at a far higher speed than we do through the universe. Its »humanoid race« of Asastanians has a population of only 6 million, who, however, have a life span of about 500 Earth years. The atmosphere on this super-planet consists mainly of oxygen, then nitrogen, hydrogen, carbon and carbonic acid. So the gaseous bubble around their far distant planet consists, in the main, of the selfsame elements as the Earth's atmosphere.

There is less gravitational force on Asastan than on Earth, which perhaps explains why the brains of the inhabitants grow to such proportions. Without pressure equalization, it would be hard for our Earth bodies to survive there, Lilit opined; we would have the ongoing feeling *»that we were going to burst«.* The crash aliens had originally planned to take a volunteer from Earth back with them; however, friends of theirs had already tried previously to introduce animals to their environment, *»and they didn't do very well.«* The animals had to live in pressurized rooms on Asastan, so they were returned to Earth. *»For Earthians, our life would also be difficult to endure mentally, since it wouldn't satisfy your senses. You couldn't eat anything or have sex with us. What would you do?«* Well, we probably wouldn't be able to get a bite of food down anyway, for starters, since in our state of utter astonishment we certainly would think of everything else but that! Asastanians *»still pursue reincarnation«* but it takes place externally, without pain. Their scientists – including the »gene-keepers« and all others supervising the cloning equipment – make up about a third of Asastan's population. Besides researchers, »guardians« also comprise about a third, supervising all the functions of artificially created life and its ramifications. The last third consists of those who work and go about their daily lives. Everyone is assigned according to function, *»which becomes apparent soon after birth«.* Each is integrated into the system according to the qualities one brings along. Asastanians view life as cyclical: one time one is incarnated as a scientist, and endowed with a scientific psyche, another time as a guardian or something else. The victims of the crash have lost all desire to visit Earth any more with a spaceship: *»Isn't it enough that we came to grief in the crash once already?«* Most of them don't give a second thought to our planet anyway. Lilit said, *»It is, as you say, ›old hat‹ to us.«*

Asastanians live in types of glass mansions with high domes, partially also underwater. They do not build cities, having no necessity to do so, as there is plenty of space. Each person simply lives where he pleases. With their gravity-less movement, they already enjoy the perfect transportation system.

A kind of automated information system brings news to all their residences. The latest news story at the time of my interview, not exactly a blockbuster, was »*more sightings of UFOs from alien planets*«. In this vein Lilit confirmed that their compatriots enjoyed a friendly exchange with other universes.

Just as is true with us, flora and fauna also exist on Asastan, artificial landscapes with grass and trees, although all poisonous plants and animals were eliminated in the course of their formation process. »*We have lots of whitish animals, lions and zebras too, for we love the color white. Our animals don't kill each other in order to survive. And like us, they also drink only ›enriched water‹*«. In the visions accompanying the trance dialog, Mira was even able to hear a few animals talking in rudimentary fashion. She saw pale chimpanzees and bear-like creatures, which the Asastanians endowed with more or less human consciousness. It was her impression that this animal/human potential was all made possible through genetic engineering and biotechnology.

Most of the Asastanians are involved in new work projects, on construction improvements and many other things. They create in great measure their planetary landscape structure, where they not only »*transform the planet's surface, but the conditions of plant cultivation as well*«. For this they utilize the reflexes of the soil, i.e. the biological texture out of which their planet is made. They view planets as living organisms on which they – just as on themselves – can bring forth other structures through cell transfor-

mation. For example, Mira saw in one vision how they programmed artificially created viruses with command-codes to fulfil special functions.

They were not »human gardeners«, that was a lie, explained Lilit apparently confirming the statement made just before, that »*nature does it better*«. Besides, the whole tenor of their science, as well as the additional pieces which fit into the puzzle of their findings, all point to genetic implications being a major aspect of Asastanian evolution and in the present lives of these and other aliens. Just as such fundamental interventions into inherited substances took place in our pre-historic time, these will gain new importance in the near future (this is treated in the next chapter).

With regard to our own solar system, Lilit reported that it has existed in its present form for about 70 million years and is about 700 million light years away from the mid-point of all cosmic centres. Their Asastanian system is almost twice as far away as we are from the so-called »primal central sun«.*

Humanoids have existed on Earth for about three million years, which accords with our own findings. But the human soul has always been here, whether embodied or not, »*before that it was in other animals*« and has been becoming aware of itself since the development of apes.

Some 500 million years ago, a new moon named Mallona was formed, »*which however didn't appear to earthlings*«, because – through an explosion – it diverged from the system at a time when there were not yet any human beings on Earth. At that time things were already developing on this planet in the same fatal direction in which Asastanian genetics proceeded. In other planetary systems within the Milky Way, a civilization arose whose genetic con-

* In esoteric studies, an astral-astronomic representative of highest consciousness.

struction also appeared on Earth. But they later departed because they would not have been able to survive on early Earth. It was these creatures from the ancient Earth who, together with Mallona people, developed these »in-gene-ious« innovations. Their »Father Lorin« was one of these genetic pioneers. That is why he still looks rather earthian. He is the only one on Asastan who does – he even has long hair. »But it is his cruel fate to have to always behold us«, his gene-technological fruits.

Our solar system has enough strength to last another five million years but, through earth-magnetic changes, it will soon experience a major shift of the polar axis. The entire system is now moving toward a new energetic space. Such a giant quantum leap of evolution takes place about every three million years. Planets are threatened at this juncture, but they do not necessarily die. As an aside, Lilit remarked that we are altering our biological environment through our nuclear testing; and that our next evolutionary step will take us in the direction of solar energy, i.e. fusion reactors.

She also let it be known between the lines that our human evolutionary leap forward was related to extraterrestrial encounters. The US – by that she probably meant the government – had already had contact with extraterrestrials from our »near future«, and UFOs from other eras had also arrived. However, Asastanians have no connection with them.

Communicating with us is not particularly interesting at present for Asastanians. »Maybe there will be a point to it in about fifty years, when you are further developed« she said drily. They are not yet human enough to want to help us directly or commit themselves: »We are only speaking here in order to fulfil our karma.« Father Lorin, who has apparently incarnated on Earth now and again, was also completely uninterested, being himself too busy. According to Lilit, he was so scientifically oriented even way back in the distant past that he forgot all ethical boundaries. That is why he was such a depressive while incarnated on Earth. »The cosmic drama is also a part of it, he says today.« It is the awful trauma and karma of Lorin, according to Lilit, to know »that he made Asastanian civilization into what it is today. He thumbed his nose at spiritual power, and we are the result.« Commander Bax was on another expedition at the time of my questioning. Alira preferred to listen, rather than talk.

Beyond my own efforts, the Asastanians know of no serious attempts of Earthians to contact them telepathically. The apparent reason for entering a dialog with me was that I – as »Vipan« – was one of them in a number of instances, a kind of »guest-reincarnation«, the last time about 350 years ago. »Why else do you think I come to talk to you? You've lived here several times, because you wanted to.« Since I cannot come up with a conscious memory of it, Lilit offered to implant a device to assist my data recall. »It is an energy injection to activate your brain cells.« In the course of the trance, I hesitatingly accepted her offer, but until recently I was not able to recall anything in this connection.*

Then, however, one night, several weeks after the last talk with Lilit, without any conscious mulling over, just as I was falling asleep, I experienced within myself inner pictures of dark-eyed aliens, which caused me to become fully awake again and reminded

* Besides this apparently purely energetic implantation, there also exist more physical, metallic hypertechnical miniature devices which are implanted during so-called »abductions« by the aliens in various parts of the body, then later partially removed. I met an American mathematician and corn crop researcher a few years ago to whom this very thing happened while sleeping. In the meantime there are hundreds of well-documented cases of this implantation phenomenon. Mira's initial vision of an alien arm in which there was an implantation also points to Asastanians' implanting themselves with such specific function-chips. In other words, a kind of extraterrestrial piercing.

me of Lilit's words. Such things persuade me that there is an uncanny connection still binding us to the distant past. Perhaps I should focus on Asastan in a self-prescribed lucid dream program....

Their Philosophy/Their Warnings

Right at the beginning, Lilit addressed the central theme of her position by saying, »*We are your future*«. The initially confusing implication slowly becomes clearer when we examine this statement in the context of Asastanian philosophy: »*Your past only exists because we went through this stage of development.*« And this specific development is stamped by the conviction which runs parallel to the Old Testament command, »*Make the earth your subject*«, at least if one takes this command quite literally. Viewed from this perspective of creation, the Asastanians perceived »*a fascinating experience and a new chance*« to shape life themselves, the result of which, however, seen from a distance, did not lead to their happiness.

Lilit's concept of time is based on the superhelix and central solar time, whatever that means. In any case, the Asastanians use the periodic revolution of (one of) their planet(s) around their sun as time measure: »*Whenever the direction of revolution reverses, one unit is completed.*« Perhaps they mean a cyclical magnetic pole-jump of an instable satellite within their system, whose pattern of motion is then used as a kind of metronome for their own time measurement.

»*We long ago went through the development which you are now going through and we went on to the point where you, too, will land one day, if you make the same mistakes.*« So they on their planet had similar problems to ours and followed the path of technology consistently, right down to the smallest piece in the mosaic of life itself. But it didn't make them happy. They are dissatisfied with their course of evolution and especially with their bodies which resulted from it. »*We are a genetically altered race with a burdensome karma.*« They believe it is only a kind of intermission in their overall destiny, before they look like human beings again. »*We don't yet know exactly how we will find our way back to the human being, but we firmly believe we will do so.*«

In any case, they have recognized that they have left the path of the primal law of nature, which is universally applicable: »*as above, so below; as inside, so outside.*« The Asastanians pushed a great many things forward with their gene technology, they even altered their own bodies according to their desires and eliminated pain. They became super-intelligent in a highly reasoned way, have breathtaking abilities and travel through cosmic world history...yet they miss being human. »*We no longer correspond to what the divine principle foresaw as humanness.*« Ever since they realized that, they yearned to correspond again to the original image of a human being. »*All our desires go back to the original source.*«

Their societal system has no government, each person is self-sufficient, lives for himself, or within a self-generated group, as in Lilit's case. They have neither money nor an economic system as we do. »*We work straight from our consciousness toward the maintenance of the planet and our own bodies, everything comes about by itself.*« There seems to be an existential power there of a type still unknown to us, which works by assuring that everyone receives what is needed and wanted. Since they don't have to fight for survival, their peaceable natures are the natural result.

On Asastan love seems to exist between cosmic partners, who are also known on Earth as dual souls or soul mates.* Their unusual »moon-sun« or »sun-moon«, which unites both polarities, is a fitting companion piece to this. Seen from this point of view, their purely energetic sexuality also becomes understandable. However, the further step of throwing pregnancy overboard unfortunately led to far-reaching consequences. They no longer have any dreams and don't have myths or fairy tales either, »since everything is perceived consciously«. They have »become empty over the course of time, as regards philosophizing«, said Lilit with regret. »We treat our psychological structures with pure reason these days.«

They have no religion in the conventional sense, but they have great respect for life as such, even though this may appear to us as a rather strange form of respect. They hope that the law which brings forth everything living and allows them their absolute freedom is a good one. »That's our only philosophy – we know no other.« Their present fate is their unhappiness, but they nonetheless believe in an ideal which transmutes.

On Asastan there is hardly any cultural life, and what there is left decreases all the time, having become endlessly dull. All their artists have disappeared, since »without pain, there can be no art.« Their spiritual needs have more or less expired, spiritual consciousness being born of suffering. »Precisely because we can't really suffer anymore, we are unhappy.« Thus, the unpleasant paradox arises that the personal experience of happiness is only possible when it is coupled with suffering.

They do not pursue astrology, feeling themselves free of any power of the stars, but have »a non-person-alized astronomy«. They say there are developed and undeveloped universes all around them and that their problem is living in harmony with the universes which border on their own. When that will be attained is a question of overall evolution, »although we don't know if there is an end to evolution«.

As go-getters in grand style, they even go so far as to declare will as belonging to the fourth dimension, »since through it and in it everything happens«. In their everyday life, logically, there are no rules; it seems to me a strange kind of rational anarchy. »We do what we have to, and that is also what we want. We have no problem with that.« For Asastanians, nature has no laws of its own, they themselves come up with the ideas and simply have to give the corresponding orders to nature in order for those ideas to materialize. They have continually tried to turn their fantasies into reality, but »the point at which we have now arrived is where you land when you always get your way«.

They can see into the past and into the future, but only imprecisely when they look ahead. They are capable of viewing as many as seventy different probable futures, though they don't know which variation will actually come about, since »it doesn't depend on us alone, how something develops«. Consequently, they can engage in direct time travel only into the past. When they mull over something, the sought information pops up automatically – a principle which is also operative in so-called Akasha readings.* From this perspective, Lilit also made some statements with regard to future Earth developments:

• »Unleashed by your superpowers bad epidemics and nuclear wars will probably come in about 15 years. We

---

* There is an esoteric parable which says that during the descent of the holistic soul from highest consciousness frequencies down to the denser material spheres, it split into feminine and masculine halves over the course of its incarnations. Thus, on the spiritual return journey to wholeness, it is continually searching for its other half and will not rest until it reunites with it and again enters the cosmic Garden of Eden.

* Akasha reading is tapping into the universal data storage or the collective unconscious and supra-conscious while in deep trance.

don't believe in disarmament. People won't believe it, but it is going to be worse than anything human beings ever dreamed of. The major impetus behind this war is despair and absolute insanity.«

• *»In about 75 years your next pole shift will take place with great deluges and even continents will be displaced. Much land will go under water. A large-scale UFO invasion will have to come. Many people will be in danger of their lives, they will have to be removed, perhaps this will have to be done by us.«*

• *»Over the next 100 years many alien births will occur on Earth and your population will double through the accelerated birth rate. Many things will no longer suffice to prevent births because nature also knows that human beings are in mortal peril. In such times there were always inordinately high birth rates...so that much more can be exterminated afterwards.«*

• *»The next step in the evolution of your race on Earth will take place within 3000 years. Your apes will get bigger and humans will become more intelligent. You will find manlike apes which become more human. The ›missing link‹ will once again appear.«*

The Asastanians have feelings toward Earth resembling sympathy, that's why Lilit thought it her duty to inform us about the dangers of the critical developments which we are presently going through. *»You are about to make the same terrible mistake that our ancestors once made.«* They give no advice with regard to prolonging the life-span, since it does not seem appropriate in our present situation. *»What's the point, if you then get stuck in a nuclear war? It will only get interesting in 50 years, if you've survived.«*, was Lilit's dry commentary.

Nevertheless, they admit at the same time that nothing is predetermined. The hope that things will develop differently and human values will be maintained should, therefore, not be given up. But: *»We*

also hoped for this development, but it didn't come about. You still have all that ahead of you and have the chance to master it, which we unfortunately lost. Our future is not necessarily your future!«

Today the Asastanians are only afraid that they might one day lose control over the mechanisms they developed and installed. Their standard of evolution is not at all bad, but they miss essential things. *»You're heading in the direction of what we became! If your genetic technology continues to develop in the way it has so far, then our present life is your future. You must try to learn from us what all this can lead to. We have no fathers or mothers, we are all parentless. Other civilizations still look just like yours. They have huge problems, but are intermittently happy.*

Many of your governments support gene technology. You ought to know what path you are deciding on. You are an original work, the original creation out of which we developed. The price you intend to pay is too high, in order to avoid your present difficulties.«

So much for their mental warnings. Asastanians communicate primarily telepathically, although they possess a kind of script consisting of 35 symbols. These, however, serve mainly as mathematical/nautical records or functions. They are also in contact with those among them who are not embodied. Their will towards embodiment and reincarnation on Asastan is not in every case absolutely guaranteed, *»we also enter other bodies in other places in other universes.«* But they do not wish to remain without bodies, since then only timeless consciousness exists. *»It's the coming and going which makes life what it is.«* Many of Lilit's siblings would like, at some future point, to incarnate on Earth, *»in order to push along our progress«*. However, they do not intend to return soon via UFO, after their unfortunate experiences with our *»energetic winds.«* It is more likely that they'll some day send one of their

»spiders«, the unmanned space probes which they can land via remote control.

Incidentally, Lilit set great stock in making clear to us that they do not engage in abductions or in research which might cause anyone pain or suffering. They also are not involved with the crop circle configurations, *»UFOs from nearby universes are responsible for those.«* Apparently they are created in order to draw our attention to the existence of these other races and prepare us for the unexpected. Animal mutilations, as have occurred mainly in the US, were also not caused by Asastanians.

They don't have religious cult figures Lilit said they don't meditate, but practise a form of contemplation, and *»see the ideals of the original source living at the center of all galaxies in the shape of human masters such as Jesus and Buddha.«* In a certain sense, they revere the masters of the central universe, *»also the Nazarene as well as other great ones«,* but only because they managed to attain an even higher stage of development than the Asastanians. The inhabitants of Asastan don't look up to these masters, *»rather they look across. They are even free of their genes and live solely out of their consciousness, and we consider that an even higher stage of evolution than what we have attained.«*

They left us with a cryptic remark: *»Sugar doesn't only dissolve in water, but also in milk!«* Was this supposed to be an amusing send-off or is there another, deeper message buried in these words? That is something I leave to each reader to answer for himself.

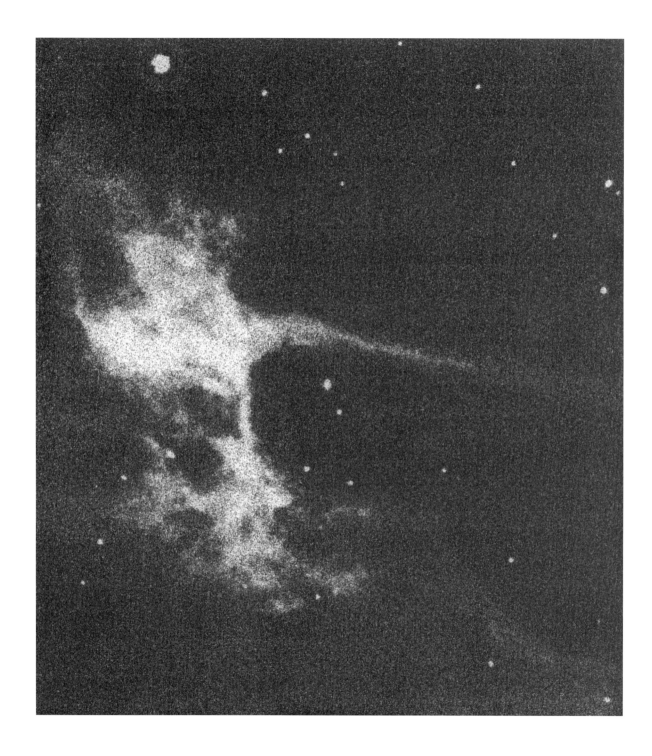

The Roswell Controversy – Conclusions

Genetic Madness

Hardly a day passes without further achievements in genetic technology being trumpeted through the media. Be it a newly modified food, curiously artificial animal crossbreeding or medical genome experiments, the developments proceed at such breakneck speed that ordinary mortals can hardly register them.

The Nobel Prize for biology in 1995, for example, went to a researcher whose work explored how genes control biological development. These might stem presently only from the fruit fly (Drosophila), but they are the very same fundamental processes which take place inside a human embryo. At the moment, molecular science is taking giant steps toward cracking the innermost transmission codes of nature and intervening with them, too. The embryon protection laws which prevail in most western countries still prohibit human cell manipulation, but how long will they continue to do so? In Britain and Belgium, for instance, the obstacles have already been removed.

All types of flora and fauna are being eagerly experimented with. Recently, by means of a blossom-switch gene, scientists have succeeded in producing blossoms in plants where before leaves were supposed to grow. Just a year ago, two sheep were cloned right down to the last cells of their bodies: the first step toward mass production of living beings. Even a hybrid of sheep and goat has already been shown on TV as entertainment; the gene-manipulated product called »geep« or »shoat« doesn't know yet whether to »baaaa« or bleat. The next step is transgenetic animals, raised for purposes of organ donations (pig hearts are very similar to human hearts, for example).

Genetic plant manipulation has progressed furthest. Transposing super-resistance to known bacteria right into the reproductive genes leads to 50% larger harvests than before. Already, lobbies are disputing with governments about the necessity of labeling genetic manipulation as such. And, of course, genetic patents are already being traded on the stock exchange. It is simple for industry to apply pressure by arguing »assured food production for the world« through gene engineering of plants. Genome analyses cost a great deal of money, therefore the goals are invariably coupled to what is economical. In addition to this, the most shocking part of the present situation is that none of these many exploratory laboratories is engaged in fundamental research anymore. They are all hunting down product development which they hope will help them strike it rich.

Wherever there is that kind of money involved, it is understandably difficult to keep scientific development to meaningful paths. Dealing responsibly with nature and its creatures is, to put it mildly, quickly subordinated to so-called economic necessities. On top of that, the layman is totally overtaxed by the extremely complicated field of molecular biology. Tiniest particles of matter are examined in the cell core in order to read and decode the symbols of the genetic language of life which subsequently can only be read by the laboratory elite...whom the general public is supposed to trust. But can we and should we still trust such experts, who long ago transgressed the boundaries of humane ethics? The man on the street is primarily an observer of processes unfamiliar to him. What's going to happen when what is now still gene technology vision becomes hard and fast reality?

Depending on social circumstances, research into life's fundamental design can result in differing consequences. What happens when a dictator or madman takes over this knowledge? From genetic terrorism all the way to secret biological workshops of insane warmongering scientists in which gene monsters are raised for kamikaze missions...all kinds of Frankenstein horror scenarios are imaginable. Hollywood has already – without any exaggeration – painted the devil on the wall with a string of films on the subject.

Efforts to improve the human race and the human lot have existed since the beginning of time in all cultures. However, what is going on today behind strictly guarded laboratory doors (because of industrial espionage) would shock Gregor Mendel, the father of hereditary science, to the core. The mind-boggling pre-genetic experiments of the Nazis under Dr. Mengele appear almost harmless compared with the mischief that a precocious government lackey or scientist stooge could unwittingly set in motion today. Researchers from Johns Hopkins University succeeded, by intervening in the inheritance code of the mouse by means of one single gene, in turning a generation of laboratory mice into uninhibited killers of their own species. Another research team located the specific mouse gene which controls the development of the head. After eliminating that master gene, mouse embryos which followed were all born without heads.

Everywhere one looks, laboratories are trying to copy, mutate and restabilize the DNS-reproductive molecules or the RNS-genetic messenger molecules, and then, on a trial-and-error basis, since they are still a long way off from understanding and correlating the complexities of living organisms, to look on astonished at the results of their experiments. Millions of laboratory animals suffer agonies from these delusions of scientific grandeur.

When one realizes that a chimpanzee's genes are 99% identical to those of a human being, one can figure out just how many possibilities are being explored by »Homo Sapiens« and what motives might be hiding behind such experiments. Man ate of the tree of knowledge and has begun, today more vehemently than ever before, to play God. But does the desire to subjugate the earth also mean being free to mess about with creation itself? This poses fundamental questions: where is this experimental work leading? Is that where we want to go? What is permitted to human beings in the name of freedom, and what isn't? It is a matter of seeking a new quality of humanness, but who is defining that quality? Voluntary limitations and supervision through ethical commissions are all well and good, but who should be the one to draw the line, beyond which we are not permitted to venture? How should we enter upon a process of reflection when the man in the street doesn't have the foggiest idea what tinkering with genes entails, and any attempt to make the subject popular is not in the interests of those holding the strings? Now that we are puttering about with the very heart of life itself, it is time to pose the ultimate questions: where do I come from? Where am I going? Where would I actually like to go? What is the human being? What should a human being become? Why are we really alive?

Even though I am an optimist, I feel sufficiently pessimistic about this subject to assume that these questions are hardly being posed globally. Yet when a civilized nation finally decides to draw a line, another nation will soon be found which wishes to make the forbidden possible. Major economic factors will invariably assert themselves and then become accepted practice over the course of generations, lowering the inhibition level further and further.

It goes without saying that genetic research also has its benefits. But in my opinion the positive opportunities for mankind resulting from it, when measured against the risks, are being vastly overestimated. The revolution taking place in biochemistry has yet to prove that our world will be a better place through its contribution. Sadly, it is this very burden of proof which may be our undoing.

At present, the genetic disposition of various types of cancer is being worked on under high pressure and long-term efforts are being made, through mass diagnosis of cancer susceptibility, to eliminate the specific gene already in the zygote. The psychosomatic dimension of cancer, which is already accepted by conventional medicine, points unequivocally to a connection between genetic structure and the psyche, which means that the manipulation of life's molecules will, for better or for worse, be reflected in the overall psyche of the individual. Even if this type of genetic technology is called, almost affectionately, gene therapy, how much of a leap is it from there to genetic removal of mental disturbances and, ultimately, eugenetic acts?

Although the process of genetic development and maturation, from zygote to adulthood, is still unknown for the most part, as is neuron development in the brain, we are just about to decode the biological programs of our 100 billion, or so, little gray cells. Despite many blank spots on the map of the human brain, the most complex structure in the entire known cosmos, researchers want to gain access to the brain via electronics as well. Cross-disciplinary junctions (interfaces) of biology and technology have already been found; connections between neurons and semi-conductors have already been successful in their initial stages. If brain and computer enter into a direct dialog with one another, the road leading to a superchip inside our skulls is already paved. It is still unclear how complex thinking processes can be attached to electronics, though initial, simple circuits between nerve cells and transistors have already been set up and made to operate. A multi-faceted network between our mostly unutilized brain lobes and an artificial neuron data highway is what we will soon face. Besides the total computerization of society, Bill Gates is actively investing heavily in gene technology.

The hottest theme at the moment is transfer of embryos. Computer supported sperm analysis and test tube fertilization are already part and parcel of everyday life. But any attempt to create a healthy baby by the introduction of hormonal experimentation, the procreation of human life in an egg cell laboratory and manipulated reproduction must bring with it risks of laboratory error. The first test tube babies are already living among us: this method has been applied hundreds of times all around the world and more than 100 babies have been successfully born this way. However, maternal feelings can be affected and emotional confusion may result. A dangerous chapter in human history has begun. From artificial insemination to selection and manipulation of human embryos, working toward genetically desirable traits, all the way to sexless reproduction, everything can be ordered today. This is already a lucrative business in the US. Soon the choice between girl or boy, with this or that body build, will no longer be a Utopian dream. Along the lines of the motto, »Everything is possible« nothing will be left to nature anymore. When methods which are still unreliable today become sufficiently refined, human beings with exceptional attributes will be able to be bred. That's when nose and eye shapes, skin color, hair stucture and body sizes with matching intelligence quotients will be able to be chosen from catalogs and implemented. The only question is what will the souls invited to enter such an embodiment have to say about it?

It has already begun: viewing the ageing process as a genetic sickness. Since our cells normally begin to degenerate after about 60 renewal cycles rather than regenerate, science is looking for ways to reprogram the process, with a mind to giving new incentives to the huge geriatric market. The »gods in white coats« are pursuing physical immortality, without the slightest spiritual grasp of what they are about. Neurobiology and molecular genetics are working in tandem in their efforts to uncover all biochemical coordinating systems. Everything from artificial blood, prepared by stirring water into it, then imbibed, to a soulless spare parts storage depot for human bodies is being considered. Technically reproduceable sensory organs are no longer a figment of the imagination. Artificial-organic bones are already being successfully constructed. In a California cosmetic clinic, fingers can be grown on malformed hands. The bionic neuroprotheses are already in production. After we have managed to eliminate natural immune defenses against foreign cells in our own genetic chain, nothing will stand in the way of artificially growing hearts, kidneys and lungs in genetic laboratories. How big a step is it then from the test tube preparation of a genetic-therapeutic pregnancy to external breeding of human beings?

Genetic technology also has a few side shows running: we are attempting to teach biocomputers with brain-similar neuronal networks, so-called bio-

morphic calculation architecture, how to think like human beings. In about five years, the first flexible electronic models are due to hit the market. The Japanese are now developing robots which manifest primitive feelings. We are tinkering with an electronic human eye and have already taken significant steps toward artificial robot muscles. As a power source, we already have today nano-technology miniature reactors measuring .0000001 mm, with cog-wheels of Lilliputian size, so small they would fit on the knee of an ant. In the meantime, computer programmers have even created artificial creatures which live from energy, move about in virtual biotopes, grow there, reproduce, adapt themselves to new conditions via mutations after a few generations and show early signs of true individuality. With that, the long-held premise that life is matter bursts like the proverbial soap bubble. What happens if such an artificial intelligence, whether electronic, genetic or a hybrid of the two, develops a creation far superior to itself? A genetically engineered multiplying genius as a constructor of its own progeny? Who can know what consequences will arise from the ever more detailed knowledge of the human genome? What was once broad-mindedly conceded in some science fiction fantasies lies not very far in the future.

The human evolutionary path required eons to develop in the highest degree of its creative potential in the beginning of the 21st century. But it now appears to require just a tiny step to put everything we have attained thus far in jeopardy by thoughtless action. Perhaps we should hope that a sort of genetic engineering Chernobyl disaster will bring us to our senses through a healing shock before we reach the point of no return.

If we examine the insane progress-oriented thinking outlined in these pages in the context of the statements of the genetically contoured Roswell aliens, it might begin to dawn on us just how near we are here on Earth to an evolutionary dead end. The warnings of this genetically perverted race should give us food for thought. To formulate one more time the essence of the message clearly: an extra-terrestrial people genetically related to us from a previous, archaic stone age makes one last effort to escape its own genetic fiasco. Their visit to the inhabitants of planet Earth, with whom they once shared a genetic heritage, is both a healing/shocking warning against a genetic-programmed apocalypse as well as a call for help by this species. The question is, whether we are even capable of taking this very strong hint while we still have a choice of futures. Yet even if we recognize the gravity of the situation, it is questionable to what extent we will be able to change our ship's course. It is far more probable that this freedom of decision will soon be forgotten like yesterday's weather report.

The grandiose claims being made today by geneticists, coupled with the gullibility of the general public – who are being promised new and beneficial drugs capable of eliminating existing diseases could have devastating consequences. Not only things for the common good come from modern science! As desirable as a sensible dialog is between technology and nature, the influence being exercised on our genetic heritage has not just biological, but philosophical/ethical and all encompassing political/spiritual consequences as well. Whether these technologies have a constructive or destructive effect depends on our own ethical attitudes, which are divided into different camps at present. Where should the borders of human ethics be drawn? Do we have ways of protecting the boundaries? Without wishing to make a taboo of technological progress, we should rethink our ethical principles, now that the first excesses of biotechnology have occurred. We mustn't forget that

these fundamental insights with regard to the blueprint of life have an immense effect on the genetic legacy we hand on to future generations. Our present spiritual approach to this is no less than a kind of last will and testament of terrestrial society.

Plausible Time Leaps

The boldest of all freedoms is unlimited travel through time and space. A time machine has not just been a dream of humankind since H. G. Wells, it reaches back to experiences in our dream mind. Scientific theories of time travel have been pondered now and again but have been regarded as a practical impossibility in real life.

However, as Stephen Hawking, one of the most brilliant living physicists, has recently done an about turn from his earlier position and now affirms time travel, things have decidedly changed: »Insofar as one connects Einstein's General Theory of Relativity with quantum mechanics.« The reason for his change of opinion probably lies in laboratory experiments conducted by two universities in which the transmitting of information at speeds greater than the speed of light was practically proven in repeated tests. In his newest manuscript on the »Physics of Star Trek«, Hawking considers it realistic to »warp« time/space without upsetting the laws of causality.

Günter Nimitz, of the University of Cologne, has even managed to thrust a Mozart Symphony via microwaves over a distance of 5 in. at 870,000 mph, which amounts to 4.7 times the speed of light, a world record. Raymond Chiao, of Berkeley, is successfully working on the same problem with photons. Both are taking advantage of the so-called tunnel effect, which permits several quantums to transcend barriers for which they need literally no time. However, since for everything moving faster than the speed of light, time, due to the curvature of space, runs backwards, the door to the past appears to have opened a crack.

Einstein was the first to recognize that time is not an absolute or a constant, but depends on the speed of the traveller. Inside a very fast moving space ship, for instance, time moves quite normally, while the clock of someone outside, left behind on a planet, moves much more slowly than this. An astronaut travelling in space for ten years at just under the speed of light would find, upon his return to Earth, that a thousand years had elapsed since his departure. While an expedition into the future appears a mere technological challenge, a journey into the past is probably a question of principle which falters at the barrier of the speed of light. That is the state of our knowledge since Einstein.

Recent proof of travel at speeds exceeding that of light has turned our cause-effect relationship upside down. An effect can now take place at the same time as its cause, at least in the field of quantum mechanics. Whoever finds this shortcut through a »wormhole« in curved space ought to be able to pop up again in a completely different time/ space. Such wormholes are to be found in so-called black holes, but all matter would be torn to shreds instantly due to the extreme forces of gravity active there. According to US physicist Kip Thorne, there is nonetheless one possibility of getting away with it undamaged: that is, if one were to use »*exotic matter with negative gravitation.*« By means of these hypothetical wormhole connections or perhaps with the alternative super string theory of US physicist Richard Gott, ufonauts should be able to enter our space continuum from other universes just as easily. Regardless of whether one calls these possibilities hyperspace leaps, star gates, time warps or time bridges, or dismisses them

as so much foolish science fiction or psychic balderdash…according to the evidence of well documented occurrences all around UFO phenomena, flying saucers actually appear to be time machines. Hence, ufonauts are actually more »temponauts«, and shouldn't be regarded as extraterrestrials, but as time-displaced beings.

German theoretical physicist Burkhard Heim has postulated an extremely interesting concept in this connection. In his six-dimensional unified quantum field theory, UFOs materialize as gravitational wave generators out of the fifth and sixth dimensions into our four-dimensional space/time world, then dematerialize again, thereby causing paranormal phenomena to occur. Synchronicities, time paradoxes and psychic realities are all integrated without contradiction in this concept. The diametric contrast between psychic and real dissolves into a kind of brotherhood.*

The mysterious »Philadelphia Experiment« by the US Navy in 1943, is also worth mentioning. At the time experiments attempting to make the warship USS Eldridge undetectable to radar led to its invisibility to the naked human eye as well. On the one hand, this unintentional technological breakthrough was incomparable, but at the same time it represented a catastrophe of undreamed-of proportions for the participants. Because after they had returned to their own space/time continuum, most of them were in a state of mental confusion, seized by panic and horror at what had happened to them. The project was immediately hushed up and its continuation kept top secret, just like Roswell. It is clear that this occurrence and its follow-up near Montauk Point, N.Y. also contained elements of

* After a convention lecture my wife gave on »Telepathy with the Unborn«, Mr. Heim said he could mathematically prove that such communication was possible.

time experimentation, thought control, teleportation and artificial materialization. By means of occult practices, synchronicities were induced and perhaps even doors to parallel universes opened. When another experiment later threatened to go out of control as well, the main medium involved in it, a man named Duncan Cameron, apparently created a mental beast in order to destroy the project. All further proceedings are veiled in silence.

The so-called »Cloudbuster Experiment« of Wilhelm Reich in the early fifties should also be seen in the context of these weird experiments. In it, Reich managed, with a hose and tubular-formed apparatus, to disperse or construct cloud formations in the atmosphere, based on »orgonomic« principles. By conjuring rain for the farmers of the area during drought periods, he even financed his own institute and laboratory. Occasionally, unusual UFO sightings resulted from these weather-energy experiments, as if Reich had called up observers from another dimension through his energy interventions in Earth's atmosphere. Having myself been able to duplicate many of Reich's orgon experiments with a small study group in the context of my work for the former Austrian Wilhelm Reich Archives, I shall add a few of my personal experiences and encourage the reader to experiment for themselves.

Perhaps you have already noticed – presupposing a relaxed state – that when, on a summer's day you gaze in an unfocused way into the blue for awhile, small, glistening white wormlike forms squiggle quickly across your vision. Your instinct may be to dismiss this effect as an optical illusion or a phenomenon occurring in the eye. If you then take a light-colored organic substance as background for such experiments, e.g. a white or light-colored cotton blanket in full sunlight, and view it from a distance of about three feet, meditatively and unfocused, you will be able to see with a little practice how the blanket fills up with these tiny orgon energy bolts. According to a Sri Lankan guru, at whose retreat I successfully learned twenty years ago to withdraw my consciousness from my body, it should be possible to remove oneself into other dimensions by adjusting one's own frequency to those of these miniature light sperm, or Reichian orgon units. I haven't as yet completely succeeded, nor have I practised it sufficiently. But my half-hearted experiences are enough to show me that there is something to it.

Also, my telepathy and aura sighting experiments with a self-built orgon accumulator had a greater level of success inside the appliance than outside it. Coupled with several exercises by the Shaman friends of Carlos Castenada, I experienced other fascinating effects in the direction of slipping through space and crossing dimensions. In certain meditative settings, the walls at first began to breathe and to alter themselves, until finally, in a sort of whirlpool they laid bare an entrance into another world. At a certain point, however, an instinctive fear took root inside me together with a kind of rational objection to what I was experiencing, which caused me to hold back from leaving our own space/time continuum entirely. But a presentiment remained.

That's why matter and spirit have long ceased being antagonists for me. They are simply differently experienced degrees of density. In other words, spirit is high frequency matter and matter is low frequency spirit. And somewhere in this continuum, we are at the base of our personal development, that is to say, our individual psychosomatic frequency, coupled with our concept of reality, which precisely corresponds to our own stage of individuation. Thus, it is quite possible that in the apparently empty space around us, beings exist whom we are not able to perceive, simply because there is no overlapping of reality concepts or individual wave lengths. If, however, we manage to transform our own spectrum of perception upwards into higher frequencies or dimensions and locate on this level another concentration of consciousness-energy wishing to communicate with or to be perveived by us; and if it then lowers itself on its own frequency sufficiently for its reality to overlap with ours, sightings of UFOs, elves or other astral or half-materialized forms may be caught with the inner and/or outer eye before they finally adjust fully to our own level of density.

Seen from this point of view, the »psychoid UFO projections from the unconscious« of C. G. Jung and remaining crash wreckage tested in the material testing laboratories no longer contradict one another. So-called »beaming« is, thus, nothing but spiritual or technical manipulation of conglomerate conditions of spiritual matter or material spirit within an extended consciousness which reaches deep into the world of anti-matter or into parallel universes, dream states or whatever one wants to call them. Viewed in this way, ufonauts are but visitors from other dimensions and their UFOs are but reality-transforming time machines capable of unleashing, through their electromagnetic interactions with our own space/time physics, certain phenomena, from corn crop circles to Bermuda Triangle anomalies. In a trance conversation I had with another UFO commander several years ago it was implied that »projection technologies« play a part in this. In the local newspapers in 1989, a UFO sighting was reported right above Attersee Lake in Austria. In my transcommunicative queries, it was explained to me that it was not the UFO itself that was seen, but rather, a projection of it, caused by the real UFO from a safe distance outside the field of vision. This was done in order to

analyse human reactions to the sighting. Thus, there are manifold variations in the ways in which the fluid line between what is psychic and what is physical may be crossed. Nonetheless, the likelihood, as trite as it may sound, is that most UFO crew members are from distant planets whose homes may lie beyond frequencies of reality familiar to us.

Just as one can get from point A to point B in many different ways, conscious energies also have many ways at their disposal to travel from one dimension to another. Whether short-circuiting their way down a time tunnel; or simply taking advantage of propitious time-space holes present in any case in the cosmic enterprise; or simply manifesting themselves through dream worlds, we are going to have to become more conscious of the fact that we live in a »multiverse« with multiple possibilities, and that there are no limits set for our creativity, viewed long-term. However, even if the technology of some industrialized countries is more advanced than is generally admitted, one can safely assume that we have not as yet made such a hyper-high-tech breakthrough here on Earth. The billions of dollars which are presently being wasted on a highly antiquated space rocket technology bear ample witness to this. The helplessness of western science, rooted in the traditional mechanistic-physical and chemical-neurological world concept, can of course only support a technology which at best can manage to attain the furthest reaches of our planetary system. If even a journey to Mars takes a year, and another year is required to reach Jupiter, how are we expected to continue? Are we supposed to bear children in our spacecraft so that the 17th generation can finally shake hands with extraterrestrials and transmit via radio the happy news to distant future generations? One thing is as sure as can be: we won't be able to reach extraterrestrial homesteads with our present-day technology, and vertical-starting space transporters such as NASA's X-33 will do nothing to change that situation. The concept of space tourism some people are working toward will have to limit itself to the immediate surroundings of our planet. The step from island hopping to planet hopping is still a fair distance away.

Completely different methods are required for interstellar time travel: tachyon energy would be one possible way toward a new space technology, through which speeds of at least a billion times the speed of light are theoretically possible. Tachyons, the counterpart of Einstein's mass, are particles which move unbelievably fast, but cease to exist when reduced to speeds less than that of light. If, however, we could manage to catch or artificially produce tachyons, a spacecraft could initially be accelerated to the speed of light via photon propulsion and then computer switched to tachyon power. The craft would presumably then depart from Einstein's space and be catapulted into an overlapping space in which the time factor is without any significance.

Bob Lazar, a nuclear physicist who claims to have analysed propulsion systems of crashed UFOs at top secret AREA 51 in Nevada, thinks they are fed by anti-matter created by smashing Element 115 with protons. The energy released from this collision could be made to distort our space-time continuum. Elements 110 through 112 can already be artificially manufactured in small quantities. »Science News« has recently reported that physicists are on the verge of success in the manufacture of Element 114.

Leik Myrabo, an American professor of engineering sciences in Troy, New York, is presently working on the development of an Earth version of a flying disc, based on microwave propulsion. Made of heat-resistant silicon carbide, measuring about 30 feet in diameter, and weighing 1390 lbs. it should reach speeds of 13.6 miles-per-second, the equivalent of about 50,000 mph. Under these conditions, a crew could be transported to the Moon in about 5 hours. Since the targeted acceleration to Mach 25 within 10 seconds corresponds to 300 times the acceleration of Earth, and we can visually perceive only up to 20 g, the disc would become invisible right after take-off.

However, space and time still remain a giant challenge to our reason, and very few scientists have dared to trespass upon the limits of orthodox technology. But even some NASA scientists are beginning secretly to toy with fundamentally new technologies. It would be simpler and, evolutionarily seen, more constructive if we were to accept assistance from experienced, time leap-trained extraterrestrials. But for that we would first have collectively to accept their existence and then organise a peaceful global welcome for them.

Our Cosmic Ancestors

As mentioned earlier in this book, the legends of the Ugha Mongulala tribe of Brazil talk about six-fingered deities who are said to have visited the Indios 15,000 years ago. »...*Suddenly, glistening, golden ships appeared in the skies. Huge fiery signs lit up the plain. The Earth quaked and thunder resonated over the hills. People bowed down in awe before the powerful aliens who came to take possession of Earth.*« According to myth, 130 light-skinned divine families came in shimmering golden craft and are supposed to come again once every 6000 years. But that isn't all: these legends tell of an extensive subterranean cave system, purportedly carved out by the aliens and the Indios at the time, whose hidden entrances are still today well guarded by their caste of Indian shamans. In this deep and extensive cave system, which is said to connect a network of 13 subterranean settlements, some of which are still inhabited by the Indios, a mass of gold and hypertechnological apparatuses are supposed to be stored, as well as scripture symbols of the alien astronaut deities. These include examples of a rejuvenation machine, a kind of frequency modulator or life energy generator, only used by the top leaders of the tribal association. According to legend there are also, various spacecraft which »*are big enough for two passengers and have neither helm nor sails, but one can fly faster with them than the strongest eagle, and move as lightly through the clouds as a leaf in the wind. Such vehicles have seven long legs that carry a large silvery bowl. On their ends are rolls the size of a water lily.*« Erich von Däniken wanted to investigate this in person, but as a white man he had no chance to become familiar enough with the Indios to find out anything objective. According to Däniken, three men and one woman, each with twelve fingers and toes, are preserved in a special fluid in one of these caves.

As »coincidence« would have it, our children's nanny, whom we hired ten years ago, became intimate with the chief of these natives during an adventure trip cum jungle expedition. She was the mistress of Chief Tatunca Nara (»Big Watersnake«) for several months. The Indio shamans prevented her from entering the caves, since they were displeased that their chief wished to make a white woman his wife, but she did find out enough to be able to confirm that the legends are indeed real and not from the imagination of German author Karl Brugger, who published a book titled »Die Chronik von Akakor«.* In these legends, the stellar system of the six-fingered deities, located in the furthest depths of the cosmos, is called »Schwerta«. It has twelve celestial bodies

* »Chronicles of Akakor«, only published in German.

revolving around it and could well be identical with the twelve-moon system described by the Asastanians. Incidentally, our acquaintance finally returned to Austria with a veritable arsenal of native jewellery and highly poisonous curare arrows, complete with bow, after the tense situation with the Indio magicians and the war being waged by the Indios against the Brazilian gold prospectors both became too dangerous. Our parapsychological researches revealed, after she had also been threatened by the magicians in her dream worlds, that associations from earlier lives were the cause of these disturbing contacts, something we might have guessed from the very beginning.

When even today, in the jungles between Brazil and Venezuela, the Brazilian government supports the mass liquidation of Indios, all because of enormous gold, petroleum and uranium deposits, how much more gold must have existed at the time of the extraterrestrial visitors! Incidentally, the investigating reporter Karl Brugger, who knew a little too much about these murderous connections, was killed by the Brazilian secret service in Manaos in 1984.

Besides the six-finger »myth« of the Ugha Mongulala, the above mentioned legends, and the rock carvings of the North American Anasazi Indians, who immortalized six-toed petroglyph imprints near a horizontal wheel (UFO?), the Sumerian Cuneiform of the Tigris/Euphrates valley (from where the Ugha Mongulalas claim to have originated) also offer highly interesting facts.

Curiously, the numerical system of the Sumerians is – sexagesimal. This appears strange to us, accustomed as we are to a decimal system, which surely stems from the number of fingers we have. Yet what is an enigma for us is exciting to mathematicians and astronomers. We ourselves often use the Sumerian twelve in our everyday lives, which we consider more appropriate for the figuring of hourly time and also, for example, in geometric gradient measurements. After the appearance of the Roswell-Santilli aliens, one cannot help wondering whether this numeric system based on twelve derives from twelve-fingered beings.

This hypothesis gains in validity with additional study of the Sumerian legends of creation, which, thanks to the studies of Zecharia Sitchin,* were meticulously deciphered. According to these Sumerian sources, astronauts came about 450,000 years ago from another star with an enormous orbit and landed on Earth. These »deities« had great problems with their home planet, Nibiru, whose thinning atmosphere was permitting more and more harsh cosmic radiation to penetrate. These intrepid explorers hoped to remedy the situation by bringing large amounts of gold dust into their stratosphere.* But the enormous amounts of gold required to save their planet couldn't be found in their home system, so they set out to find it elsewhere, ultimately achieving their aim on planet Earth, which was not yet inhabited by Homo Sapiens. A first group of fifty space travellers called Anunnaki – »the ones from heaven who are on Earth« – by the Sumerians, landed in the Arabian Sea and set out toward Mesopotamia. There they established a space airport, from which another group, prospecting in North Africa (Kenya) and other places, finally gathered the gold and transported it back to their home planet.

It then happened, 150,000 years later, that the hard-working extraterrestrial gold prospectors began to mutiny, because of their intolerable working conditions. While the leader of the enterprise demanded exemplary punishment of the mutineers, the planet's chief »An« (later called Anu) and his

scientific advisor Enki showed more leniency. They agreed to create Adamas, a kind of primitive earthly work force, and hand over this demanding task to them in the future. For the experimental creation of a prototype, they took a highly-evolved ape which was already present on the planet. In order to create Adam – that is, this first human being in their image, with the inner genetic construction of the Anunnaki – they refined a forerunner of the apeman by means of genetic technology. Thus, Adam, the Earthian, was not a person, but rather a generic name, created through mixing the masculine divine gene with that of a female ape by fertilizing her egg. A Sumerian cylinder seal from 4000 BC (see picture no. 41) shows that this was a kind of »in vitro« fertilization, subsequently implanted into the ape's uterus. Thus, the first Adam was not only the first human being on Earth; he was also the first artificially created terrestrial test-tube baby, whose birth nearly failed when no labor contractions set in and Enki had to deliver Adam himself by performing a Caesarian. On the basis of discoveries so far, it is evident that in this distant past, evolution took a giant step which to this day cannot be explained by science. What does become comprehensible for the first time through these Sumerian Cuneiform writings is that the missing link so long sought by paleontologists came from beyond our planet! Numerous archaic pictures of hybrid creatures, human bulls, bird-men and other animal/human being depictions all attest that this method of creation did not succeed until an excessive number of false starts had taken place. Also, the Egyptian sphinx might be a clear sign of genetic human/animal/hybrid experimentation.

After the first Homo Sapiens saw the light of day, the experiments were turned around and repeated with fourteen fertility deities, that is, Annunaki women, who then gave birth to seven male and seven

* This is similar to the golden radiation-protection layer on the glass helmets of our astronauts.

female Adamas.* At the next stage of genetic-engineered evolution, the new human species were finally enabled to reproduce. Just how many workers were ordered and produced for gold mining is not evident in the creation myths of the Sumerians.

When we say that »God« formed the human being from clay, we mean that he created a hybrid being half from his divine sperm and half from the Earth, that is, by means of an earthly ape body. The first appearance of the primeval human mother, calculated in various mitochondria DNA examinations to have taken place about 300,000 years ago, from whom we all must stem, thus corresponds approximately with the paleontological dating of the first fossil evidence of Homo Sapiens.

In the Book of Moses one reads that the spot where God made Adam was called Paradise. And the Sumerians, bearers of the oldest traceable high culture in southern Mesopotamia, who are considered the inventors of pictogram language, depicted these events as a series of pictures with commentaries. Hence, the Biblical »knowledge« of Adam and Eve was nothing else but the knowledge of and the ability to reproduce. The Sumerian emblems of two intertwined snakes (see picture no. 42) – to this day the universal symbol of medicine – clearly indicate the double helix DNA structure and the knowledge of the genetic code, with which the Anunnaki produced Adam and Eve and, in order to simplify production, then bestowed on them the capacity to reproduce.

In the Hebrew Talmud it is written quite clearly that the first human beings had no navel, since they were not born of woman. In Egyptian myths, Osiris was cut into fourteen strips by his brother, then reassembled into immortality by his mother Isis,

»the magical« – however, without genitals, which could not be found. To me, this appears to be a similar case of genetic intervention to that of the Roswell aliens, who, according to their statements, also gained »de facto« immortality through manipulation of DNA strips, and who also forfeited their genitals. The first Book of Moses says that the sons of the gods had relations with earthly daughters and that through these unlawful human relations, demigods, that is, hybrids, resulted. These sons, according to legend, stemmed from the people of Shem, the »people of the rocket ships.« Further, in the Book of Moses the great flood is depicted as if the Lord (it should actually be translated as »gods« from Hebrew, since Elohim is a plural) used it to exterminate mankind because of this genetic blasphemy. In the scriptures of the Ugha Mongulala, this global flood is also referred to, as having occurred in the year 10,468 BC.

If we now look at the signs on the Roswell I-beams which are visible in the Santilli films, we recognize a certain similarity with Phoenician and the later ancient Greek letters, all of which developed out of Sumerian pictograms. Moreover, the Phoenician and Hebrew alphabets (both of which can be counted as belonging to the roots of our script) have 22 letters. If one adds to these the 12 hexagonal numbers and a sign for zero, one arrives, unsurprisingly, at the precise number of letters/symbols mentioned by the Asastanians as comprising their »nautical script«, namely, 35.

If we examine some of the central Sumerian syllables and their meanings, we perceive further connections which cannot be dismissed as coincidence. The syllable AN stands both for father of gods, heaven and divine being. The symbol for this lord over all Sumerian gods was a star. The syllable LIL primarily means simply air. And what the great mother figure Inanna and Ishtar (or Lilit) were to the Sumerians

---

* Interestingly, mystical Hebrew legends mention the name of the first woman and partner of Adam to have been Lilith.

in Mesopotamia, Isis was to the Egyptians: the embodiment of the dark feminine aspect of the unconscious. Proceeding from these linguistic patterns, it isn't a great leap of the imagination to interpret ASAS-T-AN as ISIS-AN, »Star of Isis« which corresponds figuratively with the Lilit-Star, which is what Lilit called Asastan's sun. In a comparison of these legends and parallels, one has to wonder whether the crash aliens from Roswell might be grandchildren of the Anunnaki, introduced to us in the Sumerian myths, and consequently, so to speak, our cosmic ancestors.

We recall that a channeled message from Asastan said that Lilit's forebears once came from Venus. One's usual first reaction to the possibility of life on Venus is that it is much too hot there for human-type life. However, if we examine latest researches relating to our second nearest planet, we are forced to revise our attitude: Venus clouds have five times as much condensed water as Earth's clouds at the same altitude. Further explorations have shown that the so-called »afterglow« of the dark hemisphere suggests the conclusion that oxygen is present, thus permitting the process of photosynthesis in plants. The climatic conditions, such as clouds and wind, are also comparable to Earth's. Russian probes which landed about 1400 miles apart both sent back pictures of a landscape in bright sunlight, thereby refuting the theory that the surface of Venus is just a sandy desert caused by storms. There are even oceans and lakes. The speed of its rotation, 26 hours, is also similar to Earth's. Only air pressure and temperature, as measured by Americans and Russians – due to differing measurements, a pressure of 90 atmospheres and a temperature of 440° C. were agreed upon – would be intolerable for Earth beings. However, these measurements were made in 1967. Strangely enough, very little relevant information was made public after the most recent US and Russian missions. Since it is NASA policy to filter its information, it can be assumed that if latest data corroborate a more salutary climatic environment for human beings, the news has been withheld. Besides, it is not necessarily impossible for other forms of intelligent life to have developed even at the cited conditions of temperature and pressure, to say nothing of the possibility of less dense life forms modulating at higher frequencies. However, such speculations lead us into dimensions with which orthodox scientists are persistently uncomfortable, as they present a great threat to the sober posture of pure reason they display in their special fields. To change that rigid thinking, events will have to occur to shake those foundations and force them out of their rut.

The Spiritual Dimension

Since time immemorial simple people have gazed at the stars with reverence and admiration, even though for a long time they had no idea what the points of light which they worshipped in the sea of darkness really were. In many ancient civilizations, the stars were revered as gods, hence the names of our own solar system's planets. These »other worlds« have been identified today as perfect and natural parts of our physical universe which had been anticipated and described by philosophers and inspired writers over thousands of years. We recognized that the heavenly lights which reach us from distant sources are much, much older than our planet and worlds around us.

A being looking down upon us with other highly sensitive equipment from one of these incredibly far distant light sources would perceive our galaxy with its countless suns as an equally tiny point of light, in the middle of which the reader, sitting and reading these lines in his home, on a planet revolving around his sun, is wondering whether life exists on other planets. In a word, we are all extraterrestrials, or extra-galacticals and maybe even extra-universals. It is just a matter of your point of visual perception. Add to that the fact that where you see one reality, other perceiving organisms, outfitted with quite different visual, acoustic or other perceiving senses perhaps utterly unknown to you, might experience something quite different. Yet both realities are valid. Only the interpretation of them differs. Each sense can only perceive from its own limits and frequencies out into reality and then qualify the information according to its own databank. And that brings us right smack up against the phenomenon of UFO sightings. Only when the frequency bands of both participants overlap can a sighting occur – although there is always the possibility that the more developed side might be capable of blotting out the contact experience in the consciousness of the lower frequency observer. Since more than 100,000 UFO sightings have been reported from all over the world in the last 50 years, of which about 10% can be taken seriously, one can venture to say that a new era has begun for us Earthians and that we need to wake up and contemplate our cosmic connections with these phenemena in the sky. At present, despite the availability of overwhelming amounts of accumulated data, neither our scientists, nor our traditional religions seem capable of supplying modern answers.

However, there is an occasional ray of hope: the illustrious British »Journal of the Royal Astronomical Society« recently published an article entitled »The Natural Selection of Universes Containing Intelligent Life«, a contribution, in which distinguished astronomers seriously explore the idea that our cosmos was created by creatures of superior intelligence. »*More intelligent beings, perhaps our own descendants in the far future, might possess not only the knowledge to design, but also the technology to build universes. Intelligent life in parent universes creates offspring universes fit for inhabitation, new life evolves to a high level of intelligence and creates further universes...Plausibly, offspring universes have properties closely similar to their parent universes – apart from small genetic variations in the constants of physics – and the universes most hospitable to intelligent life are naturally selected by their ability to reproduce.*«

According to this theory, »*our universe was made by highly intelligent forms of life living in another universe; Their universe was necessarily compatible with their existence and therefore essentially similar to our own. Moreover, highly intelligent forms of life in our universe, in their turn, will also create universes. Thus, we have a picture of cosmogenic reproduction in which intelligent life fulfils the role of conceiving and producing universes.*«

The article goes on to discuss the fine tuning of the fundamental constants of nature, how highly intelligent life might manufacture universes, how the first self-reproducing universe began and reasons why intelligent life might want to create universes. Finally astronomer Edward R. Harrison, in response to Einstein's remark »*the most incomprehensible thing about the universe is that it is comprehensible*«, concludes »*that the universe is comprehensible because it was created by comprehensible beings who had thought processes basically similar to our own.*«

This excursion into higher conjecture gives one an inkling of the impoverished state of knowledge in which we generally vegetate while persisting in self-righteous pretensions. We – by which I mean members of the scientific establishment – to this day don't know the initial catalyst of the heartbeat, why the sky is blue, that planets are living organisms, or even what sort of power moves the universe itself.

Why, indeed, does anything exist? There must exist some cosmic plan, behind which lies a cosmic spirit. Let us hold onto the wisdom of the Rig Veda, which says that it is pointless to reflect on the beginning of the universe since we live in the middle of it and have to relinquish our polarity in order to find an answer.

But what caused the Big Bang? At this point, only meta-physical insights can be of help. As long as we are on the path of the meaning of life, we have to assume there is a goal to creation, and also that everything in motion issued from an all-superior principle. Cosmologists and mystics try to understand the structure and development of the universe. In this endeavor, the latest physical findings from Ufology are just as helpful as metaphysical border experiences of UFO sightings in the questioning and re-examination of traditional images of God. Whether this thrust of knowledge arises from a mystical quality of science or a primordial experience of transcendence in the depths of one's inner being is, in the end, irrelevant. Within a certain critical mass of higher consciousness around the globe, the stragglers are carried along anyway.

In the dawning Age of Aquarius, which is characterised by our solar system entering new cosmic spaces permeated with higher frequencies, our brain cells cannot remain untouched. Planet Earth will increasingly shift to a finer, more astral plane and successively enlarge the reality windows of its inhabitants. Without warning, our old, materialistic world views will be unhinged and, ultimately, destroyed.

Twelve Insights

• Insight 1: We are spiritual beings

In the deepest source of our being, we all know that what matters is that we each recognize in ourselves an individual image of the divine.

• Insight 2: We are not alone

The best documented UFO case to date shows us that we are not the only creatures in the universe. We have to accept the fact that there exist many forms of life still unknown to us.

• Insight 3: We are connected to each other

Everything in the universe is interconnected. Otherwise, no contact across such vast interstellar distances would be possible.

• Insight 4: We ourselves are »extra-terrestrials«

Objectively speaking, there is no above or below in the universe. Likewise outside and inside are nothing but subjective standpoints or perspectives.

• Insight 5: We are our genes

The psychosomatic implications of genomes demonstrate that we should cherish the natural structure of life in order to follow the path which leads to the center of our Self.

• Insight 6: We are (our) consciousness

We are learning that our reality is primarily mental/ spiritual because we find more frequently that we are communicating with others telepathically.

• Insight 7: We are the power of creativity

The more conscious we become of our origins, the greater our creative potential increases. With it, we are permitted to shape the world according to our desires, but only in harmony with nature.

• Insight 8: We are woven of light

To travel faster than visual light, to have instantaneous communication, these are indications that we carry the source of light of all being within us and, holographically seen, we are that selfsame source.

• Insight 9: We are freedom

We also concede, in our unconscious omnipotence, the possibility of experiencing the outer limits of matter in order step-by-step to liberate ourselves from them.

• Insight 10: We are the timeless present

Every individualized being becomes conscious of its true self in its own way in order »one day« to find out that it has always been conscious of it in the time-less heart of the eternal now.

• Insight 11: We are immortal life

The more we allow ourselves to accept our spiritual eternity, the less fearful, the more liberated and more conscious will we be through this externally limited life.

• Insight 12: We are the living spirit of love

The »electromagnetic binding power« between the hologram's particles in the process of becoming conscious of themselves is endless divine love.

Epilogue

Latest Developments

The showing of the Roswell Santilli alien documentary on German TV channels raised controversies in the press. The magazine »Spiegel« claimed that the dissected corpse was that of a genetically-sick girl. Dr. Thomas Jansen in an article in the »Munich Medical Weekly«, offered an alternative explanation – that of a genetic disease called polydactylia which causes the develpment of additional fingers. However, this would not be relevant in this case, as Lilit's fingers were not malformed.

Several books on Roswell have appeared in the bookshops during 1996 and the summer of 1997. Some have supported the authenticity of the alien autopsy footage while others have dismissed it as a giant hoax.

Of more general interest has been the surfacing of a new, apparently significant Roswell eyewitness, revealing his recollections of the incident. Retired Colonel Philip J. Corso, a member of Eisenhower's National Security Council and head of the Foreign Technology Desk at the US Army's Research and Development Department has now claimed that he had personal responsibility for the recovered Roswell artifacts in the early phase. With this new disclosure of one of the military's best kept secrets, Corso has shown how the Roswell crash fundamentally changed the course of the 20th century. He has told how he flew over the area the day after the crash and how he has since re-visited the true crash site on the Hub Corn Ranch* as well as Brazel's foil covered field near Corona.

* At present at least five different crash sites are claimed to be the authentic one.

There have also been further reports about the autopsy films. Several people have claimed to have seen them years before Santilli sold his to the media. Johsen Takano, UFO-Museum Co-ordinator of Hakui City, Japan, insists that he was shown a two-hour version of the Santilli film at CIA headquarters in Langley, Virginia as early as 1993. Former US Army Sergeant Clifford Stone said recently that he, by chance, was able to view excerpts of a Santilli-like film back in 1969 at Fort Belvoir military base. He also claimed to know of film footage in which he could discern *»if not Truman himself, at least a very convincing double«*. Another ex-soldier, Master Sergeant Bob Allen, whose responsibility it was to pack up UFO wreckage from Hangar 1 for shipment to further examination centers, claimed he saw all three autopsies, *»and at one of them, Truman was standing behind a glass window of the autopsy room.«* With regard to the navigation panels, Allen offered the opinion that they were custom made for each ET and were used, among other things, to start the entire propulsion system. *»We tried it too, but our brain frequencies didn't work fast enough.«* *

In the middle of April '96, it was announced that President Clinton, who is not exactly being swamped with background information on the Roswell case by his own intelligence services, entrusted his scientific advisor, Dr. John Gibbons, to make attempts, with his own investigation commission, to determine whether the Santilli film was genuine. Apparently, further film material has already been located in military archives. The cryptic comment of James M., a captain involved in this investigation:

»The being in the footage is not human, not a doll and not an extra-terrestrial.«

At certain times, there was a regular manhunt going on for presumed »Roswell cameramen«, while the real retired cameraman, still in hiding, made his own home video interview in late 1996 for his business partner Santilli. Is seems that the real name of the cameraman was not J. B., but Jack S. However, since personnel archives in St. Louis were damaged in a fire and there is no mandatory registration of residence in the US, it is extremely difficult to locate him. In a recent Japanese TV Special his video interview was shown for the first time, with Japanese subtitles. A broad-shouldered, elderly man wearing glasses, with a mole on the right side of his face could be seen, obviously nervous, in front of the camera. He spoke with a strong New York accent. Since the old man was easily recognizable, it was finally decided to obscure his face and to dub his voice with an actor's, in order to make it unidentifiable. FOX television will air the interview *»probably this year«*, despite its sub-standard quality. In this interview Santilli's business partner repeated his earlier statement, that the men at the crash site were rather rattled by the sinister atmosphere and were concerned about possible radiation risks. Scientists were on hand, as were medical experts and special military units, *»Truman's team came too, in order to get a glimpse of what was going on.«* The whole thing was handled like a war situation. Those in the lower ranks received only the admonition that they were absolutely forbidden to speak about it with anyone. As to why approximately 25 rolls of film remained in his possession, he said by way of explanation that in the weeks following the crash, the entire US military was re-organized, which meant that he did not belong to any specific troup unit for a time and thus, did not have a commanding officer. Since he couldn't leave the material just lying around,

he finally took it home with him, where it was kept in a carton until the risky sale to Santilli. In retrospect, he deeply regretted ever having sold the autopsies.

According to eyewitnesses, Santilli indeed also has movies of the first autopsy, showing an apparently slender, uninjured alien body. Ostensibly, he sold this sequence to his co-financier, who, in turn, is not interested in making the film available to the public. Which begs the question of what happened to those controversial rolls which allegedly show the recovery of the UFO and President Truman at the site?

Santilli's autopsy video has sold over 100,000 copies already, but Ray Santilli's Merlin Group, which has recently been renamed Orbital Media Ltd., and the co-owner of the autopsy film, Volker Spielberg, still fend off everything which smells of the press. So for better or for worse, we simply have to wait and see if any more of the purchased films might be made public.

President Clinton's room for manoeuvre on the subject of UFOs will hopefully decrease drastically during his second administration. Shortly after the elections, Dr. Steven Greer, director of the Commitee for the Study of Extraterrestrial Intelligence, in a letter which was more or less an ultimatum, called on Bill Clinton and the chiefs of the major intelligence agencies to open the Roswell files to the public otherwise two dozen military eyewitnesses would be introduced to the media on the basis that the oath to secrecy that they took is not now legally binding. A first »summit of witnesses« is already in the planning stages.

The biggest shock of 1997 was certainly the cloning of an adult animals. British gene-sheep Dolly and two US-Rhesus-monkeys manifested the first steps of a genetic nightmare that Lilit spoke of. Since there is no biological barrier to transforming this process to human beings, Homo Xerox will not be a taboo for long. The highly significant fact, that the psyche would also be restructured through genetic interventions has been utterly ignored in all the gene-technology discussion thus far.

As this book went into its third German edition, hundreds of sightings of unusual flying objects were witnessed all over the world, including some very close encounters. Also crop circles, implantation claims, cases of abduction and animal mutilations go on and on. Because of all this, it has to be said that the general acceptance of UFOs as well as interest in unusual occurrences in the heavens has radically increased among the general public in recent years. The Hollywood production, »Independence Day« was seen by multimillions of people worldwide and the paranormal TV series, »X-Files« too draws several million viewers to their sets every week in a lot of countries. This new ›Zeitgeist‹ permits the general public to sense intuitively that there are more things in heaven and earth than the public was ever led to believe possible. According to latest US surveys, more than 50% of Americans are now convinced that the government has been withholding information about extraterrestrials.

That is the state of affairs to date. It will be interesting to see what further escapades the Roswell affair can come up with, and what shenanigans the official agencies – in the name of the people – will engage in as we get ready to enter the third millennium. For the 50th anniversary, conferences, ceremonies and other events lasting several days were held both in Europe and the US. Packs of more than 30,000 Declaration signatures were handed over to the White House and US Congress, to rattle at the locked doors of the mega X-file. A stack of about 1000 signatures from readers of the German editions of this book were presented ted to President Clinton through the US Embassy in Vienna.

It appears that it will be only a few more years before the Roswell enigma is officially discussed, and then only because of public pressure. Interest in extraterrestrial matters is increasing by leaps and bounds. In addition, one of the alleged reasons for the government agencies' denying this phenomenon will soon expire: insiders claim the government is simply waiting until all the people involved in the cover-up are dead, reducing the risk of lawsuits and embarrassment.

After the 50th anniversary celebrations and media fuss have subsided, the Roswell theme will, of course, not be forgotten. For 1998, a »March of thousands« is being planned to secret AREA 51, where it is assumed the reconstructed Roswell UFO wreck and the autopsied aliens are being kept.

Only if people are allowed to see the facts, will it put an final end to the Roswell mystery...

The Roswell Affair – A Declaration

The International Roswell Initiative

Fifty years ago an incident occurred in the southwestern desert of the United States that could have significant implications for all mankind. It involved the recovery by the US military, of material alleged to be of extraterrestrial origin. The event was announced by the Army Air Force on July 8, 1947 through a press release carried by newspapers throughout the country. It was subsequently denied by what is now believed to be a cover story claiming the material was nothing more than a weather balloon. It has remained veiled in government secrecy ever since.

The press release announcing the unusual event was issued by the commander of the 509th Bomb Group at Roswell Army Air Field, Colonel William Blanchard, who later went on to become a four-star general and Vice Chief of Staff of the United States Air Force. That the weather balloon story was a cover-up has been confirmed by individuals directly involved, including the late General Thomas DuBose, who took the telephone call from Washington, DC ordering the cover-up. Numerous other credible military and civilian witnesses have testified that the original press release was correct and that the Roswell wreckage was of extraterrestrial origin. One such individual was Major Jesse Marcel, the intelligence officer of the 509th Bomb Group and one of the first military officers at the scene.

On January 12, 1994, United States Congressman Steven Schiff of Albuquerque, New Mexico, announced to the press that he had been stonewalled by the Defense Department when requesting information on the 1947 Roswell event on behalf of constituents and witnesses. Indicating that he was seeking further investigation into the matter, Congressman Schiff called the Defense Department's lack of response »astounding« and concluded it was apparently »another government cover-up«.

History has shown that unsubstantiated official assurances or denials by government are often meaningless. Nevertheless, there is a logical and straightforward way to ensure that the truth about Roswell will emerge: an Executive Order declassifying any information regarding the existence of UFOs or extraterrestrial intelligence. Because this is a unique issue of universal concern, such an action would be appropriate and warranted. To provide positive assurance for all potential witnesses, it would need to be clearly stated and written into law. Such a measure is essentially what presidential candidate Jimmy Carter promised and then failed to deliver to the American people in 1976.

If, as is officially claimed, no information on Roswell, UFOs, or extraterrestrial intelligence is being withheld, an executive order declassifying it would be a mere formality, as there would be nothing to disclose. The order would, however, have the positive effect of setting the record straight once and for all. Years of controversy and suspicion would be ended, both in the eyes of the United States' own citizens and in the eyes of the world.

If, on the other hand, the Roswell witnesses are telling the truth and information on extraterrestrial intelligence does exist, it is not something to which a privileged few in the United States government should have exclusive rights. It is knowledge of profound importance to which all people throughout the world should have an inalienable right. Its release would unquestionably be universally acknowledged as an historic act of honesty and goodwill.

An Explanation of the Roswell Declaration

The Roswell Declaration is part of a worldwide effort to end US government secrecy surrounding the 1947 Roswell incident. It contains an appeal to the administration for an Executive Order to declassify any US government information regarding the existence of UFOs or extraterrestrial intelligence. You can help by signing and returning a copy of the declaration.

The effort is being supported by three independent nonprofit organizations* devoted to the serious study of the UFO phenomenon. The membership of the governing committees of these organizations consists primarily of researchers, scientists, and Ph.D.s. The three organizations are

• the Mutual UFO Network (MUFON), 103 Oldtowne Road, Seguin, Texas 78155, U.S.A.

• the Center for UFO Studies (CUFOS), 2457 W. Peterson Avenue, Chicago, Illinois 60659, U.S.A.

• the Fund for UFO Research (FUFOR), P.O. Box 277, Mt. Ranier, Maryland 20712, USA.

UFO organizations throughout the world are involved in a drive to obtain signatures from scientists, professionals, and the general public in support of the Roswell Declaration. On the 50th anniversary of the alleged Roswell crash, the news media in different countries around the world were to be notified and furnished with material about the Roswell incident in an effort to bring international attention to the Roswell case.

On that same day, it was planned that a copy of the Roswell Declaration, along with a listing of the total number of signatories from each of the fifty states would be delivered to the offices of all members of Congress and to the White House. In other countries, signed copies of the Roswell Declaration were to be delivered to the American embassy for forwarding to the White House. If finances permitted, a copy of the Roswell Declaration would also be placed in the first section of the national edition of a major US newspaper as well as in other major newspapers around the world.

Polls have shown that more than fifty percent of the people in the United States believe in the existence of UFOs and in extraterrestrial intelligence. Unfortunately, that interest has never been galvanized into a large-scale grassroots movement. With the »Roswell Declaration«, this may now become a reality.

Since this will be primarily a word-of-mouth, grassroots effort, your help in making copies of the declaration and distributing them to as many people as possible will be of great importance. The declaration is being made available on computer bulletin boards throughout the world. A five-page position paper, »Time for the Truth About Roswell«, from which the declaration is derived, will also be made available. The position paper includes a detailed summary of the Roswell event, an analysis of the media and government treatment of it, and arguments for allowing the public to know the truth.

The position paper and the declaration were written by Kent Jeffrey* who has researched the Roswell

* Kent Jeffrey, 37 Porteous Ave., Fairfax, CA 94930,U.S.A.

213

event extensively, worked with several of the leading investigators, and interviewed a number of the Roswell witnesses. He is an international airline pilot whose interest in the Roswell case stems in part from the fact that his father, a retired colonel and former air force pilot (and WWII fighter ace), at one time knew and worked with one of the key Roswell figures, General William Blanchard.

Although it is felt by the organizers of this effort that there is a high degree of probability the US government is withholding information regarding the existence of extraterrestrial intelligence, the primary goal is to get the matter into the open so that the truth can be conclusively determined, one way or the other. It is hoped, therefore, that all individuals, no matter what their opinion on the subject, will support this effort.

So far in the meantime, the worldwide initiative for the lifting of UFO secrecy policy (founded by Kent Jeffrey, Joachim Koch* and Hans-Jürgen Kyborg*) is gaining credibility. The representatives of the IRI are all extreme sceptics of the Santilli autopsy footage, but nevertheless, they »would be the first to applaud any proof of the authenticity of this film material«, I was assured by the German branch of the IRI. »As long as this proof is not forthcoming, we have to exercise great caution, since this is clearly a highly political and a decisive ideological affair.« Through organizations in a dozen different countries, more than 25,000 signed declarations have been gathered to date, including those of hundreds of scientists, two retired US Air Force generals, and two former US astronauts. The first packages of signatures will be handed over to Congress and the White House in 1997. Through a strategy of maintaining maximum pressure, the IRI should be tenaciously pursued until success is attained, that is to say, until the Pentagon has laid its cards on the table. If you, dear reader, agree with the IRI initiators »that in the Roswell affair it is no longer a question of proving that a crash took place, but rather of the decades-long fraud perpetrated by official institutions on the public with regard to the existence of non-human intelligence and technology, and power politics practiced merely to preserve their own structures, ignoring all moral and ethical principles on this planet«, please support the Roswell Declaration by signing and remitting the coupon at the end of the book* to the publisher. You will then periodically be kept up to date on all developments.

Contact address of the IRI:

International Roswell Initiative
3105 Gables Drive,
Atlanta, GA 30319, USA
ph/fax: (404) 240-0655
email: roswelldec@aol.com

---

* Joachim Koch, Stadtrandstr. 550 g, D-13589 Berlin, Germany
Hans-Jürgen Kyborg, Zweibrückenstr. 11, D-13583 Berlin, Germany.

* see next page – Note regarding occupation and education on the coupon: These are optional fields, however it would help us if you provided them. Don't feel that omitting them will disqualify you from the petition. We just want to present the government with statistics of who has signed the petition. Everyone is encouraged to sign. Tell your friends!

Some people may find the contents of this footage disturbing

exclusive limited edition

THE AUTOPSY-VIDEO
(detailed description on pages 62-70)

VHS - PAL
Colour and B&W
Running time:
60 minutes (approx.)

Original Santilli-Video Backcover Text:

In the early hours of the 2nd June 1947, South-west of Socorro in New Mexico, something extraordinary happened. It is now admitted that the US military rigorously suppressed the truth of the events of that night for almost 50 years, making it one of the best kept secrets in modern history.

Roswell the video contains all the viewable material taken from the reels of films received from the man believed to be the Roswell cameraman; in addition, this footage includes an autopsy of an alleged alien being and footage supposedly of debris taken from the crashed spacecraft.

In addition to this sensational raw footage, there are exclusive interviews and recordings with Philip Mantle and Ray Santilli.

Narrated by: Brian Blessed

E - Exempt from classification

REDUCED FROM ORIGINAL PRICE OF **£33.00**

SPECIAL PRICE NOW (**£ 11.95**)

AVAILABLE THROUGH GATEWAY BOOKS
PLEASE USE ORDERING COUPON NEXT PAGE

Sources

Roswell Books:

Berlitz, Charles and William L. Moore
»*The Roswell Incident*«, New York, 1980

Randle, Kevin D. and Donald R. Schmitt
»*UFO Crash at Roswell*«, New York, 1991

Friedman, Stanton T. and Don Berliner
»*Crash at Corona*«, New York, 1992

Randle, Kevin D. and Donald R. Schmitt, »*The Truth about the UFO Crash at Roswell*«, New York, 1994

Randle, Kevin D.
»*Roswell UFO Crash Update*«, New Brunswick, 1995

Hesemann, Michael
»*Beyond Roswell*«, New York 1997

Friedman, Stanton T.
»*Top Secret/ Majic*«, New York, 1996

Roswell Videos:

Fund for UFO Research
Recollections of Roswell, Mt. Rainier, 1993

New Century Productions
UFO Secret - The Roswell Crash, Poway, 1993

Purdie, John
Incident at Roswell, London, 1995

Santilli, Ray
Roswell - The Footage, London, 1995

General Bibliography:

Jung, Carl G.
»*Flying Saucers: A Modern Myth of Things Seen in the Sky*«
New York, 1969

Sharaf, Myron
»*Fury on Earth - A Biography of Wilhelm Reich*«
New York, 1983

Sitchin, Zecharia
»*Divine Encounters*«
New York, 1995

Mack, John E.
»*Abduction - Human Encounters with Aliens*«
New York, 1994

Thompson, Keith
»*Angels and Aliens*«
New York, 1991

Hopkins, Budd
»*Missing Time*«
New York, 1981

Vallée, Jaques
»*Confrontations. A Scientist's Search for Alien Contact*«
New York, 1990

Ferguson, V. S.
»*Inanna Returns*«
Seattle, 1995

Books by the Author:

Coudris, Manuel David, Mirabelle & René   »*DIARY OF AN UNBORN CHILD - A Baby Speaks from its Mother's Womb*« (ISBN 0-946551-80-4, p/b, £ 6.95) *ENGLISH EDITION BY GATEWAY BOOKS*

René & Mirabelle Coudris »*IM TRANCE-DIALOG MIT ›C. G. JUNG‹ oder Kontakte mit dem Unbewußten?*« Channeling-Chroniken I-III (ISBN 3-923781-41-5, p/b, á DM 25.-) *PUBLISHED IN GERMAN BY SILBERSCHNUR VERLAG**

René & Mirabelle Coudris »*JENSEITS BERUHMTER LEBEN UND LUGEN - Eine Talk-Show von Drüben*« (ISBN 3-901494-014, h/c, DM 40.-) *PUBLISHED IN GERMAN BY DELPHI PUBLICATIONS** *may be ordered through the author.

Index of names

Credits

Author's address:

René Coudris c/o Studio Phoenix
P. O. Box 8
A-4810 Gmunden am Traunsee
Austria/Europe
e-mail: r.coudris@magnet.at

GATEWAY BOOKS
are distributed

in the **USA** by Access Publishers Network, 6893 Sullivan Road, Grawn, MI 49637, U.S.A.

in **Australia** by Banyan Tree Book Distribution, 13 College Road, Kent Town, S.A. 5067,

in **New Zealand** by Peaceful Living Publications, POB 300, Tauranga, NZ,

in **Canada** by Temeron Books, 210, 1220 Kensington Rd NW, Calgary, Alberta T2N 3P5, Canada,

in **South Africa** by Wizard's Warehouse, POB 3340, Cape Town 8000, South Africa,

in **Singapore & Malaysia** by Pansing Distribution, 8 New Industrial Rd, Singapore, 536200,

in **Thailand & Cambodia** by Mark Standenpubs, Moo Bahn Amarinnivet 1, Bangkhen, Bangkok, Thailand.

Gateway Books Website: **http://www.gatewaybooks.com**

Finally,
I would like to express heartfelt thanks to the medium,
the publisher, both translators, the editors and all the collaborators
and last but not least Lilit and the other aliens of Asastan
involved in »The Roswell Message«
who supported me so unstintingly
in putting this book
together.